CONQUERING
INFERTILITY

CONQUERING INFERTILITY

A GUIDE FOR COUPLES

THIRD EDITION

Stephen L. Corson, M.D.

Notice: Our knowledge in the clinical sciences is constantly changing. As new information becomes available, changes in treatment and in the use of drugs become necessary. The author and the publisher of this volume have, as far as it is possible to do so, taken care to make certain that the doses of drugs and schedules of treatment are correct and compatible with the standards generally accepted at the time of publication. The reader is advised to consult carefully the instruction and information material included in the package insert of each drug or therapeutic agent before administration in order to make certain that the recommended dosage is correct and that there have been no changes in the recommended dose of the drug or in the indications or contraindications in its utilization. This advice is especially important when using new or infrequently used drugs.

 EMIS-Canada
P.O. Box 47026
19 - 555 West 12th Ave.
Vancouver, B.C.   V5Z 4L6

First Edition 1983
© 1983 by Appleton-Century-Crofts
Revised Edition 1990
© 1990 Revised text by Stephen L. Corson, M.D.
Third Edition 1995
© 1995 by Stephen L. Corson, M.D.

ISBN 1-895213-20-7

Printed in Canada

ACKNOWLEDGMENTS

Thanks go to Ray Tschoepe for his straightforward artwork and to Lee Miller for her consistent word processing. Also, many thanks to readers and patients for their helpful comments. We appreciate the fact that you want a concise factual text and hope that this fulfills that request.

Contents

About the Author

STEPHEN L. CORSON, M.D., is the director of the Philadelphia Fertility Institute, and the *in vitro* fertilization program at the Pennsylvania Hospital. He is a clinical professor in the Department of Obstetrics and Gynecology at the University of Pennsylvania School of Medicine, and Editor-in-Chief of the International Journal of Fertility and Menopausal Studies.

AUTHOR'S NOTE

As a doctor who specializes in reproductive medicine, I have found that many of the patients seen for an initial consultation are understandably anxious and depressed. More often than not they also feel frustrated, angry, and may be experiencing low self-esteem as a result of their problems. Many of these strong feelings come out of the chronic ache of childlessness, but I believe that, at least some of the time, the medical community compounds the problem by failing to give full explanations for what has gone wrong and what can be done. One of the reasons this happens, of course, is that doctors are under work pressures themselves and often are unable to spend enough time with each patient to explain all the medical facts and to lend emotional support, both of which are essential elements in the practice of medicine.

This book was written not to replace your patient-physician communications, which are as essential to the cure as the therapy itself, but to familiarize you with the many methods of diagnosing and treating infertility. With this knowledge, you will be able to ask the right questions, feel assured that the tests and treatments you are receiving are indeed necessary, and play a more significant role as a partner in the medical decisions made on your behalf.

Marvelous advances in available drugs and surgical treatments, such as microsurgery and laser therapy, give you treatment options not even dreamed of a decade ago. In vitro fertilization and related treatments are the epitome of high technology applied to reproductive problems. You'll find out how these and more standard treatments and procedures are performed and what results you can reasonably expect. Also you will learn my philosophy of what works and why, and what I believe does not work.

In the treatment of infertility, no one is to blame. No one is at fault. "Blame" and "fault" are not words in my vocabulary because they are negative notions that can only worsen frustrations and disappointments; they add nothing to treatment. The key as you approach this endeavor together is to find care from a thoughtful, understanding physician or medical team, who will treat you as a couple, a reproductive entity, rather than categorize you as "the man with poor sperm" or "the woman with an ovulatory problem." And by all means avoid computer-generated programs of therapy as substitutes for thinking and feeling doctors.

The outlook for conquering infertility is favorable: about two-thirds of the people with reproductive problems eventually succeed in having a baby. If the road is long and the toll high, both financially and emotionally, don't give up easily. Infertility is a problem that frequently will yield to persistence. Don't be afraid or ashamed to seek psychological help and emotional support from professional therapists and support groups who work specifically with couples in your situation.

Since many of the exciting treatment options that you will find in this book were not available a few years ago, the job of a fertility therapist has become paradoxically more difficult. In this field we consider the diagnosis versus the age of the patients, the previous history, and the partners' willingness and ability to participate in a therapeutic program. The skilled physician will then construct a treatment plan. Like a ladder, it will begin on the first rung with a simple, noninvasive program, consistent with a reasonable expectation of success. Increasingly, more intricate steps will be taken if success does not occur in a period that is acceptable to the patient and doctor. This, then, is the real skill of practising medicine in this area - creating a partnership in a therapeutic program that is accepted by the provider and recipient alike, a program designed for success.

One way of getting into this book is to read the chapter that you think deals most directly with your particular problem. After doing so, start at the beginning of the book and read it straight through so that you have an understanding of the entire picture. As is often the case, your infertility may have more than one diagnosis.

Remember, reading this book is a first step toward taking control of your own reproductive destiny.

There is every chance that you will be successful. Most people who climb this ladder reach their goal. May you reach yours.

Stephen L. Corson, M.D.
Philadelphia, Pennsylvania

1

Fertility and Infertility: An Overview

In the United States, approximately 14 to 16 percent of all couples attempting to get pregnant have difficulty conceiving, and are defined by fertility therapists as being infertile. Sometimes their infertility is simply a matter of age; sometimes it is caused by medications, drugs, various diseases, or because of conditions present at birth. Nevertheless, about 65 percent of all couples who are seen for treatment of infertility will eventually be successful in having a baby. The goal in this book is to give you an understanding of the various therapies that are available, and to tell you not only what to expect from treatment but also how each procedure is designed to help. The material presented here will enable you to more comfortably and knowledgeably discuss your options with your doctor.

It is important in any discussion of infertility to distinguish sterility from infertility. *Sterility* means that conception is not possible. In a man this occurs when the testes no longer produce sperm. In that case, donor sperm can be used. In a woman sterility occurs when the ovaries no longer have eggs. However, with today's new technologies, a woman can accept donor eggs from another woman and carry a normal pregnancy.

As a couple, you may be infertile if the man has a low sperm count, or if the woman is approaching menopause, has infrequent

1

ovulation, or has partially blocked fallopian tubes. You can conceive without any special medical treatment, but your chances of doing so are not as good as normal functioning younger couples. Doctors often define infertility in two ways - *primary infertility* and *secondary infertility*. Primary infertility refers to failure of conception after one year of trying for couples who have never before been pregnant. Secondary infertility is defined as failure to conceive after 6 months for previously fertile couples. The two terms are not so easily defined when, for example, a person has been involved in a pregnancy in a previous relationship. The definitions of primary and secondary infertility assume that there is adequate sexual contact and exposure between partners. These terms refer to two separate issues, one having to do with sperm getting into the vagina, the other having to do with the frequency of intercourse.

Adequate Sexual Contact

To have *adequate sexual contact* semen must be deposited within the vagina during sexual intercourse. This may seem an obvious point, but there are many ways that people can express themselves sexually, and not all of them end with semen in the vagina. Here, of course, adequacy refers only to the initiation of pregnancy, and ignores all of the social and emotional factors associated with sexual function. Moreover, certain anatomical conditions and abnormalities may make it difficult to achieve adequate sexual contact. For example, some men are born with a congenital condition known as *hypospadias*. It is an uncommon condition in which the opening of the urethra, the channel through which both urine and semen pass, is located on the underside of the penis, instead of on the tip. Many men with this problem do not achieve adequate sexual contact because the semen is ejaculated outside of the vagina. Most cases of hypospadias can be corrected surgically. For those cases that cannot be cured, the man's semen can be collected by masturbation and placed into the vagina or cervix by a process known as artificial insemination-husband (AIH) as described in chapter 15, which can be a simple answer to this particular infertility problem. In fact, the couple chosen by gynaecologist J. Marian Sims to be the first Americans to have AIH was one in which the husband had hypospadias. By now, most people know that penis length has little, if anything, to do with fertility. But in couples where either partner is obese, sheer body bulk can interfere with adequate vaginal penetration if the penis is short. AIH also has been used successfully in these situations.

Frequency of Intercourse

The more sexual intercourse you have, the greater your chances of conceiving - up to a point. Most couples that I see report that they have intercourse two or three times a week, but frequency can vary considerably with each couple. Most of us know that sexual frequency for a man usually declines with age. However, the frequency of intercourse in the early stages of a marriage determines the pattern in later years. If a marriage starts out with infrequent sexual contact it is unlikely that it will increase as the relationship goes on. Although most men can regenerate normal sperm concentration within a day or two after ejaculation, sometimes because of advanced age, medication, or diseases a man may acquire in his lifetime this may not happen. If a man has a low concentration to begin with and replenishes this slowly, intercourse on a daily basis may, in fact, be counterproductive.

The stress and fatigue of one's job often interfere with tenderness and intimacy and may be a factor in reducing the frequency of intercourse. Fertility doctors frequently find that working couples tend to cluster their sexual activity around weekends and vacations. Even if intercourse is frequent during those short intervals, the chance of conception is less than if sexual contact occurred at more regular intervals. If sexual activity is low and infrequent, failure to conceive for a year or so may not be a matter of infertility at all, but may be related only to a lack of exposure.

The Age Factor in Infertility

When your doctor assesses your fertility or reproductive potential, he or she considers many factors. Most people who come for fertility consultation are in their early or mid-thirties. Nevertheless, in our practice we do see many women in their forties. This is not surprising because demographic studies tell us that people are marrying later in life, and are postponing having children. Indeed, the birth rate in women over thirty-five has increased almost 50 percent when compared with births in that age group ten years ago. This trend may make sense professionally, economically, and psychologically, but it also means that women are not having children when the chances of conceiving are best. The best biological time to bear children in a woman's life cycle, that is, the time when a woman is most likely to conceive and deliver successfully, is between the ages of eighteen and twenty-six. Studies have shown that starting in their early thirties, women become less fertile. This means that statistically it takes women in their thirties a little longer to become pregnant. Some lose this ability completely. Of course, at menopause, whatever the age, all women lose the ability to get pregnant. Spontaneous miscarriages also occur more often when women reach thirty-five. And with the passage of time, a woman may get diseases that decrease her ability to conceive, such as pelvic infection and endometriosis.

An interesting exception to these statistics is that women who are very fertile in their younger years tend to remain so even into their early forties. I used to have an arbitrary cutoff age of thirty-nine for operations to reverse tubal sterilization. Some women convinced me to perform this surgery when they were into their early forties saying that they had been quite fertile before. They were right! I can easily recall a score of women between the ages of forty and forty-two who conceived within months of tubal repair.

In general, age is usually kinder to men when it comes to fertility. Pablo Picasso became a father when he was sixty-seven years old. Charlie Chaplin was over seventy when his last child was born. There is a long list of men in their sixties and seventies who have initiated pregnancies. It is rare, however, for a woman over fifty to conceive. In fact, about 20 percent of women who have been pregnant previously can not conceive after thirty-five. Therefore, if you are over thirty-five, you should consider fertility therapy if you do not conceive after 6 months of trying whether you were once pregnant or not, particularly if your medical history is positive for anything that might impair fertility.

Miscarriages

Not all fertility problems have to do with conception. The word *fertility* in its fullest sense also means the ability to carry a pregnancy successfully to term, and to deliver a healthy newborn. Pregnancies end in miscarriages or spontaneous abortions more often than most people realize. Sometimes a woman who gets her period later than usual thinks of it as a "false alarm" when she actually has been pregnant and spontaneously aborted within the first few weeks. The new pregnancy tests are so sensitive that pregnancy can be detected even before a woman misses her period. Most doctors who order pregnancy tests 2 or 3 weeks after a missed period find that somewhere between 16 to 20 percent of normal patients miscarry. The latest studies indicate that in an average population up to 43 percent of all pregnancies, as defined by a very early positive test, are spontaneously lost. Most of these are lost before the menstrual period with no symptoms at all. Therefore, the true spontaneous abortion rate depends upon how early the pregnancy test is done. Most early pregnancy loss results from either poor implantation of the fertilized egg (called a blastocyst) in the wall of the uterus or faulty chromosomal division in the cells of the embryo. Tissue cultures taken from spontaneously aborted embryos show abnormal chromosome pattern in 50 to 60 percent of cases. For the most part, this is nonrepetitive, and does not indicate that either partner has a chromosomal defect that will cause other spontaneous abortions. If you have repeated spontaneous abortions, you should consult a fertility specialist to see what can be done to correct the problem.

What Are Your Chances?

Infertility for a period of time, as you know, does not rule out the possibility that you will eventually conceive. Figure 1.1 shows the fertility rate among all couples trying to get pregnant - not necessarily infertile couples. Studies show that 25 percent will achieve their goal in the first month. By 6 months 60 percent will. By the end of a year, 85 percent of couples will be pregnant. Of those remaining, about 1 in 10 will conceive during the next year without any therapy, and for several years afterward about 5 percent of the remainder will conceive without therapy. After this the rate of conception with no therapy is 2 percent each year.

As you read this book, remember that it is the couple, not the individual, that is the basic reproductive unit. Very often one partner's high fertility potential will offset a minor problem in the other. For instance, a very fertile woman with excellent cervical mucus that provides a good environment for sperm can compensate for a man

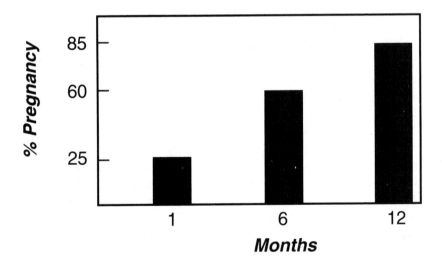

FIGURE 1.1   Cumulative pregnancy rate in an unselected population.

with lower than average sperm motion (motility). One interesting study showed that 10 percent of men who were screened before having a vasectomy sterilization procedure, and who claimed to have no problem in fathering children, had a semen analysis considered to be poor. Another 10 percent had less than ideal semen. The conclusion here was that the women they impregnated were fertile enough to override reduced seminal function.

Finding the Right Doctor

Because every couple is unique, no simple, standard, step-by-step approach to the problem of infertility exists. There are dozens of esoteric tests at your doctor's disposal, and most of them are expensive and often uncomfortable. Learning that you are infertile may be psychologically threatening. Therefore, it is important to find a good therapist who has the experience, intuition, and sensitivity to get to the heart of the problem without the burden of unnecessary tests. You want a physician who will weigh the selection of tests against the cost in discomfort, irritation, and dollars. Remember that there is no one correct approach to fertility evaluation and treatment. You want a physician who is well trained and experienced. Any competent physician should not mind if you seek a second opinion, if for no other reason than to be reassured that the testing procedures or therapies he or she recommended are reasonable. At the same time, you should be patient about therapy and not expect a medication or procedure to necessarily bring about pregnancy in the next month.

Coping with the Psychological Pressures of Infertility Treatment

We live in a society of instant gratification; if we want something, we pull out our credit cards. We are goal-oriented and want results - now. It's a world where contraception is easy to use and efficient. People come to expect that they will get pregnant just as easily as they were able to keep from getting pregnant. It comes as a painful surprise for many to learn that getting pregnant is not easy. This disappointment leads to anxiety and makes the pursuit of pregnancy an unnecessarily unpleasant experience. There is no doubt that infertility takes its toll on the psyche, but couples should realize that most likely they will eventually get pregnant. As a couple pursues pregnancy, it is important for them to pace themselves. They should try not to spend too much emotion on any one loss or misfire. There will be disappointment before joy and lots of visits to the doctor's office, but hopefully, in the end, the temperature charts and the many diagnostic tests and procedures will have been worthwhile.

2

Female Reproduction: An Anatomy Lesson

Most people reading this book no longer view conception as a simple union of sperm and egg; they are aware that conception is a complicated biological process. You can look at the intricate elements of female reproduction from many perspectives. I like to begin with hormones because these substances exert great influence over how well, or how poorly, the reproductive systems of both women and men function. In this chapter you will learn the anatomy of the female reproductive system and how each part of that anatomy functions to achieve conception. We'll look at the major female reproductive organs, and consider some typical disorders that can prevent conception.

Hormones: Important Regulators

Hormones are chemicals that regulate the body's internal activities. There are many different hormones, each controlling one or several specific activities. The hormone insulin, for example, helps control the rate at which the body burns sugar for fuel. Growth hormone controls the growth of body tissues, and thyroid hormones are generally responsible for your overall metabolic health. A hormone is released (secreted) by a gland and carried by the bloodstream to the appropriate target cells it is designed to influence. The target cells are covered with *receptors* (binding sites), which have a specific surface structure designed to capture that specific hormone from the bloodstream and bind it to the receptor. A hormone will attach only to a receptor that has exactly the right chemical and physical structure. (The lock and key analogy shown in figure 2.1 serves to illustrate this point). When doctors treat certain conditions with synthetic hormones and medications, we apply this same principle: The synthetic drugs compete with the natural hormones for these binding sites in order to treat disease or to readjust the body's response to excessive hormonal stimulation. Once the hormone is bound to the cell, it enters the cell and exerts its designed action from within, or, in some cases, causes the cell to release other chemicals as a response to the binding.

The two principle female sex hormones, estrogen and progesterone, are secreted by the ovaries. *Estrogen* is a blanket term for many similar hormones. Estradiol is the one most important to fertility. Estrogens, in general, produce all those obvious physical characteristics that distinguish a woman from a man, such as breast

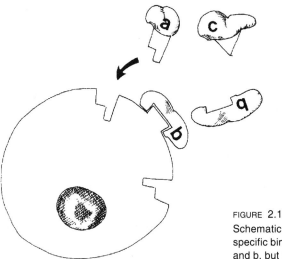

FIGURE 2.1
Schematic drawing of a cell having specific binding sites for hormones a and b, but not c.

development or the shape of the hips and thighs. *Progesterone* prepares the uterus to accept a fertilized egg and acts to relax the uterus so that it can grow during pregnancy. The remaining actions of estrogen, progesterone, and other hormones will be described where appropriate.

The Female Reproductive System
The Vulva

The major parts of the female reproductive system are illustrated in figures 2.2 and 2.3. The external genitals include the outer lips (*labia majora*), the inner lips (*labia minora*), and the *clitoris*, called the *vulva* collectively. The hairy outer lips contain fatty tissue which acts as a cushion. The two inner lips meet in front of the *urethra* (the channel for urine) where they cover part of the clitoris. During sexual arousal the clitoris becomes engorged with blood and erects, like a man's penis. Stimulation of the clitoris produces orgasm. You may have heard that the rhythmic contractions of pelvic muscles during orgasm help to propel the sperm upward toward the uterus. However, there is no scientific proof that orgasm has any positive effect on reproduction.

The Vagina

The vulva opens into the *vagina*, a muscular tube through which menstrual flow (*menses*) passes down from the uterus and through which sperm migrate upward. A membrane called the *hymen* lies across the vaginal opening behind the vulva. The hymen usually has more than one opening that allows menstrual blood to pass. People have traditionally regarded the unpenetrated hymen as the only real sign of virginity. But this idea is medically incorrect. Strenuous physical activity or early use of tampons can enlarge the opening of the hymen without sexual intercourse. Near the bottom of the vaginal canal just behind the opening of the vulva are two glands called Bartholin's glands, which secrete mucus that lubricates the vagina before and after intercourse.

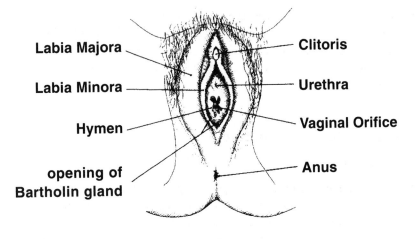

FIGURE 2.2 External female genital anatomy.

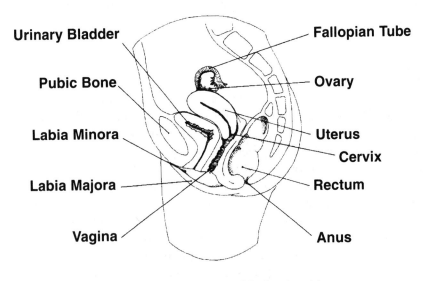

FIGURE 2.3 Cross section of the female pelvis.

PHEROMONES

The cells in the vaginal lining contain large amounts of starch called glycogen. Bacteria that are normally present in a healthy vagina ferment the glycogen, causing the vagina to become acidic. This fermentation process may also be important for the production of chemicals known as *pheromones*. These are organic acids that have a distinct pungent odor and appear in the highest concentrations around the time of ovulation.

Pheromones play an important role in reproduction in animals. In monkeys, for example, the pheromone odor identifies to the male those females who are fertile. Experiments have shown that if castrated male monkeys are smeared with vaginal secretions from female monkeys, they attract other males. Pheromones also seem to explain why women living together tend to develop synchronized menstrual cycles as a consequence of the cycling centers in the hypothalamus becoming "in phase." This may be a very primitive way of regulating reproduction in a tribal society. It is thought that chemical signals, in this case the pungent odor of the pheromones, are transmitted through olfactory nerves to the brain. A message is then sent to the hypothalamus and pituitary in the brain which regulate the ovary. If this is true, then the sense of smell may play some role in human reproduction.

VAGINAL HEALTH

Various bacterial infections can alter the normal acidity of the vaginal lining. So too can douches, artificial lubricants and certain medications, none of which should be used without good reason. Under normal conditions many different kinds of bacteria are found in the vagina. Infection is said to occur if these bacteria overgrow, or if new hostile bacteria invade the tissue. Infections require treatment not only of themselves, but also because certain bacteria and other organisms can kill or immobilize sperm. The organism responsible often can be specifically identified in the laboratory from a sample of vaginal secretions. Your doctor can then prescribe the appropriate antibiotic to treat the infection. Some couples routinely use artificial lubricants during sexual intercourse, but most women aged fifteen to forty-five don't need these because they self-lubricate sufficiently during arousal. Most fertility therapists discourage the use of artificial lubricants, especially around the time of ovulation, because they may act as impediments against sperm. You certainly don't want to use petroleum-based jellies (Vaseline, for example) in the vagina because not only may they irritate the vaginal lining, they may also have an adverse effect on sperm. Douching with bicarbonate of soda has frequently been prescribed to offset excess vaginal acidity. Since water and mucus do not mix, the cervical mucus is unaffected by this, and most fertility therapists believe that vaginal douching as a fertility aid has little to offer.

The Cervix

THE ROLE OF CERVICAL MUCUS

The cervix telescopes into the top of the vagina. It contains a channel leading to the interior of the uterus. The cervix normally has alkaline mucus that protects the sperm from the acidity of vaginal secretions. Sperm can survive in this mucus for as long as three days. The mucus is produced in small sacs, or *crypts*, which line the walls of the cervix (figure 2.4). These crypts serve as reservoirs for sperm. Hours after intercourse (coitus), the crypts continue to release the sperm upward into the uterine cavity.

Both the quantity and reproductive quality of the cervical mucus change during the menstrual cycle. Early in the cycle just after menstruation, there is a relatively small amount of rather thick mucus, so thick that it acts as a barrier to sperm. But as a woman approaches ovulation, the amount of estrogen in her body steadily increases. Estrogen causes the cervix to produce greater amounts of mucus which becomes less thick, more watery, and has a higher salt content. This thinner mucus is very elastic, and a sample of it can sometimes be stretched to about seven inches without breaking. This elastic quality is known by the German word *spinnbarkheit*. Around the time of ovulation, when mucus has just the right proportion of water and salt, its molecules line up in such a way as to form channels, known as *micelles*, through which sperm can easily pass

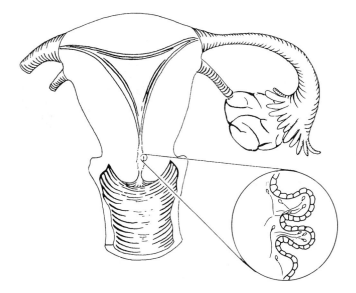

FIGURE 2.4   Cervical crypts that secrete mucus and serve as reservoirs for sperm.

(figure 2.5). After ovulation, rising levels of progesterone cause the mucus to thicken again, and the amount of mucus present in the cervix decreases. Thus, to determine whether mucus is of good reproductive quality, the physician must take a sample from the cervix near the time of ovulation. Many women, in fact, can predict impending ovulation just by the character of their mucus discharge.

DEALING WITH CERVICAL INFECTIONS

Some women do not produce cervical mucus of sufficient quantity or quality for conception to occur easily. This may be related to infection of the crypts that produce the mucus. Often this is associated with a continuous discharge - *cervicitis*. Most cervical infections can be treated with antibiotics. Those that are resistant can be routed with a freezing technique known as *cryocautery*, which does not cause scarring or other permanent damage to the cervix. Severe cases can be treated with a laser or electric loop. Unfortunately, a common

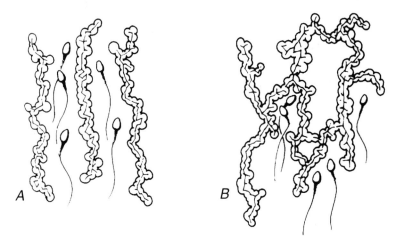

FIGURE 2.5   Microscopic appearance of protein strands in cervical mucus. (A) Appearance at the time of ovulation with channels favoring efficient sperm penetration and migration upward, (B) Unfavorable maze-like configuration found at other times during the menstrual cycle.

reason for poor cervical mucus is *iatrogenic*, that is, caused by physicians. Some gynecologists indiscriminately cauterize or biopsy the cervix causing damage. Cervical cautery with a hot instrument should not be used casually. When cervical biopsies are necessary, the smallest biopsy consistent with adequate diagnosis and proper treatment should be taken. A cervical *eversion* is fairly common in women who use oral contraceptives and in those who have recently given birth. This is an outturning of the cervical lining into the top of the vagina, resembling the rolling up of a cuff on a pair of jeans. Doctors frequently mistake the eversion for an *erosion* or cervical ulcer. They then "treat" the cervix by hot cauterization with an instrument similar to a soldering gun, or with an electric loop. These procedures may permanently destroy the cells that produce the mucus.

In perhaps 3 percent of infertile women, the mucus may actually act as a contraceptive because it contains sperm-specific antibodies. These antibodies can cause the sperm to stick together (*agglutinate*) and lose motility. Specific treatment for this and other cervical disorders will be discussed in chapter 8.

The Uterus

Above the cervix is the body of the *uterus*. This hollow muscle normally weighs about 2 ounces. But during pregnancy the uterus undergoes amazing growth and develops a special arrangement of blood vessels that allows nutrients to pass through the placenta to the fetus without mixing the blood of the mother and the fetus. During labor, the full muscle power of the uterus is seen when it pushes the baby into the birth canal.

UTERINE STRUCTURAL ABNORMALITIES

In the developing fetus, the uterus begins formation as two rudimentary pouches in the pelvis. These segments gradually migrate toward each other and begin to fuse together. The common wall between them disintegrates to form a single cavity, as shown in figure 2.6. Some women are born with a congenital condition that makes them sterile, called *Rokitansky syndrome*, in which the pouches have neither joined nor fully developed. Women who have this syndrome are born without a vagina. A functioning vagina can be created to allow for sexual intercourse, but no surgeon can create a uterus for these women. Technology does exist, though, to allow a woman with this condition to have the eggs taken from her ovaries so that they may be fertilized and carried by another woman. Although it is technically possible to transplant a uterus, just as the heart, liver, lungs, and kidneys can be transplanted, the risk to the patient and the need to give powerful immunosuppressive agents to avoid rejection of the implant make this operation completely impractical.

Two lesser disorders involving the migration of the rudimentary portions of the uterus are the *bicornuate uterus* and the more commonly seen *septate uterus*, both illustrated in figure 2.6. In both types, there are two cavities that usually are joined near the cervix instead of one. Approximately 2 percent of all women will have a two-chambered uterus. This does not necessarily mean that they will have difficulty carrying a pregnancy. And certainly this has very little to do with their ability to conceive. In fact, the vast majority of these women will have no reproductive problems at all. We don't

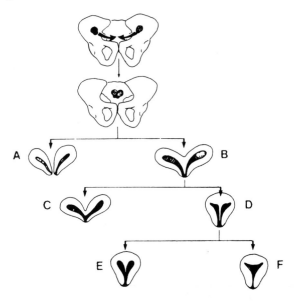

FIGURE 2.6   Steps in formation of the embryonic uterus. Top, migration of each half from a lateral position to the midline. (A) Two separate uteri and cervices as a result of failure to fuse, (B) Normal fusion beginning from bottom to top, (C) Bicornuate uterus from partial failure of fusion, (D) Proper complete fusion, (E) Septate uterus resulting from persistence of septum, (F) Normal uterus.

know why some of these women have difficulty in carrying and others suffer repeated pregnancy loss. Therefore, the decision for surgical repair is made primarily on the reproductive history of the woman rather than the appearance of the uterus.

A woman with a bicornuate uterus frequently has a cervix that cannot withstand the pressure of the enlarging uterus and begins to prematurely dilate, or expand. Once detected, however, a simple treatment with *cervical cerclage*, or banding, during pregnancy usually is sufficient to result in a healthy newborn. This is done by putting a thick suture around the cervix that looks like a purse string when tied. If, on the other hand, pregnancies are repeatedly lost at an earlier stage, surgical correction of the defect with formation of one cavity is necessary.

For the patient with a *septate uterus*, the two rudimentary portions of the uterus migrate and fuse normally, but the common wall between them fails to breakdown. Pregnancy wastage (a term that covers losses ranging from early spontaneous abortion through severe and fatal premature birth) tends to occur earlier in the septate uterus than in the bicornuate uterus. This is especially true if the fertilized egg implants on the common wall, or septum, which has a poor blood supply. Surgical repair of this condition is highly successful and can often be accomplished on an outpatient basis. Patients with a bicornuate uterus are hospitalized because the procedure requires more extensive surgery.

DES SYNDROME

Exposure of the fetus to large doses of synthetic estrogens, as well as those made naturally in the body, may lead to malformations of the vagina, cervix, uterus, and fallopian tubes. It should also be noted that these same malformations can happen even in cases where the mother took no such drugs. The well-publicized diethylstilbestrol (DES) syndrome is not only caused by DES but also by other synthetic estrogens that used to be administered early in pregnancy in the belief that they helped in high-risk pregnancies, particularly as a treatment for recurrent abortion. Women whose mothers used DES may have small, irregular, and often T-shaped uterine cavities. Their cervical canals are disproportionately long compared with the uterine cavity, and they often require cerclage to bring a pregnancy near term. Women with gross DES cervical abnormalities have a threefold increase of pregnancy loss over other women. Because of tubal changes that are also related to DES, the risk of ectopic pregnancy may be as high as 10 percent. DES daughters may have greater difficulty conceiving than do their peers. Doctors believe that one possible reason for this is that the cervical abnormalities impede sperm migration through the cervix.

THE ENDOMETRIUM

The lining of the uterine cavity is called the *endometrium*. After conception the fertilized egg (blastocyst) implants itself in the endometrium where there are many blood vessels and glands to supply nourishment.

At the beginning of the menstrual cycle the endometrium is rather thin and the blood supply not plentiful. As the patient's menstrual cycle continues, rising levels of estrogen made by the ovary cause the endometrium to become thick and lush, a process called *proliferation*. During this phase, the blood vessels increase in size and number and the glands develop. When progesterone levels that are manufactured by the ovaries rise after ovulation, about mid-cycle, the glands begin to secrete their nutrients. If pregnancy does not occur, progesterone production ceases. The thickened endometrium cannot sustain itself without progesterone stimulation and it begins to slough off, causing a woman's monthly menstrual flow. The endometrium then returns to its previous basal state to begin the cycle again under the direct influence of the ovary. The uterus is quite capable of responding normally until a woman is well into her sixties. The adverse effect of age on reproduction is ovarian, not uterine.

MENSTRUATION WITHOUT OVULATION
It is important to mention that the presence of a menstrual flow does not necessarily mean that ovulation has occurred. Lacking progesterone, the estrogen-primed endometrium will shed itself at irregular intervals, which may be longer or shorter than the usual normal menstrual cycle associated with ovulation. If a woman has bloating just before her period (usually an effect of progesterone), the odds are that she has ovulated. But, because some women who have this symptom do not ovulate, and because most women who regularly ovulate do not have the symptom, its usefulness as a reliable indicator of ovulation is limited.

The endometrium is subject to infection and inflammation (*endometritis*), which, if severe enough, can result in scarring to the point that the patient has *amenorrhea* (no monthly period). Endometritis can result from infections (usually sexually transmitted ones), intrauterine devices, or following abortion or delivery. I have also seen endometritis when none of these causes could be found.

The doctor can diagnose this condition by looking into the uterine cavity through a telescope-like instrument, called a hysteroscope, that is placed through the cervix. Many doctors rely on a simple biopsy to make the diagnosis. Treatment with oral antibiotics for 3 or 4 weeks is highly successful.

The endometrium may fail to develop properly if it doesn't receive enough hormonal stimulation from the ovaries. When this occurs after ovulation, doctors call this *inadequate corpus luteum* or luteal phase deficiency. This means that not enough progesterone is being produced or that the endometrium is not capable of responding to normal amounts of progesterone. When endometrial tissue is found in other parts of the body, doctors call it *endometriosis*. The condition may be painful, or lead to infertility, or both. While endometritis is an uncommon cause of infertility, *endometriosis*, which sounds similar but is quite different, is found in 30 to 40 percent of the women seen for infertility. (For details see chapter10).

The Fallopian Tubes

Branching out from the top of the uterus are two oviducts, or *fallopian tubes*. (See figures 2.7 and 2.8 for a cross-section of the fallopian tube). The portion closest to the uterus is called the *isthmus*. It has a narrow canal, called a *lumen*, that is just wide enough for a fertilized egg to pass through to the uterus. Closer to the ovary, the tube and its lumen begin to widen. The wider part is called the *ampulla*.

Inside each fallopian tube is a delicate lining of folded tissue called the *endosalpinx*. Special cells in this lining secrete a fluid that both nourishes and helps to transport sperm and eggs. The fluid also "activates" sperm, making them capable of fertilization in a process called *capacitation*. The endosalpinx also contains numerous special cells that grow thin, hairlike filaments that protrude into the lumen. These filaments, called *cilia*, beat in a coordinated wave toward the uterus. This action, coupled with the contraction of muscles in the tube, move the egg toward the uterus. Remember, though, that sperm swim against this gradient in order to get upstream. The distance is only about 6 inches, but it's like a swimmer trying to swim the English channel against the tide!

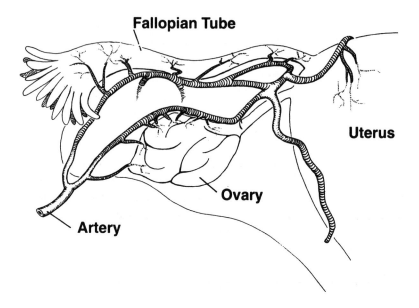

Fallopian Tube

Uterus

Ovary

Artery

FIGURE 2.7   The fallopian tube, its blood supply, and its relationship to uterus and ovary.

The funnel-shaped opening of the ampulla has tentacle-like projections called *fimbria*. These sweep over the surface of the ovary in movements that quicken at the time of ovulation. The job of the fimbria is to pick up an egg as it emerges from the ovary. Since the egg is covered with a sticky coating, this pickup mechanism is usually more efficient than you might think. However, tubal infections, whether caused by sexually transmitted disease or not, can damage the fimbria, which are very delicate.

TUBAL INFECTIONS
Tubal infections may reduce fertility in a number of ways. They can destroy the cells that secrete the fluid necessary for transport and nourishment. Moreover, cells that contain cilia that are damaged

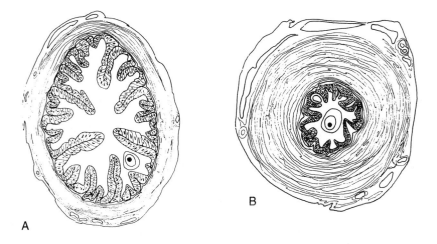

FIGURE 2.8   Cross-section of a fallopian tube. (A) An egg in the ampulla which has a large, multifolded lumen, (B) The narrower isthmic portion of the tube.

by infection regenerate poorly, if at all. This can make it impossible for the egg to move because the egg relies on the cilia to transport it through the tube. This can occur even if the tube is open (patent). Infections can leave bands of scar tissue, called adhesions, in and around the end of the fallopian tube, and these can interfere with the capturing of an egg from the ovary. If the fertilized egg is caught in the tube it could lead to a tubal or ectopic pregnancy. The first bout of tubal infection that is severe enough to cause fever and pain will leave about 15 percent of victims with closed tubes, and that figure doubles with each additional episode despite vigorous intravenous antibiotic treatment.

It is important to remember that the fallopian tube is much more than a tunnel for sperm and eggs. It must be able to move eggs and to secrete fluid. We know that the isthmus is not really necessary for reproduction. The entire section can be removed, as is often done in sterilization-reversal operations, without affecting fertility. But loss of more than 50 percent of the ampulla results in severe infertility in most cases. Unfortunately, surgical attempts to replace damaged fallopian tubes with a tube made from the bladder, bowel, or synthetic materials have not been successful.

The Ovaries

The female gonads, or *ovaries*, are located apart from the fallopian tubes, just within reach of the sweeping fimbria. These, of course, contain the eggs, known as *gametes*. Each egg, or *ovum*, is encased within its own sac, called a *follicle*. Women are born with a finite number of eggs, about 400,000. This supply diminishes naturally over time, and this reduction actually begins before birth. Most women exhaust their supply of eggs by the time they reach their late forties or early fifties, and when there are no more eggs in the ovary, menstruation ceases and menopause begins. The eggs are used up whether you fertilize them or not. The use of birth-control pills neither stores the eggs nor accelerates the rate of loss.

OVULATION

Ovulation is the release of a mature egg from the ovary. To understand ovulation, you need to know about two hormones, both of which are produced by the pituitary gland: *follicle stimulating hormone* (FSH), and *luteinizing hormone* (LH). These hormones are called *gonadotropins*, a word that means "gonad stimulators." You may find it helpful to refer to figures 2.9 and 2.10.

Before puberty, a girl's reproductive organs lie dormant, except for a brief period of activity shortly after birth. This is due to stimulation by hormones that have passed across the placenta from the mother to the fetus. Throughout childhood, a region within the *hypothalamus* (a part of the brain) is slowly maturing. When maturation is complete, usually between the ages of nine and thirteen, the hypothalamus secretes a hormone called *gonadotropin releasing hormone* (GnRH), which acts on the nearby pituitary gland. In response to GnRH, the pituitary gland begins to produce and store FSH which it releases in slowly increasing amounts. FSH stimulates

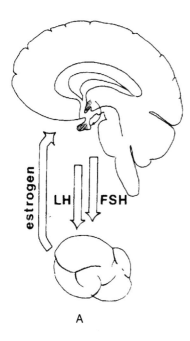

A

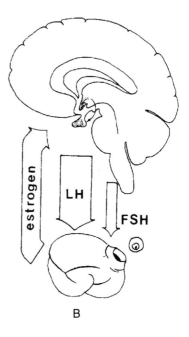

B

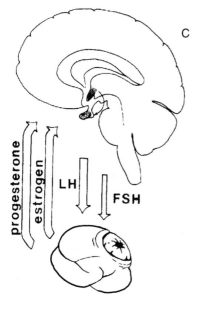

C

FIGURE 2.9 Cyclical hormone events in a menstrual cycle. Brain and pituitary above, ovary below. (A) Early in the follicular phase, estrogen secretion begins, (B) Increasing estrogen levels bring about an LH surge, causing ovulation, (C) Progesterone production inhibits LH release. If pregnancy does not occur, the corpus luteum disintegrates, progesterone production ceases, menses follows and the cycle starts anew.

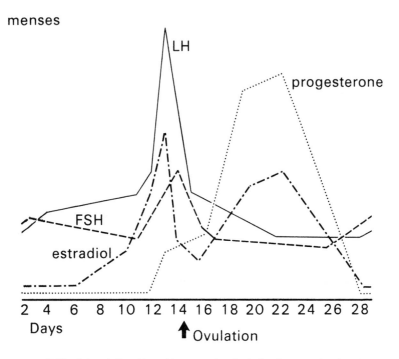

menses

LH

progesterone

FSH

estradiol

2 4 6 8 10 12 14 16 18 20 22 24 26 28
Days   ↑ Ovulation

FIGURE 2.10   Interrelationships of hormone levels during the menstrual cycle.

the ovaries and causes follicles to develop. We do not exactly know why, but usually only one follicle fully develops and forms. Within the fluid surrounding the egg, a hormone called *inhibin* is made which then feeds back to the pituitary to say, "I have had enough stimulation for now," and FSH stimulation lessens. This "feedback" mechanism between the secreting organ and its hormonal target organs is common in the body. In many ways it is similar to the relationship between your home heating-cooling unit and the thermostat on the wall that regulates the system.

A young woman's first menses is called *menarche*. The first few cycles are usually anovulatory (without ovulation) because the reproductive system's hormonal release has not been synchronized to bring about ovulation. Soon however, the system gets itself into sync, and the ovary, stimulated by FSH, begins to produce steadily increasing amounts of estrogen. If the estrogen levels rise at the proper rate, the pituitary gland then releases a sudden surge of LH, which accelerates development of the follicle, and also triggers a change of metabolism within the follicle so that estrogen production starts to fall and progesterone production starts to increase. As the follicle approaches the surface of the ovary, the overlying cells thin out and disperse; the follicle ruptures releasing its fluid content and ovum to be picked up by the waiting fimbria. Occasionally two or more eggs will develop to maturity, giving rise to multiple births. Fertility drugs, as we shall see later, are used to fool the body and to stimulate the ovaries in such a way as to produce more than one mature egg.

CORPUS LUTEUM: THE PROGESTERONE FACTORY

The ruptured follicle on the surface of the ovary turns yellow as a consequence of the naturally occurring steroids which are being used in what has become a metabolic factory to make progesterone. That structure then becomes a functioning gland called the *corpus luteum*, which literally translated means "yellow body". The increasing amounts of progesterone help prepare the endometrium for implantation of the blastocyst. If conception occurs the developing cells surrounding the fetus will secrete a special hormone that will keep the corpus luteum active in making progesterone, thus preserving the endometrium. This new special hormone is *human chorionic gonadotropin* (hCG), the detection of which is used as the basis for the pregnancy test. If conception, however, does not occur, the corpus luteum ceases production in about 14 days. Progesterone levels fall, and the uterus begins to break down its rich lining and sloughs it off, causing a menstrual flow.

After menarche, the menstrual cycle is hormonally controlled by the "feedback" mechanism mentioned earlier. It has recently been shown that DES patients are more likely than other women to have feedback problems. I don't know if this is due to an effect on the ovaries or to the central nervous system control centers. The elapsed time from the start of the menstrual cycle to the occurrence of ovulation may differ within the same woman from cycle to cycle. For example, a woman may ovulate on day 12 of her cycle in one month, and day 16 in the next month. This amount of variation is normal.

HOW TO DETERMINE IF YOU ARE OVULATING

An easy and inexpensive way to determine when ovulation has occurred is to chart *basal body temperature* (BBT) each morning when you wake up. This is a time-honored method of evaluating ovulation, but suffers from the fact that it tells when ovulation **has** occurred, but cannot predict it. This procedure, which is discussed in chapter 5, works because progesterone has the effect of increasing the basal body temperature. The rise in temperature depends upon the rate of increase in progesterone secretion from the ovary as well as the sensitivity of the body's thermostat. Therefore, there are a number of normal but different patterns of temperature increase. Because this thermostat is easily affected by activities, such as getting out of bed and eating, the temperature must be taken immediately upon awakening. Women who work at night will have no problem in keeping the BBT if they get up at the same time each day. If you have irregular work hours, you may find the method unreliable. However, as figure 2.11 shows, although the time between menstruation and ovulation may vary, the progesterone secretion phase of the cycle usually lasts about 14 days. New methods of urinary testing with kits available over the counter in a drugstore are much more accurate in *predicting* ovulation than the temperature charts. If you look at figure 2.10 again, you'll see that LH rises abruptly just prior to ovulation. The beginning of the rise is usually between 24 to 32 hours before natural ovulation. The urinary test kits are set to identify the beginning of this surge to allow for an accurate prediction of impending ovulation. The kits have a simple-to-read color end point, which makes self-testing easy and accurate. This is certainly a helpful technique for couples having insemination therapy, but is also useful for timing intercourse and for making sure that cervical mucus testing is done at the proper time. Serially performed ultrasonic examinations are accurate, but they are not as

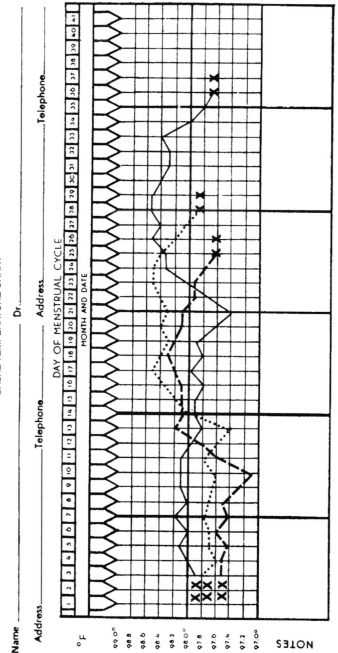

FIGURE 2.11   Basal body temperature (BBT) charts showing three normal patterns above and an anovulatory cycle below. Note that elapsed time between ovulation and the next menses averages 14 days regardless of when ovulation occurs in the cycle.

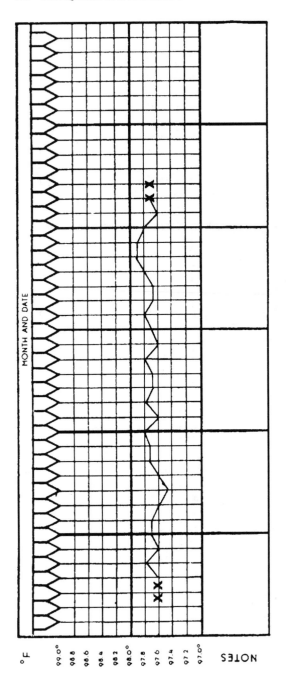

FIGURE 2.12   A BBT chart showing lack of elevation, and hence, indicative of anovulation.

cost effective. Ultrasound has shown us that *mittelschmerz* (middle-pain, in German) may occur 24 hours before, during, or after actual ovulation, and often not on the side where the patient has pain. Ultrasonic studies also have demonstrated that some women seem to ovulate on one side most of the time and that ovulation need not alternate from side to side each month.

By comparison, figure 2.12 shows a flat, or monophasic, pattern, suggestive of anovulation.

3

Male Reproduction: More Anatomy

A man's reproductive mechanism is less complex than a woman's. In fact, sperm production and delivery seem simple compared with the many physiological events that must occur during the female cycle. Since there is less separation of sexual and reproductive function in a man's anatomy than in a woman's, male infertility and sexual dysfunction often are linked. Nevertheless, the apparent simplicity of male reproduction can be deceptive. Male infertility is often *idiopathic* (without known cause). Our ability to diagnose and to treat male infertility has lagged behind the advances in treating female infertility

The Male Reproductive System

A man has most of his reproductive organs outside the abdomen (figure 3.1 illustrates the major parts of the reproductive system). Throughout the entire length of the penis is the *urethra*, an internal canal that carries both sperm and urine from the body. The penis also contains a mass of spongy erectile tissue. When the arteries that supply this tissue with blood open, and the veins become closed, the penis expands to erection. Man's principle reproductive organs are the two *testes*, or testicles. These produce both sperm and the

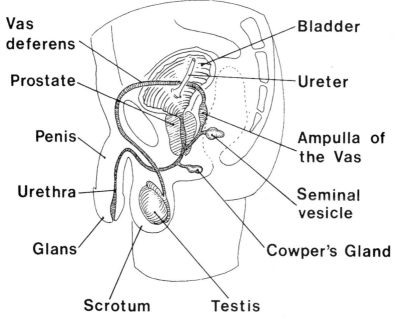

FIGURE 3.1 Male reproductive anatomy.

male sex hormones, the most important of which is *testosterone*. At puberty, testosterone causes changes in a boy's voice, facial hair, body build, and genital structure. If an otherwise healthy man loses one testicle through injury or surgery, there usually is no decrease in fertility, even if there is a decrease in the total number of sperm present in the semen released at orgasm (*ejaculate*). The ability of the sperm to move properly, and the ratio of normal to abnormal sperm, are far more important indications of fertility. We'll go into the qualities of sperm and their importance in chapter 5.

The Testes and Heat

The testes are heat sensitive and are regulated to remain about 4° F cooler than the normal body temperature of 98.6° F. Too much heat can temporarily or permanently damage the structures that produce sperm. The fleshy sac that contains the testes, called the *scrotum*, helps to maintain the proper temperature. When exposed to a warm environment, the scrotum holding the testes sags farther away from the body. The increased surface area created by the relaxed scrotum moves the testes farther from the body and serves to disperse the excess heat. The scrotum contracts when cold, pulling the testes closer to the body for increased warmth. The blood vessels that supply the testes also help regulate temperature by widening or narrowing as needed. Some children are born with testes that have not descended from the pelvis into the scrotal sac. An undescended testicle must be corrected early in childhood to prevent irreparable heat-induced damage. A testicle may not descend because it is already abnormal. Even early surgical intervention may not help in this circumstance. Some occupations expose men to excessively high scrotal temperatures. Many athletes, for example, wear unventilated protective cups and spend hours in hot whirlpool baths. Long-distance truck drivers must sit for hours on unventilated seats. These occupational factors can lead to infertility. More will be said about these hazards in chapter 12.

Production and Transportation of Sperm

Sperm are produced within the narrow, tightly coiled tubes called *seminiferous tubules*. A normal man under the age of forty produces about 125 million sperm a day (figure 3.2 shows the structure of a testicle and its ductal system). The walls of the tubules (there are many) contain cells known as stem cells. When a stem cell divides, one of the two new cells remains in the tubule wall to divide again at some point in the future. The other new cell eventually becomes a *spermatozoan* (the technical name for a sperm). It enters the passageway of the tubule and attaches to one of the many *Sertoli cells* (figure 3.3), which provide nourishment for the immature sperm. After a brief time in contact with the Sertoli cell, the sperm moves through the tubule to the *rete testis*, which serves as a collection point for sperm from the hundreds of tubules. The rete testis is linked to the *epididymis* by ducts.

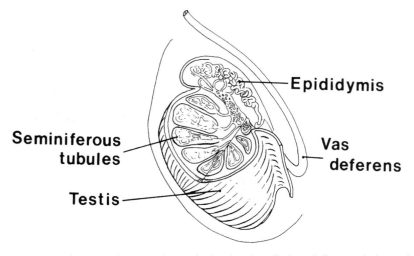

FIGURE 3.2 Cross section through a testis showing the coiled seminiferous tubules and the ductal system transporting sperm away from the testis.

Because sperm in the rete testis are still not yet mature enough to move properly on their own, they are pushed through the ducts by muscles in the ductal walls. But pregnancies have occurred when sperm, collected surgically from the rete, have been used during *in vitro* fertilization. It is within the epididymis that the sperm finally mature. The tightly coiled epididymis would measure about 20 feet if it were stretched out. Sperm spend almost 2 weeks moving through the epididymis helped along by muscles in the epididymal walls.

From the epididymis, the mature sperm move to the *vas deferens*. This mostly straight tube, about 14 inches long, rises out of the scrotum and connects with the *seminal vesicle* in the pelvis. The seminal vesicle does not store sperm as was previously thought. Its main purpose is to supply, along with the prostate gland, an alkaline fluid (semen) which surrounds the sperm. Sperm production takes about 72 days from the time primitive sperm leave the tubule wall to the time they arrive, fully matured, for storage in the vas. This is why after treatment, there is a delay in seminal improvement as seen in the semen analysis. Often this lag can last for 3 months or more following medical or surgical forms of therapy.

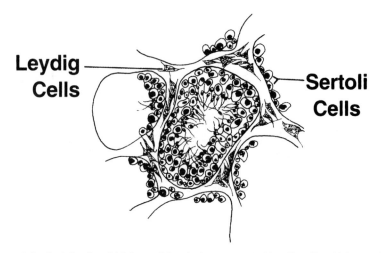

FIGURE 3.3 Sertoli cells, which "nurse" developing sperm, and Leydig cells, which secrete testosterone.

The vas is the structure that is cut and sealed during *vasectomy*, the male sterilization procedure. Closure of either the epididymis or the vas results in *azoospermia*, or lack of sperm in the ejaculate. Some men are born with blockage in the vas, usually on both sides. DES has been implicated as a cause of congenital blockage of the seminal ducts in some men who were exposed to this drug in utero. Blockages can also result from inflammation following infection or the genito-urinary tract. As will be discussed in chapter 5, to determine what has caused azoospermia, the semen can be tested for sugar (fructose test). If fructose is not present, ductal obstruction is the problem; if fructose is found the ducts are open and the conclusion is that sperm are not being produced.

The seminal vesicle and the *prostate gland* supply most of the seminal fluid, which is highly alkaline. The alkalinity of this fluid enhances sperm motility and also serves as a source of nutrition. Because the prostate gland is vulnerable to infections, it is a common culprit in mild infertility. The actual amount of sperm (germ cells or gametes) in the ejaculate is less than one tenth of the total volume.

Unlike a woman, who is born with a fixed number of eggs, a man produces billions of new sperm during his lifetime. Although men experience no cyclical hormonal-related events such as ovulation, they do have a hormone-activated control cycle which involves FSH and LH (see figure 3.4). In men, FSH stimulates the tubules to produce sperm. The Sertoli cells, in addition to serving as nutritional sources for the developing sperm, also produce a hormone called *inhibin* that shuts down FSH production. This is similar to the

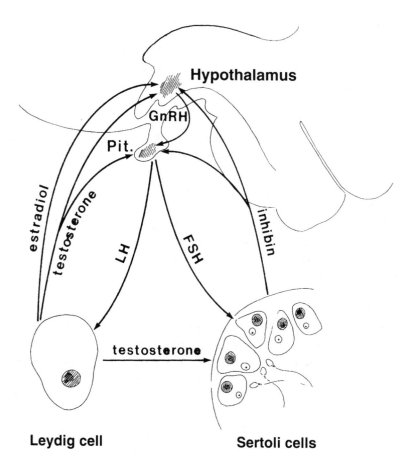

FIGURE 3.4 The male reproductive hormonal control system.

feedback mechanism in women. When more sperm are required, inhibin production drops, which then causes FSH levels to rise, resulting in the formation of more sperm.

LH stimulates the *Leydig cells* (figure 3.4) in the testes to produce testosterone. When the level of testosterone rises, the level of LH drops. When LH drops, so does testosterone, which in turn causes LH to again rise. In this way proper testosterone levels are maintained.

Sperm Delivery: Intercourse and Ejaculation

What effect does frequent coitus have on male infertility? The answer is that it increases the chances for conception - up to a point. A problem can arise if coitus is so frequent that a sufficient number of sperm cannot be replenished. Most young men can replenish their sperm count in 24 hours or less. Some men with low fertility, however, may take 3 or 4 days to do this. In the normal male approximately 100 to 125 million sperm are produced daily. Many sperm are needed to cause conception although only one sperm normally penetrates an egg. For every 14 million sperm ejaculated into the vagina, only 1 to 10 will reach the end of a fallopian tube! It's a mistake to think that by abstaining for long periods of time from coitus, men with low sperm counts can build up their counts and thus become more fertile. The buildup is counterproductive because sperm motility, which is even more vital to conception, begins to suffer if more than 8 to 10 days elapse between ejaculations. What's more, sperm concentration usually begins to level off after about 5 or 6 days of sexual abstinence. A certain percentage of the sperm in each ejaculate normally show no motility or have an abnormal appearance, or both. Fertility decreases if a high proportion of the sperm in the ejaculate are abnormal (figure 3.5 shows a normally formed sperm as seen in a specimen stained for viewing under a microscope).

To deliver sperm into the vagina, the man must be able to relax and involuntarily contract certain key muscles that control erection and ejaculation. It is not surprising that certain conditions and neurological diseases can cause problems. The nerve damage caused

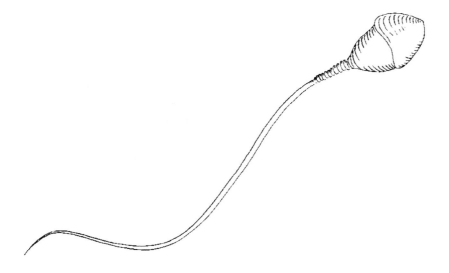

FIGURE 3.5 Appearance of a
normally formed sperm.

by diabetes mellitus, for example, can lead to *retrograde ejaculation*, a condition in which semen is ejaculated back into the bladder rather than out the urethra. This happens because the diabetic process damages the nerves that control the muscles that normally block the entrance to the bladder during ejaculation. This same malfunction can be induced unwittingly by surgery. Drugs commonly cause ejaculatory problems. Some tranquilizers and antidepressant medicines may interfere with ejaculation or erection or both. Drugs used to treat high blood pressure and gastrointestinal diseases also pose a problem. Recent work has shown that calcium channel blockers, used in treatment of cardiovascular disease interfere with the capacitation step necessary for final sperm activation. Popular drugs used to relieve ulcers and colitis affect sperm production, motility, and sometimes lower the sex drive. Marijuana causes a decrease in testosterone production, which may not only lead to reduced sperm numbers but also to a diminished sex drive.

In healthy young men, however, this effect is usually seen only with sustained use. New evidence suggests that heavy smokers have a greater chance of having decreased sperm concentration than non-smokers. The use of steroidal preparations by athletes, particularly football players and weight lifters, has led to severe infertility. Like the estrogen in birth-control pills, a small amount can be a stimulus, a larger amount an inhibitor. Damage to the testes can result from long-term use of steroids. It is important for you to be frank with the doctor about your medication or drug use because even a seemingly unrelated drug may be responsible for your infertility. Write down all of the drugs you are taking regularly - from pain killers to prescription drugs to recreational drugs - so that the doctor gets the whole picture.

4

Normal Initiation of Pregnancy: Facts and Fallacies

What really happens at the moment of conception and immediately thereafter? There are so many popular notions that it is important to separate facts from myths.

How It Happens

The process of sperm migration through the female reproductive tract is complex. Fertilization usually occurs in the ampulla, the outer, wider portion of the fallopian tube. Sperm reach the ampulla within a half hour after ejaculation. On their own, sperm do not move fast enough to reach the ampulla within that time. Therefore, by a process which is not yet understood, they must be moved along with the assistance of the woman's transport system within her tube. This is even more amazing considering the fact that the cilia beat with a wave *toward* the uterus! Sperm can live in the tube for as long as 5 days, although 2 or 3 is probably more common. This explains why conception often results from intercourse performed well *before* ovulation; under normal circumstances the ovum enters the tube to find live sperm already there waiting for it. But even if no sperm are present in the tube, that egg maintains its fertilization potential for 12 to 20 hours *after* ovulation. So the notion that extremely accurate and strict timing of intercourse around the time of ovulation is essential for fertilization to occur is a fallacy. A regimented timetable for intercourse, which does not improve chances for conception unless there is a problem with sperm survival, is simply counterproductive because it places a great deal of stress on both partners. If the egg is not fertilized, it disintegrates and is absorbed by the body. This also is true for women whose tubes are blocked by disease or previous sterilization.

When sperm encounter the ovum they surround it and secrete enzymes that break down the protective coat of cells around the egg. This is why it takes a certain number of sperm to surround the egg to cause fertilization, even though only one sperm actually enters the egg. After the layers of the ovum are sufficiently "softened," the head of one sperm penetrates the egg. At the moment this happens, a special mechanism within the egg is triggered, which prevents other sperm from entering. (If more than one sperm enters the egg, we have a condition known as polyspermic fertilization, which leads to an excess of genetic material within the egg. That embryo will have too many chromosomes and will be spontaneously aborted).

Soon after fertilization, the embryo travels down the tube to the junction of the isthmus, where it spends about 3 or 4 days developing. It divides into first 2 cells, then 4, then 8 and so on. After 4 or 5 such divisions, the embryo enters the uterus to implant within the endometrium. By this time the cell mass has an inner fluid-filled cavity and is known as a *blastocyst*. If for some reason the endometrium is not lush enough, the embryo will not "take" and early abortion occurs - so early that the woman may never know she was pregnant. If the embryo does implant, additional blood vessels develop within the endometrium at the site of implantation. This causes bleeding in about 20 percent of all pregnancies, and a woman may mistake this bleeding for menses. When a woman in this situation later learns of her pregnancy, she thinks the gestation is actually a month younger than it really is.

Women often experience some groin pain very early in the first pregnancy because the growing uterus stretches the ligaments that hold it in place. These ligaments have never been stretched before.

The pain is actually a healthy symptom because it indicates uterine growth.

Attempting Pregnancy

What actions improve your chances for conception? Certainly sufficient coitus around the time of ovulation is helpful as long as the husband leaves enough time between ejaculations to produce sufficient sperm to fertilize an egg. It is difficult to put a number, or count, on what is meant by "sufficient" sperm because men with extremely low sperm counts have been able to initiate pregnancy. Since healthy sperm can live in the fallopian tube for 2 days or more, intercourse at 36- to 48-hour intervals around the time of ovulation usually is sufficient to ensure an adequate number of sperm in the fallopian tube.

Aside from the BBT (basal body temperature) method mentioned in chapter 2, is there any way for a woman to tell when she is ovulating? Many women experience lower abdominal pain around the time of ovulation. This *mittelschmerz* may last for 12 to 36 hours and usually occurs just before or just after ovulation. Some women notice increased vaginal mucus, which actually comes from the cervix and can also identify a change in mucus elasticity. The new at-home urinary LH kits, which we mentioned before, have been a real boon to timing ovulation. Intercourse on the evening of the day or the following morning when the kit first shows a change in color will make it possible to have sperm in the fallopian tube when the egg is shed. However, even this hormonal shift does not prove positively that ovulation has physically taken place. The only actual proof of ovulation is pregnancy itself. We can be fooled sometimes. The hormonal shift may occur but the egg may mature without being physically extruded from the ovary. This phenomenon, called "intrafollicular ovulation," or "luteinized unruptured follicle syndrome," is seen most often in infertile women but may occur from time to time in normally fertile women. The diagnosis is made with serial ultrasonic examination just before and after presumed ovulation.

Role of Coital Position

Coital position usually does not affect fertility, except in couples who have physical handicaps, or if a man has an extremely low semen volume. Pillows under the woman's buttocks may be pleasing, but it's not a fertility aid; neither is the advice to lie in bed for 30 minutes following intercourse. If semen leaks out of the vagina after intercourse, this is perfectly normal. It does not reduce your chances of conceiving. In fact, if a woman says that semen never runs out of her vagina after intercourse, doctors are concerned that there is extremely low seminal volume or that the man may have retrograde ejaculation.

Ovarian Function

Contrary to popular belief, the ovaries do not necessarily alternate function; that is, the ovary that produces the ripe follicle in one cycle may or may not be the one to produce a mature follicle during the next cycle. In fact, many women ovulate predominantly on one side. Only ultrasonic studies can document this. If the tube on the side of ovulation is normal, there will be no interference with fertility. Women who have one ovary will, of course, always ovulate from that side. Some women who have lost an ovary on one side and a fallopian tube on the other can conceive by a process known as *transmigration*, illustrated in figure 4.1. In transmigration, the egg released by the remaining ovary is carried by fluids normally present in the abdominal cavity to the tube on the other side. This is, at best, an inefficient method of transporting eggs, and these patients are frequently infertile.

TWINNING

Conceiving twins can occur in two ways. With nonidentical twins, two follicles rather than one ripen during a cycle. The two eggs are then fertilized by separate sperm, not even necessarily from the same coital experience, or even from the same man. Some ovulation-inducing drugs, as will be described in chapter 7, increase the chance

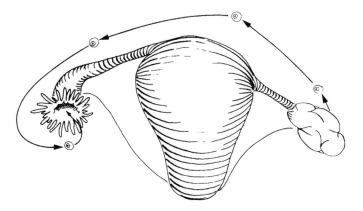

FIGURE 4.1   Illustration showing transmigration of ovum in a patient with one tube and one ovary on opposite sides. The ovum is carried passively by fluid normally present in the body cavity.

for nonidentical twinning. Identical twins occur when a single fertilized egg splits into two separate embryos. The two infants that result originate from the same egg and the same sperm cell. A set of twins of opposite sex are easily identified as nonidentical. If you have twins of the same sex, and really want to know if they are identical, sophisticated blood tests are available.

SIZE OF THE UTERUS
The size of the uterus usually has little to do with fertility unless a change in size results from some abnormal process. For example, the DES uterus is usually small and misshapen, and even if the patient is successful in conceiving, there may be a problem carrying the pregnancy. A large uterus may contain *myomas* - tumors of the uterine muscle. They can distort the cavity causing premature labor or abortion. A "tipped" uterus, one that lies deep in the pelvis, usually results from lax uterine ligaments, in which case there is no negative effect on fertility. If, however, a tipped uterus results from a disease process, endometriosis for example, that pathology itself may be responsible for compromised fertility.

Does The "Pill" Cause Infertility?

Many women are concerned about the long-term effects of birth-control pills on reproduction. There don't seem to be any except that former pill users on the average take a few more months to conceive than women who were protected by a diaphragm or condoms. Women who stop using the pill have no greater difficulty conceiving in the long run and carrying a pregnancy to term than women who never used it.

However, recent studies have emerged suggesting that birth-control pills may pose a breast cancer risk. It seems that the longer the use, the greater the risk, especially when started at a young age. These studies are at odds with the overwhelming information available from all over the world that has found no link between use of birth-control pills and breast cancer. The pill has been the most studied drug of the twentieth century and has been used clinically for more than twenty-five years. Even allowing for the latent period between pill use and cancer diagnosis, it seems unlikely that oral contraceptives are the *cause* of breast cancer, although these agents may accelerate tumor growth in some women. In a special review of the entire subject, a committee specially selected by the Food and Drug Administration found no reason to include a warning in the package relating pill use to increased breast cancer risk.

A career woman who plans to use contraceptives for a long time may actually aid her fertility prognosis. By putting her ovaries in a state of metabolic hibernation, she is reducing her risk of endometriosis. The other added benefit is that pill users have a substantially lower risk of getting ovarian and endometrial cancer. The reason for these statistics may be that the pill interrupts incessant ovulation. Only one hundred years ago, when contraception was inefficient or nonexistent, women in the reproductive age group rarely experienced long intervals of incessant ovulation. They usually were pregnant or breastfeeding, which means that they were not ovulating or menstruating for long periods of time. In a sense, their ovaries were resting. Once mechanical (condoms, diaphragms) birth control became available, women who were not interested in getting pregnant could experience years of uninterrupted ovulation.

Women may not be "bioengineered" for this and perhaps that is why certain serious disorders, such as endometriosis, have become so widespread.

The pill is often given to women with certain mild ovarian hormonal disorders to regulate their menstrual cycles. In such cases the appearance of regular menses may mask some undiagnosed problem within the reproductive system controlling ovulation. When these women stop taking pills, they may be infertile, but the reason for this is because they have reverted back to their previous abnormal status. Women *do not* become more fertile than normal after going off the pill; there is, in fact, no "rebound" effect. However, if pregnancy occurs in the first cycle after the pill was discontinued, there is a *slightly* increased chance of twinning due to a pituitary "overshoot" of gonadotropins when the suppressive effects of the contraceptive pill are removed. Hence, the increase is in fraternal twins because of multiple ovulation. Use of the pill does not later increase the risk of spontaneous abortion. Of course, the pill should not be taken during pregnancy itself, since the hormonal content may cause a variety of fetal abnormalities.

Effect Of Orgasm On Fertility

Female orgasm itself has no known effect on fertility. However, if sexual intercourse brings little or no pleasure to either partner, the frequency of coitus falls off as do the chances of getting pregnant. Women who view coitus as a threatening event may be prone to tubal spasm which may prevent sperm from passing to the end of the tube. I say "may" because no one has ever proven this. If intercourse is associated with pain, perhaps from a pelvic inflammation or endometriosis, spasm can also occur. If sexual dysfunction is psychological, then clearly a sexual counselor can be of great help. If the marriage is stable in other respects, artificial insemination with sperm from the husband may be tried.

The Adoption Myth

There is a popular fallacy that adoption "relaxes" women who have trouble conceiving and restores fertility. We all know of couples who adopted after a long period of infertility and who then conceived. For every 5 couples in that situation there are 95 couples who have remained infertile following adoption. Five percent of infertile couples will get pregnant each year without any treatment, but this rate drops off to 2 percent with continued infertility. Adoption certainly does not improve diseased tubes or reduce the effects of endometriosis. Long-term studies by Dr. Emmet Lamb of Stanford University on infertile couples who adopted show no significant effect of adoption on subsequent fertility. A close working relationship between your fertility specialist and a well-trained psychologist or psychiatrist is essential if you are experiencing great anxiety over this issue.

5

The Fertility Investigation: What Happens?

Although you've read the two definitions of infertility in chapter 1, you should not adhere too rigidly to definitions. Instead, you should decide for yourself when to seek treatment. And you should base that decision on age, the length of time you've been trying to get pregnant, how anxious you are about it, and anything pertinent in your medical history that might be preventing you from conceiving. If you've decided to get the advice of a fertility specialist, you will learn in the next few pages what will happen, which diagnostic tests will be performed and what the doctor hopes to learn from them. But first, a few comments on the current state of fertility therapy seem appropriate.

Seeking Treatment

Unfortunately, where you live may very well be a factor in the quality of treatment you receive. If you live near an urban center, you are going to have access to many specialists and to facilities where the latest techniques may be applied. If you live in a rural area sophisticated treatment is harder to find. Rural couples cannot be expected to travel many miles for each of the many office visits required in a step-by-step work-up. While the family doctor can be helpful in providing preliminary tests, you'll still have to consult a specialist, at least once, to obtain a diagnosis and most important, a plan of treatment.

Your health system or plan may also influence the course of your fertility investigation. The Canadian system, in which the provincial governments administer healthcare, works well in referrals to appropriate specialists, but it does impose some limitations upon the couple's choices. So, too, do many prepaid health plans in the United States. For example, a Health Maintenance Organization (HMO) refers patients only to specialists who belong to that group. Patients with special problems must be referred to outside consultants, who are paid by the HMO. Patients must rely on the judgement and professional integrity of the HMO physician, who decides when and if additional expertise is needed. Patients are, of course, free to seek therapy outside of the group plans, but this will be at their own expense.

The Experts

Who are the fertility therapists and where do they practice? The obstetrician-gynecologist is usually the first to be consulted about fertility problems. But the practice of obstetrics carries inherent difficulties in office scheduling and fatigue (too many middle-of-the-night deliveries), and it does not mix well with the more orderly practice of fertility therapy. This is not to say that an obstetrician cannot be an expert in this area. However, most "fertility doctors" who are gynecologists have eliminated obstetrics from their practice.

The American Board of Obstetrics & Gynecology has organized a division of reproductive endocrinology and infertility with its own approved training programs and examinations for certification. This is a rather recent development, however, and the number of people so certified is still small. Many experts in the field have practiced fertility therapy for years and are not formally certified, so lack of certification does not imply a lack of expertise.

A number of medical specialties now address increasingly narrowed areas of fertility. For example, many urologists have gone on to specialize in *andrology*, the study of sperm production and transport. Some internists have become specialists in *reproductive endocrinology*, and focus on the role of hormones in reproduction. These specialists must then refer couples to other specialists for diagnostic tests and therapy outside of their own areas of expertise. The involvement of many specialists in the investigation may be acceptable within a large fertility center, but this fragmentation of care is expensive, and is frequently unsatisfactory to the patient. In most cases, a competent fertility specialist will be able to oversee and conduct the investigation and therapy without resorting to multiple and frequent referrals. Large fertility clinics, often associated with university centers, can offer up-to-date services and techniques. In addition to offering specialists in each area of fertility, they also have sex therapists, psychologists, and specially trained nurse practitioners to deal with the "total problem" of infertility, which may include emotional distress. Sometimes your fertility expert will see something in your history or sense anxieties and urge you to see one of these other specialists rather than leave it up to you. Within a large clinic you'll have the experts you'll need, but there are also drawbacks - lots of paperwork and office memos that bog down therapy. Another factor to be considered is that in a university-centered clinic, there are young physicians in training who will participate in your care at various levels.

How do you go about getting help? The American Society for Reproductive Medicine [1] can help provide information and a list of physicians in your area who have indicated interest in this field. RESOLVE [2], a lay group headquartered near Boston with many local branches throughout the United States, maintains a list of local physicians who have been judged by these critical consumers to be particularly competent in matters of fertility. RESOLVE also publishes a newsletter and holds regular meetings for its members.

[1]   Write The American Society for Reproductive Medicine, 1209 Montgomery Hwy., Birmingham, AL 35216-2809.
[2]   Write RESOLVE, Inc., 1310 Broadway, Somerville, MA 02144-1731

Certainly word-of-mouth referral is a good way to find a therapist who is competent, successful, and just as important, approachable. Gynecologists or urologists also may make a direct referral to an infertility physician or team.

The Basic Tests

Many fertility centers adhere to a fixed plan or workup, a regimented procedure designed (one hopes) to touch all bases in a systematic approach. This fits well into computer programs, and effectively handles a high volume of patients, but the therapy tends to become rather mechanized and impersonal. I believe that each case requires its own approach to diagnosis and treatment, and that you shouldn't have to rely on a computer to plan out the most appropriate strategy. Often a good history will immediately point to the problem. Work-ups should be systematic and complete, but flexible. In our practice, my associates and I send each couple questionnaires (figure 5.1) to be filled out at home before the first office visit. The man and woman fill out separate questionnaires. We frequently get two different answers to the same question, particularly in the area of sexual function. On the first visit, both partners are interviewed together. In that way, we get to know each couple and the general features of their case before the investigation really begins. We review the medical history in depth at this time, and request any medical records that will fill in the diagnostic picture. Then the basic tests are performed, unless they have been done previously, before deciding if other studies are needed.

Evaluation of Male Fertility

The fertility investigation of a man hinges largely upon a single procedure - the semen analysis. The series of tests performed on semen specimens tells us most of what there is to know about the state of sperm production and delivery.

FIGURE 5.1   Fertility history questionnaires that we use to obtain detailed information on each couple seeking treatment.

Fertility
Questionnaire
For Women

Date _____

Name _____

Address _____

_____

Birthdate _____

Husband's name _____

Telephone number at home _____ At work _____

Other name and number to be called in emergency _____

Insurance Information

Insurance company _____ Identifying numbers _____

Referring physician and address _____

Age at first menses _____ Date of last menses (first day) _____

Usual menstrual interval _____ Usual duration of bleeding _____

Cramps (please circle) Yes   No   Minimal   Moderate   Severe

Do cramps start before or after bleeding? _____

Are cramps always present?   Yes   No

Background Information

Please underline or circle all responses that apply and fill in blanks.

Chronic headaches, history of head trauma, seizure disorder, problems with sense of smell, visual disturbances, dizziness, loss of balance.

Rapid or marked changes in weight, increased thirst, changes in appetite, increased sweating, chronically warm or cold, history of painful swallowing, change of voice or hoarseness, insomnia, fatigue, tremors, craving for salt, loss of scalp hair, growth of hair on face or body in new places or in excess, change in size of clitoris, diagnosis of thyroid disease, diabetes, history of breast secretions or milky discharge from nipples.

History of acquired or congenital heart disease, scarlet fever, rheumatic fever, diagnosis or treatment of high blood pressure.

History of pulmonary (lung) disease such as tuberculosis, pneumonia, chronic bronchitis, emphysema, lung cysts or tumors.

History of gall bladder problems, hiatal hernia, ulcer, appendicitis, colitis, regional enteritis, pancreatitis, jaundice, hepatitis, liver problems.

History of anemia, need for transfusion, arthritis, kidney infections, nephritis, Bright's disease, urinary tract abnormalities, frequent urination, auto-immune diseases.

History of any other serious or chronic illness (describe) _____

Duration of marriage? _____ Duration of infertility? _____	
Either partner previously married?	Yes No
Children from prior marriage?	Yes No
How long to conceive? _____ (male) _____ (female)	
Outcome of pregnancies:	
Delivery, miscarriage, abortion Delivery, miscarriage, abortion	
Year _____ Year _____	

Complications: Yes   No   Complications: Yes   No
Fever: Yes   No   Fever: Yes   No

Previous methods of contraception: Pill   Condoms   Foam   Diaphragm   IUD   Withdrawal   Rhythm   None

If pill, were menses regular before?   Yes   No

If pill, were menses regular after?   Yes   No

How long to resume menses when pills stopped? _____ weeks

If IUD, was device removed to conceive?   for complications? (describe) _____

_____ other? (describe) _____

Usual frequency of sexual intercourse per week _____

Lubricants used: Yes   No   Specify _____

Does husband ejaculate during intercourse?   Yes   No

Does ejaculation occur outside vagina?   Yes   No

Does his semen leak out when you stand?   Yes   No

Do you douche before or after?   Yes   No

Is intercourse (coitus) painful to either partner?   Yes   No

Do you achieve orgasms?   Never   Rarely   Usually   Always

Has artificial insemination ever been suggested?   Yes   No   Husband   or   Donor

History of Syphilis   Gonorrhea   Pelvic infection?   Yes   No

Do you work?   Yes   No

Type of work _____

Exposure to chemicals or x-ray in work or in hobbies?   Yes   No

Smoking habits: Yes   No   Pack/day

Alcohol: Yes   No   Drinks weekly   Yes   No

History of use of marijuana, opium or other addictive drugs:

Medications used now or recently _____

Allergies _____

History of therapeutic x-ray treatment (not for diagnosis) or anti-cancer drugs or drugs for arthritis: Yes   No

Family History: Father   Alive   Dead   Cause _____   Age _____

                   Mother   Alive   Dead   Cause _____   Age _____

                   Sister(s) _____ Age(s) _____   Brother(s) _____ Age(s) _____

History of family infertility caused by endocrine (hormonal) disorder?   Yes   No

Previous hospital admission (any reason) Medical/Surgical

                Where   When   Reason

1. _____

2. _____

3. _____

History of psychiatric treatment: Yes   No

Name of Doctor _____

Previous Infertility Studies

Drug treatment: Yes   No   Hospital Admission: Yes   No

Temperature charts? Yes   No   Normal: Yes   No

Husband had semen analysis: Yes   No   Year   Normal: Yes   No

Post-coital test for sperm survival in cervix: Yes   No   Normal: Yes   No

X-ray of tubes and uterus: Yes No Year Normal: Yes No

Laparoscopy (telescope in abdomen): Yes No Year Normal: Yes No

D & C to examine uterine lining: Yes No Year Normal: Yes No

Hysteroscopy (telescope in uterus): Yes No Year Normal: Yes No

Immunologic testing for sperm allergy: Yes No Normal: Yes No

Hormonal tests: Yes No Results, if known _____

Chromosomal (genetic) studies   Tay-Sachs screening

Sickle cell screening   Thyroid tests

Skin test for tuberculosis   Year____   Skull x-ray   Year ____

Diabetes test   Others ____

Previous Infertility Treatment

Any procedure on cervix such as biopsy, cauterization, cryosurgery (freezing): Yes No

Any procedure on uterus, vagina, tubes, ovaries, or operations for inflammatory or infectious pelvic diseases, operations for adhesions or endometriosis: Yes No

Stimulation of ovulation with oral or injectable agents such as estrogens, Clomid HCG, Humegon, Pergonal, others: Yes No

Treatment of endometriosis with drugs: Yes No

Treatment of tubes with medication via uterus: Yes No

Artificial insemination: Husband Donor Yes No

Use of fertility-promoting douches: Yes No

Fertility Questionnaire For Men

Date _____
Name _____
Address _____

Height _____ Weight now _____ Greatest weight _____
Hair color _____ Eye color _____
Ethnic extraction _____
Birthdate _____
Telephone number at home _____ At work _____

Background Information
Please underline or circle all responses that apply and fill in blanks.

Rapid or marked changes in weight, increased thirst, changes in appetite, increased sweating, chronically warm or cold, painful swallowing, change of voice or hoarseness, insomnia, fatigue, tremors, salt craving, loss of hair other than on scalp, decreased beard growth, history of thyroid disease, diabetes, increase in breast size or sore nipples.

History of acquired or congenital heart disease, scarlet fever, rheumatic fever, diagnosis or treatment of high blood pressure.

History of pulmonary (lung) disease such as cystic fibrosis, tuberculosis, pneumonia, chronic bronchitis, emphysema, lung cysts or tumors.

History of liver or gall bladder disease, cirrhosis, jaundice, pancreatitis.

History of arthritis, auto-immune diseases, kidney infections or stones, gout, urinary tract abnormalities, other serious or chronic diseases.

Do you ever suspect that you have fathered a child outside this marriage?   Yes   No
How long ago? _____

Have you ever had reason to doubt your fertility outside this marriage?   Yes   No

Are you circumcised? Yes No

If no, does foreskin retract easily? Yes No

Have you ever been treated for gonorrhea, syphilis, prostatitis, or infection of testicles and/or seminal vesicles? Yes No

Has there been a recent change in libido or sexual drive? Yes No

Do you have difficulty in maintaining erection? Yes No

Do you ejaculate in vagina without difficulty? Yes No

Is urination or ejaculation painful? Yes No

Usual sexual frequency weekly (all outlets) _____

Has a doctor ever told you that you were infertile? Yes No

Has a semen analysis ever been performed? Yes No

When? _____ Where? _____ Results? _____

Has artificial insemination ever been suggested to achieve pregnancy with your sperm? Yes No

With donor sperm? Yes No

Any history of hernia repair at any age including shortly after birth? Yes No When? _____

History of mumps? Yes No Age _____

Any history of undescended testes? Yes No

Final outcome, if yes _____

History of injury to testes? Yes No

History or diagnosis of varicocele (varicose veins in scrotum)? Yes No

Treated _____

History of treatment in past to promote fertility? Yes No

Specify _____

History of genitourinary surgery?   Yes   No

Present means of employment _____

How long has this type of work been performed? _____ Years

Have you ever been employed in occupation with sustained high temperatures?   Yes   No

Have you ever been a professional driver, or do you drive long distances as part of your employment?   Yes   No

Type of underwear worn: Boxer Shorts   Jockeys

Tobacco: Cigars Cigarettes   Pipe   Amounts Daily

Alcohol - Drinks weekly _____

Drugs

History of use of marijuana, opium or other addictive drugs: Yes   No

Medication used now or recently _____

Allergies _____

History of therapeutic x-ray treatment (not for diagnosis) or anti-cancer drugs or drugs for arthritis?   Yes   No

Family History: Father   Alive   Dead   Cause _____

                  Mother   Alive   Dead   Cause _____

                  Sister(s)   Age(s) _____

                  Brother(s)   Age(s) _____

Any history of family infertility or endocrine disease? Yes   No

Specimen Collection

The semen specimen may be collected during an office visit or at home and delivered to the laboratory. The patient masturbates into a sterile wide-mouth jar. The first few drops of semen usually contain the most vigorous sperm, and the jar's wide opening helps prevent loss. Ideally, the specimen should be collected 2 to 4 days after the last ejaculation. If the specimen is taken sooner, the sperm count may not have yet been fully replenished. Don't wait as long as 7 days because the count does not increase, and the wait can cause a decrease in sperm motility. If you cannot ejaculate in an office or laboratory setting, the specimen can be produced at home, so long as you can get it to the laboratory within 2 hours. The jar should be kept next to the body so that the sperm will not lose motility from low temperature.

There are a few men who cannot be persuaded to produce a specimen by masturbation under any circumstances. Interrupting coitus at ejaculation to collect the specimen is not a particularly good method because semen leaks out before the first throbs of orgasm are recognized. Ordinary rubber condoms are unsatisfactory for collection because rubber adversely effects sperm motility. However, there are special plastic sheaths made for specimen collection during intercourse, and they can be readily obtained from a physician or pharmacy. Although some religions forbid masturbation or the use of sheaths, we have found that most members of the clergy accept this practice when it involves fertility enhancement.

After collection, the semen is tested in a laboratory to determine reproductive quality. Before describing these tests, however, it is worth stressing that they should be performed by technicians with experience in semen analysis. A technician who performs these procedures only occasionally may not get consistently accurate results.

Semen Volume and pH

The first step in the analysis is to measure the amount of semen in the ejaculate. A single ejaculation normally contains between 2 and

5 mL of semen, depending on the frequency of ejaculation. Less than 1 mL may be associated with infertility because few sperm will reach the cervix, even if sperm *concentration* is normal. As an analogy, although the concentration of sperm may be normal, the amount of fluid (semen) through which they must swim becomes like a small puddle in an almost empty reservoir (the vagina). High volumes of semen, 7 ml or more, can also indicate infertility, but for reasons that remain unclear.

Low semen volume may be the result of retrograde ejaculation, which can have any number of causes. Diabetes, for example, can damage the nerves controlling the bladder sphincter. This muscle normally blocks the entrance to the bladder during ejaculation, but failure results in the semen being passed into the bladder rather than through the urethra. Certain medications that affect the nervous system, particularly those used in treatment of high blood pressure, may also cause retrograde ejaculation, or lack of ejaculation. Many cases of retrograde ejaculation occur following urologic surgery, and cannot always be avoided, particularly when the bladder and prostate gland are involved.

SEMEN PH
The pH of the semen is also assessed. A normal pH - about 7.5 to 8.5 - is in the alkaline range, nature's counterbalance to normal vaginal acidity. Rarely is diet responsible for changes in the pH.

COUNTING SPERM
Sperm counts are performed by placing some of the specimen in a glass counting chamber, the same device doctors use in doing white blood cell counts. If the technician is skillful, repeated counts on the same specimen will not vary by more than 15 percent. But if you are tested on another occasion you *normally* can be expected to show a variation of 40 percent or more, even with adequate time between tests. If you are infertile, the variation can be even greater. Therefore, several analyses may be necessary to gauge your expected range. Automated semen analyses are becoming popular. The system uses

a recorder and a video camera attached to a microscope with a computer that has been programmed to differentiate sperm by size and shape.

How many sperm does a man need to be fertile? Many specialists consider 20 million per mL of semen as the acceptable lower threshold of normal fertility. But many normally fertile men have counts below this arbitrary figure. Forty years ago 60 million sperm per mL was considered normal. Twenty years ago, experts adjusted the figure down to 40 million per mL. Since the methods of counting haven't changed until recently, why the lower sperm counts? One contributing factor may be the environmental stresses under which people live. In animal colonies, conditions of crowding and stress reduce overall fertility of the population, perhaps as a built-in defense mechanism. This may work in humans as well. If so, men aren't the only ones affected. We know that stress can also produce ovulatory disorders in some women. There is a seasonal variation in sperm concentration with a decrease in the summer months but usually only to a minor extent.

A second factor may be the various poisons that are part of our contemporary life-style. It wouldn't surprise me if industrial pollution will prove to have an adverse affect on fertility. It is well known that medications are capable of causing disturbances in sperm production and maturation. Therefore, it is not unreasonable to assume that some of the industrial pollutants that we drink, eat, and breathe might have the same effect. The fact is that most studies in this area have concentrated on the risk of cancer rather than the effects on fertility. We all remember when aniline dye and asbestos exposure related malignancies were reported. Heavy alcohol consumption can dampen the sex drive and, by affecting the liver, can alter testosterone metabolism that leads to seminal problems. Cigarette smoking may lower sperm concentration in some men. Chronic use of marijuana can also diminish the sex drive as well as reduce testosterone and sperm production. Although the testes have a tremendous reserve capability, continuous assault by a variety of toxic agents may overcome their ability to compensate for these factors. Nevertheless, as we have said before, men with very low sperm counts have proven to be fertile without any special therapy. This underscores the fact that the sperm count is not the most important thing measured in semen analysis.

Sperm Motility

More important than sperm number is sperm *motility*, the inherent ability of sperm to swim in seminal fluid or through the female reproductive tract. When we analyze motility, what matters most is the total percentage of moving sperm, not the total number of sperm. You can have a very high sperm count, but if only 40 percent of your sperm are motile you can still be infertile. On the other hand, you can have a lower count with 60 percent of the sperm motile and be fertile. No one really knows why this is so, although theories abound.

During the motility analysis, we make an estimate of the percentage of motile sperm. These sperm are then graded for their vigor on a 4-point scale. The laziest swimmers receive a 1, the fastest sperm a 4. An overall score of 3 or more is considered normal. Sperm are also graded on their *progression*, the ability of the sperm to swim in a purposeful fashion. Sperm that swim in erratic circles or in figure-of-eights do not contribute to fertility. The sperm of some men will show good motility for 2 hours after ejaculation, but motility may then decline dramatically over the next few hours. Therefore, to get a more accurate picture, motility should be evaluated over at least a 6-hour period. At normal room temperatures, there should be no more than a 25 percent reduction of motility in 6 hours.

Using the new video-computer semen analysis, we can look at sperm in a video frame and see how they move in a way that is not available to the human eye. We now know, for example, that the flagellum (tail) of the sperm normally beats 7 or 8 times per second. And on slow motion we see that normal sperm move in a complicated wave form. Sperm normally move with the head at an angle to the rest of the sperm body and tail. Too much or too little of this side action is thought be of significance. The computer can also measure the velocity of the sperm in a straight line and also in what is called a curvilinear fashion and assess quickly the ratio between the two. It is hoped that this knowledge will allow us to make diagnoses and offer treatments that will lead to more pregnancies from men whose sperm motility is abnormal.

Viability and Morphology

Viability refers to the percentage of sperm in the specimen that are actually alive. Motile sperm are obviously alive, but so too are some of the nonmotile sperm. A special stain that distinguishes living from nonliving cells is used to arrive at the viability count. For good fertility the count should be 60 percent or better.

Morphology refers to the appearance of sperm. Figure 5.2 illustrates normal and some common abnormal sperm forms. The minimal satisfactory percentage of sperm showing normal morphology-ratio of length to width; neck piece appearance, characteristics of the tail - and other factors depends on the reference system utilized by the individual laboratory. The old parameters of at least 60% for morphology and motility have been reduced to about 40% in laboratories using revised World Health Organization (WHO) criteria, and if one uses Kruger scoring system, normal morphology as low as 14% may be acceptable. Thus, it is important when comparing semen analyses to note that different laboratories may have widely divergent criteria. The computer programs for analyzing morphology are not as good as the eye of a trained observer and his microscope. No one has ever shown that sperm morphology has anything to do with congenital birth defects in the offspring. Conversely, the sperm morphology of men known to carry chromosomal defects is no different from anyone else's. Such defects are caused by abnormalities at the level of the gene, a scale far too small for any optical microscope. Therefore, men who have a relatively high percentage of abnormally formed sperm need not worry that pregnancy, if it occurs, will carry with it an increased risk of having an abnormal child.

Viscosity, Clumping, and Agglutination

Semen is normally very viscous (thick) after ejaculation, and may remain so for up to 30 minutes. We think that this viscosity enhances the ability of semen to remain in contact with, and feed sperm into, the mucus-filled cervix, by first forming a "plug" over the cervix. Then enzymes in the semen thin it out until it becomes watery. Many doctors believe that if enzyme activity fails and the semen remains

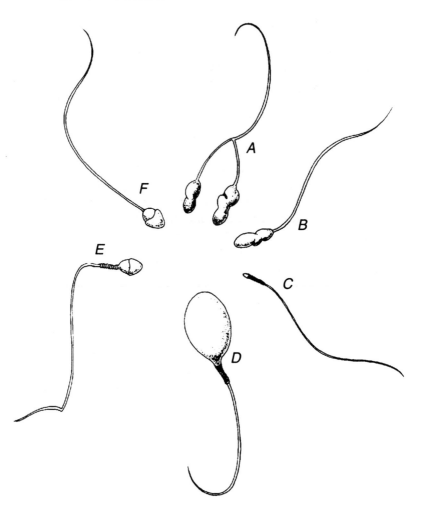

FIGURE 5.2 Various abnormal sperm forms commonly seen, including (A) Double-headed variety, (B) abnormal neck, (C) Microsperm, (D) Macrosperm, (E) Tail abnormality, (F) Normal.

thick, sperm will be delivered into the cervix less efficiently, and fertility will suffer. If sperm under a microscope seem to stick together in clumps, it could signify a chronic infection in the genito-urinary tract. An infection of the prostate gland can produce such clumping. Somewhat different from clumping is *agglutination*, in which the sperm adhere to one another in a head-to-head or tail-to-tail fashion. Agglutination suggests that a man's immune system is producing antibodies to attack his own sperm, as if the sperm were disease-causing organisms. Such immunologic causes of infertility are discussed in chapter 14.

Fructose Test

A complete absence of sperm in the ejaculate may be caused either by a failure of the testes to produce sperm or by blockages of the ductal system that prevent sperm from entering the ejaculate. The fact that the epididymis produces a type of sugar, fructose, provides a convenient method of finding out what is really happening. If fructose is absent from the seminal specimen, we assume that the ductal system is blocked.

Medical History and Physical Examination

If the semen quality is less than satisfactory, physicians look first to the medical history to uncover the cause. We know certain illnesses and surgical procedures can affect seminal quality. These include:

Mumps. Mumps, in a man, can cause severe testicular pain. If a man gets mumps after puberty, he may become infertile or even sterile permanently, and usually he remembers the incident.

Testicular torsion. This is an acutely painful condition never forgotten by those who experience it. Torsion occurs when the testicle twists on the vas, blocking the flow of blood to and from the testicle. It is not very common, but if not promptly corrected by surgery, permanent sterility can result.

Undescended testis. Even if this condition is surgically corrected early in childhood, the testis may not function normally in adulthood.

Epididymitis, or infection of the epididymis. If the infection is not promptly treated with antibiotics, the epididymis can become blocked by scar tissue.

Inguinal (groin) hernia operations. These operations may result in inadvertent and undetected damage to the vas.

Prostatitis. A common infection of the prostate gland, which can affect the motility of sperm if the condition becomes chronic.

Vasectomy reversal. About half of the men who have had a vasectomy have antibodies against their own sperm and, thus, reversal of the sterilization may not be successful even though sperm once more appear in the semen.

Radiation treatments or chemotherapy for cancers. These treatments can cause long-term or permanent sterility, depending on the doses received and the duration of therapy. Today many men have been cured of lymphomas and Hodgkin's disease and other related illness with chemotherapy treatments not previously available. Unfortunately, many of these drugs are toxic to the testes. Often sperm production is affected for a relatively short period of time, but the damage may be permanent. It may be possible at the time that the diagnosis of illness is made to collect sperm and to freeze it before treatment begins.

In utero causes. Exposure in utero to drugs such as DES can affect seminal quality.

Medications or drugs the patient might be taking can have an adverse affect on sperm production or delivery. Among those are anti-inflammatory agents, antibiotics for urinary tract infections, ulcer medications, anti-hypertensive drugs and drugs used for colitis and enteritis.

Testosterone Production

If I think the patient may have decreased testosterone production, I'll ask about changes in voice, beard growth, sex drive, and feelings of overall well-being. The patient's body build, hair distribution, and muscular development may sometimes be a tip-off that special hormone tests are needed. The tests may include evaluation of serum testosterone, FSH/LH, and prolactin. If prolactin, a hormone found in both sexes, is elevated in the man, it could block the release of gonadotropins (FSH/LH), and lead to reduced testosterone, thereby interfering with sperm production and motility.

Clinical Examination: What to Expect

It makes many patients less anxious if they know in advance what to expect from the clinical examination. Physicians look at and palpate the penis, testicles, epididymis, and prostate. We want to rule out such conditions as a varicose swelling of the scrotum, discussed in detail in chapter 12, scarring from previous epididymal infection, or an ongoing prostate infection. The examination to rule out varicocele is done with the patient standing. The doctor will probably estimate or measure the size and consistency of the testicles. One or both testicles may be smaller than normal, suggesting some degree of degeneration. This is important because sperm production is related to testicular size. Normally, the right testicle is lower than the left for the simple reason that men seem to walk better that way! The doctor will inspect to be sure that the urethra opens at the tip and not underneath (hypospadias). The epididymis and the vas deferens are checked for areas of firmness which, if found, would indicate chronic infection. Extreme tenderness would tell the doctor that there is an acute infection. The prostate must be felt through a rectal examination. A tender gland or one that is spongy (what doctors call "boggy") usually indicates infection.

Evaluation of Female Fertility

History and Physical Examination

What will your examination entail? Your medical history may tell of conditions or illnesses that are contributing to infertility. Particularly important are details of past pregnancies, if any. Abortions or full-term deliveries, even if uncomplicated, may have laid the groundwork for infections that may have affected your reproductive tract.

During the physical examination doctors look at body fat, muscles, and hair growth and their distribution over your body. These observations may provide clues to hormone imbalances. A milky discharge from the breasts of a nonnursing woman may indicate elevated levels of prolactin, which, like other hormone disorders or imbalances, can interfere with ovulation. We worry about strenuous physical conditioning because a major loss of body fat can cause a dramatic reduction of gonadotropin release leading to decreased estrogen production and total amenorrhea. Long-distance running tends to produce this result more than aerobic exercise. On a less dramatic scale, excessive physical conditioning may lead to anovulation or less than normal ovulation cycles. We look for surgical scars on the abdomen because previous surgery could have left as its aftermath pelvic infection and adhesions, either of which might interfere with tubal function. A gynecological examination rules out an abnormal vagina which could prohibit sperm from making adequate contact with cervical mucus. We want to make sure that you don't have endometriosis, tubal or ovarian abscesses, or uterine myomas. Because the cervix may be the site of infection, we sometimes take cultures during the vaginal examination to be certain there is no infection present.

Ovulation Detection

BBT CHART
A woman who regularly menstruates on a 26- to 34-day cycle probably ovulates normally, but one cannot be sure. The easiest way to detect whether, and perhaps when, ovulation had occurred is for a woman to maintain her own basal body temperature (BBT) chart. The good part is that it doesn't hurt, it's free, and its accurate. But bear in mind that the chart is not used to predict ovulation, but to demonstrate that you've ovulated in the preceding cycle. Each day upon awakening, even before leaving the bed, take your temperature orally and record it on the chart. When ovulation is about to occur, there usually is a lower than normal temperature, as illustrated in figure 2.11. However, not everyone has a drop before the characteristic rise over the succeeding days. As you know, the rise

in temperature is due to increasing levels of progesterone production. The accuracy of the BBT chart can be thrown off by any number of things, including any illness that causes temperature elevation. If you are a person who keeps irregular waking hours, such as an airline stewardess or an emergency room doctor on a night shift, your charts will be more difficult to interpret because your biorhythms are disturbed.

URINARY LH TEST KITS

The urinary LH test kit is not fooled by rhythm disturbance. These kits are available over-the-counter. They are extremely accurate and useful in predicting ovulation so that patients can time intercourse if it is important to do so because of seminal problems or infrequent coitus. They also allow the doctor to more accurately time inseminations, progesterone assays, and endometrial biopsy. Although the instructions on the kit may state that the first morning urine is preferred, this is not true for all women. In our experience the late afternoon or early evening specimen has been more accurate. There is not a great difference either way, and it is more important to test at the same time each day. Testing should begin about 3 or 4 days before anticipated ovulation, which is calculated by subtracting 14 from the end of the menstrual cycle. Thus, a woman who normally has a 33-day cycle should ovulate around day 19 and should begin her testing on day 15 to allow for a normal cyclical variation.

ULTRASONIC PELVIC EXAMINATION

Many, if not most, fertility practices have in-office ultrasonic capability. The older methods of abdominal examination which require a full bladder in order to produce quality images have given way to vaginal probes, which have greatly simplified the examination. When the process is performed serially around the time of expected ovulation, confirmation of actual, physical ovulation can be made as the clear large follicle changes its appearance on the screen to a smaller, less regular structure with more ultrasonic echoes. Perhaps equally important is the use of ultrasonography to determine the thickness of the endometrium at the time of ovulation since there is evidence that this is prognostic for pregnancy in that menstrual cycle.

ENDOMETRIAL BIOPSIES

An *endometrial biopsy* is a minor office procedure in which a tissue sample is removed from the uterine lining and examined to determine if ovulation has occurred, and if the lining of the uterus is normal for that stage of the cycle. New instruments have been developed which make this an almost painless procedure. Gone are the older techniques that were, admittedly, an unpleasant process. Most endometrial biopsies are taken in the last 6 days or so before the expected menses. Patients often worry that the biopsy will interfere with pregnancy initiated in that cycle. Although this can theoretically happen, statistically there is no greater chance of miscarriage if a biopsy is performed during the cycle of conception. The biopsy specimen is very small, and the chance of that being the exact site of the implantation is extremely unlikely.

FSH AND LH MEASUREMENTS

One of the most helpful recent developments in the female fertility survey is a simple blood test which can accurately predict not only the ability to conceive from an ovarian point of view, but also the early abortion rate. While men normally produce sperm daily even into old age, women are born with the most eggs they will ever have. When this reservoir is exhausted, menopause occurs. But for the five-seven years prior to this time, the individual is highly infertile - unlikely to conceive and likely to abort - based both on oocyte quantity and quality.

Thus, for women destined to be menopausal at 51 (the average age in North America) fertility may be retained at 45, but not so for one who will cease menstrual function at 44; she may be irrevocably infertile at 38 (except for a donor egg pregnancy).

Testing for estradiol and FSH levels on the 3rd day of the menstrual cycle gives a surprisingly good estimate of reproductive potential.

As ovarian function wanes, FSH levels increase in an effort to provide more ovarian stimulation and thus FSH serves as a marker. The follicular or early phase prior to ovulation is usually shortened. Therefore, if estradiol is unusually high on day 3 of the cycle, this will tend to decrease FSH values which otherwise would be high; therefore, it is important to measure both in order to have a valid result. In addition, there are data to suggest that elevated LH values early in the cycle are associated with an increased potential for abortion. We now screen all women over 35 years of age who enter our practice regardless of the assumed reason for infertility. We also screen those women who have responded poorly in the past to any type of ovarian stimulation. Telling a 32 year old woman that she is highly unlikely to achieve a successful pregnancy without an egg donor is shocking to the couple and grueling for the physician, but identification of these individuals with premature or incipient ovarian failure is preferable to years of unsuccessful therapy. Note that all other parameters of ovarian function may be within normal limits at this time, including temperature charts, progesterone levels after ovulation and the endometrial biopsy.

BLOOD TEST TO MEASURE PROGESTERONE LEVELS

Another method of establishing whether ovulation has occurred is to measure the progesterone levels in the blood because elevation of progesterone is a presumed indicator of ovulation. In a nonpregnant cycle, progesterone production usually peaks about 7 or 8 days after ovulation. Therefore, in a 28-day cycle with probable ovulation on day 14, progesterone levels should be sampled on day 20 or 21 of the cycle. It is important to know the progesterone levels because they provide more information about ovulation. If the progesterone level is lower than normal it may mean that there hasn't been enough hormone produced following ovulation, and that the endometrial lining may not have developed sufficiently to receive the growing embryo.

This relationship is not always so simple. Some patients have normal progesterone values, but unsatisfactory endometrial biopsies. Others may have low progesterone values and an endometrial biopsy that is normal. We can sometimes see the exact site of ovulation on the ovary - a cherry-red spot called a *stigma* - with an instrument called the *laparoscope* (discussed later in this chapter). Ovulation determination alone is certainly not sufficient reason to do a laparoscopic examination. But if laparoscopy is performed as part of the fertility workup during the luteal phase of the cycle, the doctor usually will be able to see the stigma if it is there.

Hysterosalpingography: An X-ray Examination

Hysterosalpingography, or HSG for short, refers to examination of the uterus and fallopian tubes by X-ray. A special dye that becomes visible on X-ray photographs is passed into the uterus through the cervix. If all is well in the reproductive tract, the dye will fill the uterus and spill out of the fallopian tubes. The HSG can reveal structural defects in the uterus or blockages and other disorders of the tubes. There is some discomfort experienced with this test, but it is transient, and no worse than menstrual cramps. Most doctors are aware of this discomfort and try to be gentle in carrying out the procedure. We inject the dye slowly so that it doesn't cause the kind of pain that could induce tubal spasm, and we try to avoid using instruments to grasp the cervix in a traumatic manner because that always causes some discomfort. Risks are few, since the instrument used to inject the dye is not inserted deeply into the uterus.

The HSG has some inherent drawbacks and inaccuracies. It is not really useful in detecting adhesions around the ends of the tube. HSG is really a basic screening test and, if it reveals abnormal results, more definitive tests are necessary. Another drawback of HSG is that the procedure itself may reactivate dormant infectious organisms in the tubes. If you have a history of tubal infection, prophylactic antibiotics may be prescribed to prevent reinfection that could be triggered by this procedure. If the tubes are found to be abnormal, antibiotics are given after the test to prevent infection.

Until very recently, all of the dyes used for this study contained high levels of iodine. Women who were allergic to shellfish risked a serious allergic reaction to the dye. A new type of dye is now available that lessens this problem. The test is performed early in the menstrual cycle, or immediately after the menses to avoid X-ray exposure to the fetus. Another reason the test is done then is that later in the cycle the endometrium thickens around the opening of the tubes. This can lead to a misdiagnosis of tubal closure.

The Rubin's Test

For many years doctors used the *Rubin's Test* to check for tubal blockage. The test presented problems for both patient and doctor. Carbon dioxide gas was passed through the fallopian tubes causing shoulder pain as the diaphragm became irritated. Pain in the shoulder was the sign of a normal test. Tubal spasm was common and the results were misinterpreted as tubal blockage. Add to this the fact that the test does not allow doctors to detect whether one or two tubes are open, and it is easy to understand why most fertility therapists have given up on this method of diagnosing tubal problems.

Post-Coital Testing

The fertility doctor must find out if the sperm survive once they come into contact with the cervical mucus. This is done by using a painless procedure called the *post-coital test*, in which a sample of the mucus is collected after intercourse and examined under a microscope. After intercourse, the woman comes to the physician's office for the mucus sample to be collected. How long afterward is a matter of some debate among fertility therapists, but most prefer to take the mucus sample between 4 and 12 hours after coitus. My own opinion is that a post-coital test that is done 1 or 2 hours after intercourse does not give as much information as one performed after a longer interval. Many patients can show good initial sperm survival soon after coitus only to have it become abnormal in the next few hours. The mucus can be taken from the cervix with a number of devices: a syringe, a pipette, or a specially made forceps. The pH of the mucus is then tested. Ideally, it should be neutral, around the pH of 7 or slightly basic, 7.5. Not infrequently the cervical mucus is acidic. If the pH is less than 6.5, there is usually a deleterious effect on sperm survival in such an acidic environment. The elasticity of the cervical mucus is measured at this time. One should be able to stretch the mucus out in an unbroken strand of 6 inches or more. The mucus should be clear and copius. It is important to perform the test at the right time. In some women good cervical mucus may last for only 12 hours; in others it can last for days. Performance of the test just after an LH kit color change assures proper timing.

How are the results of the post-coital test interpreted? All doctors agree that more than 20 motile sperm in a field magnified 400X under a microscope is a good result. Most doctors would agree that fewer than 5 motile sperm is a poor result. When very few sperm are seen, it means that either a low number of sperm have entered the vagina or that the sperm have been carried off by *phagocytes* in the cervix which treat the sperm as foreign material. Large clumps of sperm stuck together or sperm with quivering motion suggest the presence of sperm antibodies either in the man or the woman. Your specialist will have his own interpretation of the results, and you should be guided by him or her. If the post-coital tests are poor, the problem may be with the sperm, mucus, or both. The *Kurzrok-Miller test* helps to identify the source of the problem. A sample of mucus is taken and placed on a microscope slide with semen from the husband and semen from a fertile donor. A comparison is made between how well the husband's sperm and the donor's sperm penetrate the wife's mucus. The other half of the test involves using mucus from another ovulating fertile woman. The two sperm specimens are added and the results are compared. Artificial cervical mucus as well as mucus taken from the cervix of an ovulating cow can be used as a standardized medium for testing sperm motility. When bovine or artificial mucus is used, sperm velocity can be measured along a graduated capillary tube.

Second Level Tests

Hamster Egg Penetration Assay

In this assay, hamster eggs are harvested and the protective coating around the eggs is removed with enzymes (figure 5.3). The husband's sperm that have been specially prepared are incubated with the eggs for 2 hours. The eggs are removed and examined to see if they have been penetrated by the sperm. This is a very sophisticated test system, difficult to perform, expensive, and not standardized. Is this test worth the trouble? The answer is that with all of these drawbacks, it has much to offer. First, the end point of the test is a biological one, rather than a reading in a machine. If the man has a normal semen analysis and a normal post-coital test, doctors too often conclude that the reproductive problem lies with the woman. The hamster test has taught us that this is not always true. The test is not infallible, but men whose sperm penetrate none of the hamster eggs are statistically less likely to impregnate a woman. Many women may be subjected to every type of treatment imaginable only to find, after a hamster test was performed, that the sperm are inefficient at egg penetration. Standard semen analysis correlates poorly with the results of the hamster assay. Some men who appear to have quite normal semen analyses will frequently have no egg penetration whatsoever, and vice versa. My associates and I have looked at 227 patients in whom the hamster test was performed and found that pregnancy occurred twice as frequently over a 30-month interval when the test was normal compared with abnormal results. These results were true regardless of any accompanying problem or its treatment in the woman.

We have found in our *in vitro* fertilization laboratory that sperm from men with normal hamster egg assays will fertilize 86 percent of normal appearing human eggs. But only 41 percent of the eggs will be fertilized by men whose sperm failed to penetrate any hamster eggs. These men are infertile, but not sterile. Thus even with *in vitro* fertilization the hamster test gives valid information. At present there is no specific treatment for someone with a normal semen analysis and a poor hamster test result. The actual mechanism may be one of

Hamster Egg Penetration Test

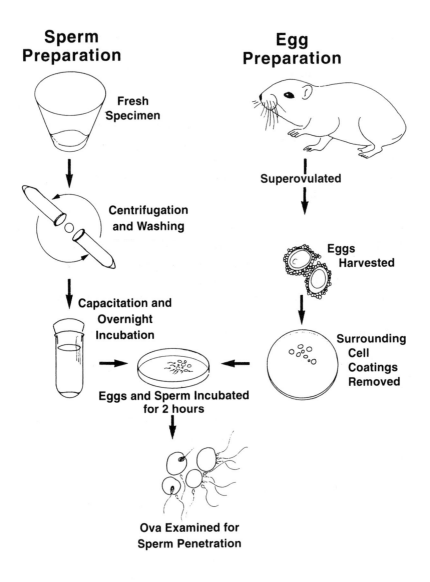

Sperm Preparation

Fresh Specimen

Centrifugation and Washing

Capacitation and Overnight Incubation

Eggs and Sperm Incubated for 2 hours

Egg Preparation

Superovulated

Eggs Harvested

Surrounding Cell Coatings Removed

Ova Examined for Sperm Penetration

FIGURE 5.3 Testing human sperm with the hamster egg penetration procedure.

poor sperm activation (capacitation), or some enzyme abnormality on the sperm head itself.

If some of the sperm are of good reproductive quality, doctors try to perform some maneuver that will get more of these sperm higher up into the woman's reproductive tract, such as intrauterine insemination. If this does not work, we can try surrounding the egg in the laboratory with many times the number of sperm normally present - in vitro fertilization (IVF) - or by putting sperm and eggs in the fallopian tube with a laparoscope. Doctors call this latter procedure GIFT, an acronym for gamete intrafallopian transfer. One of these methods usually works. If not, we now have the option of inserting a sperm directly into an egg during IVF.

Acrosomal Reaction Test

The acrosomal reaction allows the sperm head to shed its envelope, a prerequisite for fertilization. Special staining techniques allow for evaluation of this process and promise to supply additional information as to the functional level of the sperm. Sometimes men with normal analyses fail to undergo this necessary step.

Male Tests

Testicular Biopsy

If the semen analysis tells us that a man has reduced sperm numbers or a high percentage of abnormally shaped sperm, a safe and easy way to find the possible causes is by testicular biopsy. In this procedure a snip of tissue is removed from the testicle and examined under a microscope. Although many men find the mere thought of this alarming, the procedure causes little discomfort and can be performed under local anesthesia. Much valuable information can be obtained from this very tiny tissue sample. The biopsy can tell how well, if at all, sperm are being produced. It tells whether there is any inflammation or scarring in the tubules. It also gives information about the different cell populations within the testes.

For example, some men have the Sertoli cells lining the tubules, but no sperm at all. This is known as the "Sertoli cell only syndrome" and unfortunately cannot be treated. Some biopsies show *maturation arrest*, in which young sperm do not develop beyond a certain level of maturity, even though the cell population in the testes is normal. Unfortunately, treatment for this problem is usually unsatisfactory, although direct insertion of one of these immature sperm into an egg can cause a normal pregnancy.

Testicular biopsy should be performed routinely on men who lack sperm in the semen. Even if the fructose test uncovers a blockage in the ductal system, the physician cannot assume that sperm production is normal. Congenital abnormalities and damage resulting from infections often affect more than one area of the male reproductive system. For this reason a biopsy is usually performed routinely before any corrective surgery on the ductal system. If the biopsy reveals any incurable abnormalities of sperm production, useless surgery can be avoided. If surgery is planned to repair a block, a *vasogram* - an X-ray technique similar to the HSG performed on women - can be done. The vasogram uses a special dye that is visible on X-ray and points out the exact location of the obstruction.

Hormonal Analyses

Until recently, hormonal analyses of infertile men were considered a waste of time and money, largely because so little was known about the relationship between hormone levels and fertility in men. Much remains to be learned, but there are a few things that hormone analyses can now tell us. High levels of FSH and LH in the blood indicate a failure of testicular function that rarely responds to hormone therapy. In fact, a high level of these gonadotropins represents the body's futile attempt to stimulate testicular function, a situation that sort of parallels ovarian failure at menopause, except that the testes continue to make testosterone even if sperm production ceases.

On the other hand, low levels of gonadotropins may indicate a malfunction in the pituitary gland or hypothalamus. Under this set of circumstances, sperm production is poor because the testes, while healthy, are not receiving the stimulatory message from the central nervous system. Low levels of gonadotropins suggest that hormone therapies, like those described in chapter 12, will stimulate the testes and result in improved fertility.

Testosterone is produced by both the adrenal gland and the Leydig cells in the testes. It is not known how well the blood level of this hormone relates to the amount of testosterone found within the testes. It is known that intratesticular testosterone is important for sperm motility and development. Serum testosterone can be measured to identify men whose testosterone production is decreased. Like a detective, the experienced clinician uses every clue, every increase or decrease in hormone levels to help solve the mystery of infertility. An increase in prolactin, for example, is not only important in women, it is also important in men because it interferes with the release of gonadotropins (FSH and LH), creating a fall in testosterone production which, in turn, leads to a decrease in sperm production and motility. Many hormones have a cause-and-effect relationship and we try to be alert to them. Sometimes the only clue to increased prolactin is a lowered sex drive. One can easily be misled by this complaint because so many emotional and physical factors may be involved.

Female Tests

Endoscopy

The female workup includes several types of *endoscopic* procedures. These procedures allow the physician to visually inspect the internal organs of reproduction. Some women don't have to have these procedures done. For example, if an ovulatory defect is diagnosed and treated and if the results of HSG are normal, this test can be withheld initially. The fertility therapist might come back to the test if pregnancy does not occur after the ovulatory problem has been corrected.

LAPAROSCOPY

Laparoscopy, illustrated in figure 5.4, is performed while the patient is lying on her back under local or general anesthesia. The telescope (in this case called a laparoscope) is inserted through the navel area after carbon dioxide gas passed through a needle into the abdominal cavity, has elevated the abdominal wall. It lets the doctor see the internal reproductive organs, liver, gall bladder, appendix, and other organs merely by rotating the laparoscope. A dye test can be performed through the cervix. Additional instruments inserted through a separate incision can be used to perform various therapeutic and biopsy procedures. The gas is removed at the end of the operation.

Laparoscopy can be performed as outpatient, same-day surgery. However, if extensive therapeutic surgery has been performed during these procedures, the patient may have to stay in the hospital overnight. Of course, laparoscopy poses a theoretical risk to the intestines, major blood vessels, and the bladder, but in practice accidents are rare.

FIGURE 5.4 Diagram of laparoscopy.

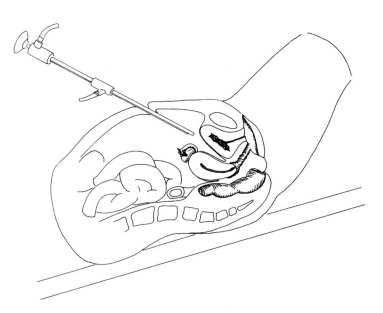

I recommend that the patient consider laparoscopy early in the work-up under the following circumstances:

1. Unexplained infertility in excess of one year
2. Infertility in women over thirty-five
3. Any abnormality seen on a hysterosalpingogram
4. Failure to conceive after apparently successful ovulation induction for 6 to 8 months, or after well-timed donor inseminations for 6 to 8 months.
5. Suspected endometriosis
6. Infertility with previous abdominal surgery
7. Prior to planned tubal repair (it can then be carried out under the same anesthetic)
8. Infertility with a history of pelvic infection

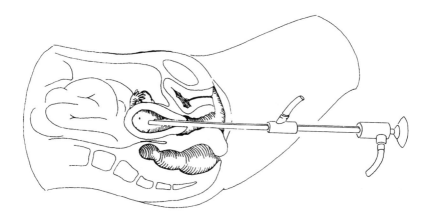

FIGURE 5.5   Diagram of hysteroscopy.

HYSTEROSCOPY

Hysteroscopy, illustrated in figure 5.5, is an endoscopic procedure which allows the doctor to see the uterine interior. Hysteroscopy is recommended when the HSG results suggest the presence of uterine anomalies such as adhesions, septum formation, polyps, or myomas. Some surgical procedures can be performed during hysteroscopy to remove or correct abnormalities. These therapeutic procedures are usually done on an outpatient basis in an operating room. Diagnostic hysteroscopy is usually done in the office under local anesthesia. Laparoscopy and hysteroscopy used together in the operating room provide a thorough diagnostic evaluation of the reproductive system. Hysteroscopy is also of great help to the patient whose scarring is so extensive that it has prevented menstrual flow. Scar tissue can be removed and estrogens given to encourage the remaining normal uterine lining to overgrow areas of scarring.

TUBOSCOPY
Recently very small diameter telescopes have been developed which allow for direct inspection of the interior of the fallopian tube. Tiny instruments passed down an operating channel can be used to cut adhesions within the lumen of the tube.

Hormonal Testing

Because of the expense involved, I order specific hormone tests only when necessary as indicated by the patient's medical history or findings during the physical examination. Even if a health plan or insurance carrier covers the cost, the consumer ultimately pays in the form of higher insurance rates. So-called routine endocrine testing may add $600 to $1000 to the cost of the workup and is, in my opinion, unnecessary.

THYROID TESTS
Thyroid disorders are rarely a cause of infertility. However, if the woman has problems that indicate a thyroid disorder, or if she presently has symptoms that indicate an overactive or underactive thyroid, she should by all means have the simple test to measure the amount of thyroid hormone in the blood. The pituitary hormone, thyroid-stimulating hormone (TSH), which gives the stimulatory message to the thyroid, is often a more sensitive indicator of thyroid function than thyroid hormone itself. Some patients temporarily

have an overactive thyroid because the gland is inflamed. Many of these patients subsequently revert to a condition of hypothyroidism, or underactive thyroid. Therefore, the finding of thyroid overfunction or underfunction depends upon when we examine the patient. Most thyroid conditions can be medically treated. But some patients may need a total or partial thyroid removal, which will require oral thyroid replacement medication. A decrease in thyroid function is sometimes associated with increased levels of prolactin; if we find elevated prolactin, we have to check that the thyroid gland is working properly. The interplay of hormones can be quite tricky.

MEASURING FSH AND LH LEVELS

If a woman fails to ovulate, it may be necessary to measure the levels of follicle-stimulating hormone (FSH) and luteinizing hormone (LH). Such a test is called for if the attempts to induce ovulation, described in chapter 7, should fail, or if the woman is totally amenorrheic (has no periods at all). A low level of FSH in the blood means that for whatever reason, the pituitary gland or hypothalamus may be at fault, and additional tests may be needed. On the other hand, if the FSH levels are high, the ovaries are not responding to maximal stimulation by the gonadotropins. This condition is actually a premature menopause, and all of the symptoms of menopause may be present, including hot flushes and increased perspiration.

Measuring LH levels is useful in identifying the Stein-Leventhal syndrome, also called *polycystic ovarian disease*. Women with this condition tend to have excessive body hair, are frequently obese, and fail to ovulate. Many of these women, but not all of them, have ovaries enlarged by numerous cysts, which is why it is called polycystic disease. The normal ratio of LH to FSH is disturbed with the LH being dominant. Women with this syndrome respond to ovulation-inducing techniques described in chapter 7.

MEASURING ESTROGEN LEVELS

If one of my patients is not menstruating I try to determine if she is producing enough estrogen. We cannot always determine this simply by measuring the amount in the blood because estrogen levels fluctuate too much during the menstrual cycle. Doctors therefore frequently use a method called *progesterone challenge* to evaluate estrogen production. The patient is given an oral or injectable dose of progesterone. If there has been sufficient estrogen stimulation of the endometrium, uterine bleeding will occur when the effect of the progesterone wears off. If the patient fails to bleed, we know that either the estrogen levels are chronically low, or that the endometrium is unresponsive to this challenge test.

MEASURING TESTOSTERONE AND OTHER ANDROGENS

The ovaries and adrenal glands normally produce small amount of androgens, or male hormones, including testosterone. Overproduction of these hormones can block ovulation. If excessively high levels of androgens are present in the blood, we then have to determine whether it is the ovaries or adrenal glands that are responsible. This is done by measuring the levels of other hormones produced by these organs. The adrenal glands produce many different hormones, and if they are present in high amounts, the problem lies with these glands. The diagnosis can be reinforced by measuring the rise and fall of blood androgen levels as the adrenal glands and the ovaries are alternately stimulated and suppressed with appropriate drugs as discussed in chapter 7. In rare cases, tumors in the ovary or in an adrenal gland produce large amounts of testosterone leading to voice change and beard growth in the woman. Surgery is needed to remove the tumor.

PROGESTERONE TESTING

Progesterone is measured after ovulation to determine if the ovaries are functioning properly. The test is done between 5 to 8 days after ovulation when progesterone will be at its highest. If the findings are consistently low, it is an indication that the corpus luteum is not working properly and, in fact, this poor function may be responsible for infertility or early pregnancy loss.

DETERMINING PROLACTIN LEVELS

The hormone prolactin, secreted by the pituitary gland, prepares the breasts to produce milk. But nonnursing women should have normal levels of this hormone in the blood. High concentrations can interfere with ovulation. In measuring prolactin, the doctor must be aware that blood levels can be temporarily elevated from fear, fondling of breasts, thyroid disease, pregnancy, certain drugs (especially tranquilizers), and that prolactin levels are higher after eating and as the day progresses. Therefore, in our practice we draw prolactin levels early in the morning usually before the patient has eaten, and we do remind the patient to avoid breast stimulation that morning. Truly high prolactin levels can be treated with drugs. If, however, the excessive levels are caused by a pituitary tumor, surgery may be required. Small pituitary hormones sometimes yield to drug management, but tumor regrowth is common when the drug is stopped.

Carbohydrate Metabolism Tests

Diabetes mellitus in a woman can increase her chances of pregnancy loss. Advanced diabetes is easily diagnosed because the symptoms of that disease are so pronounced and affect more than just fertility. But subtle diabetes, especially early in the disease, can be an undetected cause of repeated pregnancy loss. There are tests that can alert us to diabetes in its early stages, by monitoring the amount of glucose (sugar) and insulin in the blood. Then we can control the blood glucose levels with diet and medication, and greatly improve the patient's chances for successful pregnancy.

Additional Second Level Tests

CHROMOSOMAL ANALYSIS

Chromosomal abnormalities rarely prevent conception, although they may be responsible for repeated abortion. If such abnormalities are suspected, both partners must be tested. Blood samples are taken, and the cells are grown in the laboratory so that chromosomal analysis can be performed.

Chromosomal abnormalities that are important in infertility usually involve *translocation*, which means that a piece of chromosome has broken off and attached itself to another, or that two chromosomes have exchanged genetic material (chapter 17). The malformations that result from translocation are usually so profound that the embryo does not survive. Exceptions to this rule include the Down Syndrome (which used to be called mongolism) and certain conditions involving the sex chromosomes which result in offspring with altered sexual developments and other anatomic irregularities.

When should a chromosomal, or *karyotype*, evaluation be considered? With two consecutive early losses (before 12 weeks), the chance that either partner has a chromosomal problem is less than 1 percent. After three consecutive losses, that chance is 3 to 5 percent. Karyotype evaluation for uninsured patients cost as much as $500 each. So the decision to perform a chromosomal analysis is based, in part, on the partners' history of reproduction, the age of the couple, their degree of anxiety, and the family's genetic history. Test results usually take 2 or 3 weeks to obtain. Unfortunately, no specific therapy has been devised for patients with these chromosomal irregularities. Pregnancy is a gamble. Eventually, with persistence, the right combination of genetic material will usually come up, and a normal infant will result. Most often, however, patients go through the ordeal of repeated pregnancy losses before achieving success. This is somewhat different from the patient who carries a gene, either dominant or recessive, for a specific disease process which might be inherited by the offspring. Let me emphasize that most chromosomal changes result in an all or none phenomenon. If the chromosomal material is unbalanced, the effect is so great that abortion almost always occurs. On the other hand, if the normal chromosomes are involved in fertilization the child is absolutely chromosomally normal. Finally, the offspring may be a balanced translocation carrier, as was one of the parents. This child is normal but has the same risks of increased miscarriage later in life as one of the parents.

IMMUNOLOGICAL TESTING

The body, by nature, fights invading agents, infectious or otherwise. Some women's bodies perceive sperm as a threat and produce an antibody to reject these invaders. The result, alas, is infertility. Fortunately, this form of infertility is rare. An antibody reaction is suspected if the results of post-coital testing show adequate sperm numbers, but poor motility and/or clumping in the presence of good mucus. To add to the problem, neither semen analysis nor post-coital testing is specific for the diagnosis of immunological infertility. It is a mystery why all women don't form antibodies to sperm considering the fact that sperm deposited in the vagina work their way into the fallopian tube and abdominal cavity. The protein coating the sperm is foreign to the woman. Whatever the safeguards are to prevent antibody formation, they occasionally break down and we don't know if the reason has to do with the sperm or with the immunologic response of the woman. But the fact is that some women make antibodies directed against sperm - usually against all sperm - but occasionally just to the husband's sperm.

In some rare instances men manufacture antibodies against their own sperm. Normally, sperm do not enter the blood stream. However, occasionally infection, trauma, or the reversal of a sterilization procedure can create a pathway for the sperm to get into the blood and trigger this antibody reaction. Thus, the man's immunologic system treats his own sperm as foreign invaders. A semen analysis might seem normal at first in these cases, so we have to continually be on guard for the telltale signs: the agglutination of sperm, poor motility, and disordered patterns of sperm motion.

I find the best test for this is the *immunobead system*. In this test, antibodies made in a rabbit against human antibodies are used to coat plastic spheres which are placed with the sperm to be tested. If the sperm are covered with human antibodies the spheres will attach and are easily seen in the microscope. The number of motile sperm to which spheres are attached can be quantitated in the laboratory to see if there is a significant problem. Immunologic infertility is relatively rare, but must be considered a source of infertility when other more common possibilities have been ruled out or when post-coital tests are repeatedly poor (see chapter 14 for diagnosis and therapy).

MICROBIOLOGIC CULTURE

Certain microorganisms are associated with infertility and repeated pregnancy loss, or both. One such organism is known as *ureaplasma urealyticum, or T-mycoplasma*. This organism is like a bacteria in some respects and resembles viruses in others. It is possible to identify these microorganisms by taking a smear from the cervix and growing a culture from it in the laboratory. But culturing is a difficult and expensive procedure. It's not surprising that you find many physicians treating infection with a broad spectrum antibiotic, such as tetracycline, without bothering to identify the responsible organism. Ureaplasma urealyticum is one of the organisms that cause "ping-pong" infections which travel from one partner to the other. Therefore, both partners should be treated even if one of them doesn't have symptoms. In North America 30 to 40 percent of all cervical cultures will be positive for this organism. Therefore, it is not surprising that many fertility experts have serious doubts that this organism is truly responsible for reproductive difficulties. But because treatment is simple, we tend to treat, whether clinically significant or not.

There is no question that a positive culture for *chlamydia trachomatis* should be treated. This is an organism that is known to cause more tubal infection and damage than gonorrhea. It is more likely to be culture positive in women with a thick mucoidlike cervical discharge. The organism may be present either in the complete absence of symptoms, or it may cause severe pelvic pain and fever. If the patient has the infection, it confers no immunity thereafter and, like ureaplasma, this tends to be a "ping-pong" infection, and all sexual partners will need to be treated. A blood test can determine if the patient has had contact with the organism in the past but results don't tell us if the infection is presently active. Cultures are expensive and difficult. For that reason, we've turned to the chlamydial antigen test which can read a cervical smear to tell us whether or not the organism is currently present. Fortunately, treatment with a form of tetracycline is simple, inexpensive, and effective.

6

Psychological and Emotional Aspects of Infertility

The patients we see obviously want a remedy for infertility. And surely most of what the patient and doctor do together deals with biologic cause-and-effect, the "mechanics" of reproduction. But infertility always has an emotional dimension, and therefore emotional issues must be considered as well.

Why Have Children?

Most people go to a physician when they become concerned about their own health or appearance. But a woman whose tubes are scarred and closed from a long-forgotten infection faces no health risks. A man with a low sperm count can enjoy a healthy life. What motivates an infertile couple to consult a specialist? The answer may be partly biological. Other mammals apparently have a reproductive instinct, since sexual activity is confined to those times when the female is able to conceive. Humans, on the other hand, are the only species outside of pigmy chimpanzees to engage in sex anytime during the monthly cycle. Does this mean that humans have no reproductive instinct? Or do they have a reproductive instinct, but one that exists separately from sexual desire? Some sociological and physiological studies indicate that the latter is more

91

likely to be the case. Is there such a thing as "maternal instinct" or "paternal instinct"? My gut reaction is yes. Whether this instinct is physiological is unclear, but what is clear is that men and women have strong emotional needs for children.

Various cultural pressures can intensify the desire for children. In some early societies, infertile couples were regarded as people to be avoided, because it was thought that they brought bad luck. In Western culture, fertility is given the stamp of approval by the Bible. We are charged to "be fruitful and multiply." In the old testament, Rachel, Leah, Hannah, Sarah, and Elisabeth were women who finally became fertile after God smiled upon them. The implication is that God does not smile upon those who are infertile. Infertility, then, carries a stigma of unworthiness based on religious doctrines. Orthodox Judaism and Roman Catholicism prohibit use of contraceptive devices. In India, some religions forbid coitus except for the explicit purpose of procreation.

In our practice we have heard many reasons for people wanting children. Some couples simply feel a need to perpetuate the family name. That motivation is by no means unique to our culture. As I found on a trip to China, people take pleasure in tracing their families back over 1000 years. Maybe that is why the Chinese government's policy of limiting a family to only one child has not met with enthusiasm, pitted as it is against this strong tradition. I have seen couples for whom pregnancy is an end in itself. The altered hormonal levels experienced during pregnancy produce in some women a general feeling of well-being. Some women enjoy the solicitude shown by family and friends during pregnancy. Men regard their pregnant mates as proof of their own virility. Some couples seem to want children so that they can live vicariously through them. They hope that their offspring will achieve goals they are unable to attain themselves.

We always consider the reasons why people come to us. Not all of their reasons seem psychologically sound. Is it healthy for a woman to want pregnancy primarily to deny the aging process or because she feels useless? Is pregnancy a good reason to hold a mate in a shaky marriage? There may be dozens of misguided reasons why people want children but the truth is that the overwhelming majority of patients we see have very legitimate and healthy reasons for wanting a child. When the reasons seem less than acceptable (admittedly a value judgement), the couple is referred for psychological evaluation and counseling before specific infertility treatment is begun.

Psychology and Fertility: Effects on Each Other

We know the desire to have children may result from various cultural and psychological pressures. Many of us in the field wonder about the relationship between emotions and fertility. If there is such a relationship, however, it is certainly ill defined at this time. For example, it is often claimed that tension and stress impair fertility. We know that sudden psychological trauma, such as the death of a loved one, can temporarily interfere with menstrual and ovulatory functions, as well as dull the desire for sex. Theoretically, emotions can induce a spasm that interferes with tubal function, but hard evidence to support this contention cannot be found. Stress and tension do not interfere with fertility in a predictable manner. Rape victims, to cite an extreme example, can suffer the added indignity of pregnancy. Male sexual drive and performance are often affected by tension and emotional stress, sometimes leading to augmented sexual drive, other times depressing sexual function. Certainly pre-existing or concurrent psychological problems may interfere with fertility. Alcoholism, for example, may coexist as a consequence of lowered self-esteem and depression. This may lead to decreased sexual activity from the effect of alcoholism or from the emotional strain. Men with borderline potency may begin to have difficulty in achieving and maintaining an erection after learning that they have an abnormal semen analysis. Treatment itself can also be the source of major stress. Women with irregular ovulatory function may react to the stress of diagnostic procedures and therapies by becoming anovulatory. About 20 percent of women who enter our donor insemination program temporarily will not ovulate. Donor insemination is also stressful to the husband, who can quickly turn feelings of inadequacy into sexual dysfunction, or even overt depression. Psychological counseling is particularly important here.

With the stress of infertility, women who have recovered from anorexia often take up their self-induced starvations again. Expensive infertility treatments, such as *in vitro* fertilization, not only strain people's finances but their emotions as well. It is a shattering experience to not conceive after going through intensive daily therapy, testing, egg retrieval, and embryo replacement. A strong relationship is needed to survive this experience.

Today, many couples postpone having children for years so that both partners can establish careers. When they finally decide that the time has come to start a family, panic may set in if they do not conceive rapidly, especially if they are in their mid-thirties or older. Up until that point, many of these people felt they were plotting their own destinies, and they assumed that when they were ready they would conceive without difficulty. It comes as a shock to them when they cannot.

The Psyche of Infertility

A common reaction to the diagnosis of infertility is denial. This is a normal psychological mechanism that allows the psyche time to adjust and "reprogram" itself to a new set of circumstances. Denial becomes pathological only when it becomes persistent and self-defeating. The diagnosis of infertility usually comes as more of a surprise to a man, because he experiences no warning signs such as menstrual irregularity.

In time, denial often turns into anger. "No, not me," becomes, "Why me?" The person might blame his physician, thinking his or her previous medical care was responsible for the present situation, or a parent, who had not responded promptly or properly to symptoms of a childhood disease that later resulted in infertility. Eventually some of the anger is directed inward, causing feelings of worthlessness. An increasing number of women have voluntary abortions prior to marriage, or even early in a marriage because it is not a convenient time to start a family. If infertility arises from complications of a previous abortion, the self-anger and guilt felt by the woman can be severe enough to require professional psychological or psychiatric care.

The infertile couple often experiences a surge of optimism once they and their physician agree on a course of treatment. This makes disappointment all the more intense if pregnancy does not occur within a short time after therapy has started. Despair and frustration can cause the couple to become isolated from family and friends. Feelings of guilt and shame may arise as they try to evade disturbing questions from parents and friends. This emotional upheaval often puts an even greater strain on the marriage. Although the partners try to be mutually supportive, this may be difficult, especially if the responsibility for infertility is perceived to rest solely with one partner. In some cases, the other partner becomes so overly supportive to the infertile partner that he or she feels suffocated by compassion and can never live comfortably with the diagnosis. It is quite common for sexual activity to cease entirely for a time after a diagnosis of infertility. If the man is the infertile partner, he may become impotent for a while or, conversely, seek to prove his fertility outside of the marriage. We've seen many women lose their ability to achieve orgasm. I can't tell you how many times I've heard couples say that they "no longer see the point of sex if no children will result from it."

Although their pain is real enough, couples who have never conceived can be said to suffer grief without an object. Much more catastrophic is the experience of the couple who, after a long interval of infertility, finally conceive only to lose the long-awaited pregnancy through spontaneous abortion. This grief has an object. It is difficult for those who have never been in this situation to understand the intensity of emotion directed toward a mass of cells within a blood clot. But the feelings are real, intense, and completely understandable.

Seeking Help

With so much emotional turmoil, what can a physician trained in infertility do for the patient? Patients want someone who is communicative, supportive, and, above all, honest. No one is going to be helped if the doctor gives a prognosis that is more optimistic than the situation justifies. It is our custom to have regular conferences with couples to review treatment strategies and prognoses. I realize that semen analyses, coitus by appointment, and temperature charts are all additional sources of stress. So when they are no longer necessary, I'm quick to discontinue them. Physicians should refrain from using inherently pejorative medical expressions, such as "inadequate luteal phase," "hostile cervical mucus," and "seminal deficiency" because they can only add to the couple's anxiety and guilt.

In truth most fertility specialists are not equipped to treat the emotional side of infertility if it becomes a major issue. An association that was started by infertile couples, RESOLVE, [1] is an excellent source of information, and group support. At their meetings infertile couples can meet others who have intimately shared the same experiences. Some of the members of RESOLVE have succeeded in conceiving. These couples provide hope as well as emotional support. Couples can also receive aid from the growing number of psychologists and psychiatrists with special interests and expertise in treating the taxing emotional side of infertility. A psychiatric referral is made when the degree of stress seems to be interfering with the enjoyment of everyday life. With help, couples learn to cope with the infertility problem in a healthier way and go on with their day-to-day activities in a much smoother fashion, even if the therapy is not working at the moment.

[1] RESOLVE, Inc., 1310 Broadway, Somerville, MA 02144-1731

7

Ovulation Induction

Ovulation is the key to conception. About 30 to 40 percent of all infertile women fail to ovulate at all (*anovulation*) or fail to ovulate consistently. For ovulation to occur (as pointed out in chapter 2), the body must produce different hormones in proper sequence in the right amount and at the right time. It's no wonder, then, that hormone imbalances of one sort or another cause a great proportion of ovulation disorders. Most of our efforts to induce ovulation are directed toward correcting these imbalances.

Causes of Ovulation Disorders

A malfunctioning thyroid gland can interfere with ovulation. But since the thyroid regulates the rate of metabolism for the entire body, the symptoms of thyroid disorders are usually so dramatic that the diagnosis is made prior to consultation for infertility. Empiric use of thyroid hormones in the absence of a demonstrable disorder has no role in the treatment of infertility.

An overactive adrenal gland can also result in infertility. These important glands, one on top of each kidney, secrete about 40 different hormones, including testosterone. If a woman has too much of this "male" hormone it interferes with normal ovulation. It's our job to determine whether the adrenal glands or the ovaries are producing the testosterone that is responsible for elevated levels of this hormone. In some cases both the ovaries and the adrenal glands are responsible. If the adrenal glands are malfunctioning, their activity can usually be easily suppressed with prednisone or other oral agents. If the problem is a pituitary tumor the hormone ACTH will be overproduced and act on the adrenal glands. This is treated by removing the tumor with a surgical procedure. We now have advanced diagnostic tests, such as computerized X-ray (CAT scan), and magnetic resonance imaging (MRI, as doctors call it) that can diagnose even a very small tumor in its earliest stages.

In some women, estrogen levels do not increase at the proper rate during the menstrual cycle. As a result the pituitary does not release enough LH to induce ovulation. We can correct this with oral doses of estrogen taken in small, gradually increasing amounts to stimulate the normal train of events depicted in figure 2.10. There is a positive feedback mechanism here: increasing doses of the proper amount of estrogen will provoke LH release, but high doses given in a steady fashion, such as with birth-control pills, will suppress LH release. Figure 7.1 illustrates use of an estrogen starting with 1 pill daily and progressing to 3 daily for ovulation induction over a period of 9 days. Because of the well-publicized DES syndrome, many women are now understandably reluctant to take estrogens. But in the treatment described here no estrogen is given to patients after ovulation or during pregnancy. This method of ovulation induction used for 40 years has proven to be quite safe.

The polycystic ovarian syndrome, formerly known as the Stein-Leventhal syndrome, is a term used to describe an anovulatory woman who usually has irregular menses, excessive body hair, and who is frequently obese. The ovaries typically are enlarged and contain numerous small cysts just beneath the ovarian surface. Before endocrine tests became widely available, diagnosis was made based on the findings mentioned above. Today, the diagnosis is often made on a hormonal basis: The syndrome is said to exist when the level of LH in blood is at least two and one half times that of FSH, although both may be within their respective normal ranges. The physical findings often are dependent on ethnic group, and many women with the telltale hormonal shift are neither obese nor hairy. Many

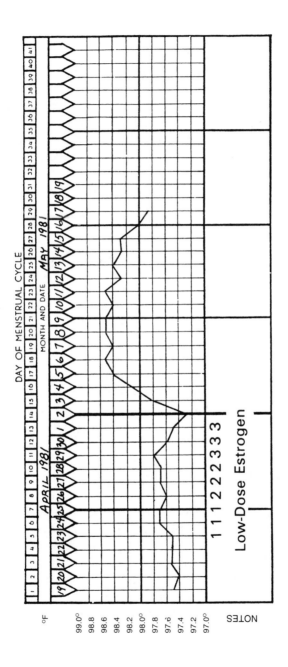

FIGURE 7.1 BBT recording of an ovulatory cycle with use of serially increasing oral doses of estrogens.

authorities argue that the ultrasonic appearance of the ovary is even a better indicator of polycystic ovarian syndrome (PCOS) than hormonal patterns. These ovaries may have small cysts just beneath the surface and give rise to the "necklace" sign seen as a ring of small cysts around the periphery of the ovary.

Not infrequently, the excessive hair growth is a consequence of increased production of testosterone in the ovary. Blood levels of testosterone usually are normal or slightly increased. Since treatment for anovulation frequently begins with clomiphene citrate regardless of specific hormonal findings, identification of this subgroup of anovulatory women is not always necessary. If pregnancy is not immediately desired, the patient is usually placed on birth-control pills in order to stop (temporarily) the disordered hormonal production.

In the discussion that follows concerning the many drugs used for ovulation induction, we will give some specifics as to prescribed dose and duration of treatment. It is important to realize that many drugs are prescribed differently in actual practice than are set down in Food and Drug Administration (FDA) regulations. Therefore, with some of the agents to be discussed below, even though they have been used for over a quarter of a century, we find that the actual way the drug is used in many cases is different from the FDA-regulated original use. Some women, for example, fail to release enough LH at the proper time, even though their estrogen levels seem to increase at a normal rate. For 30 years this problem has been treated with the hormone *human chorionic gonadotropin* (hCG), a use that while not approved by the FDA, has worked in practice. Remember that LH serves a dual purpose: It causes the ripe ovarian follicle to release its egg, and stimulates the corpus luteum to secrete progesterone. After conception, LH levels drop off, but progesterone secretion persists because the blastocyst secretes hCG (which is the basis for the pregnancy test) to keep the corpus luteum active. In practice, hCG administered by a physician will cause a ripe ovarian follicle to ovulate, often within 24 to 36 hours, as shown in figure 7.2. In other words, hCG works as a surrogate for LH, and it is readily available for clinical use while LH is not. Because hCG remains active in the body longer than LH, it takes only a single injection to induce ovulation.

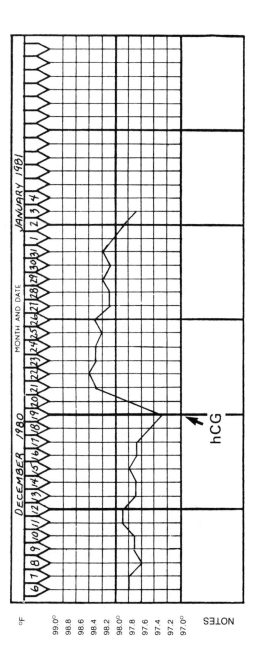

FIGURE 7.2 BBT recording of an ovulatory cycle in which hCG has been used to trigger ovulation.

Drug-Induced Ovulation

Today, as for the past 25 years, the drug most commonly used for ovulation induction is *clomiphene citrate* (Serophene or Clomid). Clomiphene citrate works by occupying estrogen receptor sites in the hypothalamus to prevent estrogen from binding to these sites. This fools the body into thinking that estrogen levels are lower than they really are. The hypothalamus then instructs the pituitary to release even greater amounts of FSH (follicle stimulating hormone) and LH (luteinizing hormone) which in turn accelerate the growth of an ovarian follicle. Figure 7.3 illustrates the use of Serophene. Note that the drug is usually administered from day 5 to day 9 of the cycle. We can start this earlier or later depending upon the patient's menstrual history. The FDA approves dosages from 1 to 2 50 mg pills each day for 5 days, but physicians often will use doses that far exceed this. In difficult cases, clomiphene citrate treatment has been combined with hCG, although this use, as we've said, has not been approved by the FDA either. Clomiphene citrate has been found to induce ovulation in 60 to 70 percent of women who hadn't been ovulating, although their pregnancy rate is 40 to 50 percent. Women who haven't been able to menstruate without medication usually respond poorly to this drug. But even if we eliminate these women from our count, we still find that the pregnancy rate is much lower than the apparent ovulation rate. The reasons for this seem to be that when ovulation is induced with clomiphene citrate it sometimes produces hormones in the wrong sequence. Also, we know clomiphene citrate sometimes reduces both the quantity and quality of cervical mucus, probably by affecting those cells in the cervix which secrete mucus. This antifertility effect limits its usefulness. Because of these antimucus effects, we have to repeat the post-coital test, even if the patient had normal findings before we started her on this drug. The test tells us if we have to substitute another drug for the clomiphene citrate. Clomiphene citrate also may increase testosterone in the blood. The ovaries of many women who require clomiphene citrate secrete rather high amounts of testosterone to begin with. The clomiphene citrate stimulates more LH release, which in some ovaries causes more testosterone

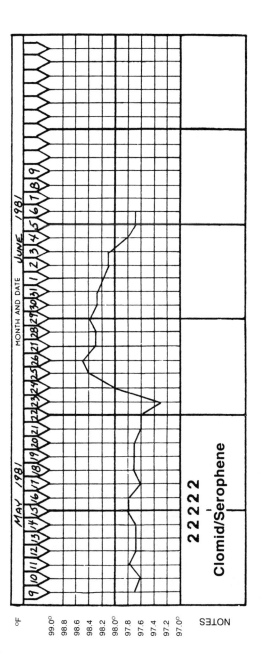

FIGURE 7.3 BBT recording of a typical clomiphene citrate-induced ovulatory cycle.

production. So if the patient secretes even more testosterone, the quality of cervical mucus gets worse, and this, in turn, decreases sperm survival. Once detected, poor cervical mucus can be treated as we will describe in the next chapter.

Clomiphene citrate can produce some unwanted side effects. But, fortunately, we know from long clinical experience that this drug does not cause birth defects. Don't be alarmed if you experience temporary bloating or mild depression. Some women have reported temporary hair loss. Others - especially if they wear contact lenses - have experienced ocular effects, such as seeing halos around lights. During therapy, the curvature of the eye changes slightly, so that the lens may fit a little too tightly. The effect doesn't damage the patient's eye or have any permanent effect on her vision, but most women feel more comfortable switching to prescription eyeglasses during this time. Hot flashes may also be experienced, and while bothersome, it is actually a good sign, because it tells us that FSH and LH are being released from the pituitary. All of these symptoms disappear soon after the clomiphene citrate is discontinued, and ovulation normally occurs 5 to 9 days *after* the last pill.

Clomiphene citrate is not an ideal drug. It sometimes releases such high levels of pituitary hormones that the ovaries become enlarged. You can tell when enlargement has occurred because you get a heavy feeling and discomfort in the lower abdomen. Fortunately, the enlargement is usually mild and temporary. The ovaries return to normal size when clomiphene citrate is discontinued and no permanent effect occurs. But when enlarged ovaries are found, further therapy is withheld until the ovaries have returned to normal. Then the dose is lowered in the upcoming cycle. Pelvic examination is usually sufficient to determine if there is significant enlargement. Some doctors like to monitor ovarian size with ultrasound on a routine basis when using this drug.

As a result of an excessive release of gonadotropins, clomiphene citrate may stimulate the ovaries to ripen more than one follicle. If conception occurs it may result in multiple births. Twinning occurs in about 6 percent of women who conceive during a course of treatment with clomiphene citrate. This is about 7 times greater than the twinning rate among women who are not on this drug. However, the chances of twinning are not related to the dosage taken. Triplets are rare.

Human Gonadotropins

We have said that clomiphene citrate works by causing the woman to produce more FSH and LH. But some women don't respond to this treatment because of a malfunction in the hypothalamic-pituitary control center. For these women a preparation containing human FSH and LH can be administered directly via intramuscular injection. *Humegon/Pergonal* are the trade names for one of the most widely used preparations. It is the most powerful ovulation inducer available. The use of Humegon or Pergonal should be reserved as the hormonal treatment of last resort for several reasons. For one, it is exceedingly costly. For another, Humegon/Pergonal causes the therapist to walk a tight wire between a dose large enough to induce ovulation and a dose so large that multiple gestations and large ovarian cysts result. The patient must be monitored with blood tests and ultrasound. This is inconvenient for the patient because she must come to the doctor's office daily for about a week or so. At a certain estrogen level and follicular size, Humegon/Pergonal is no longer needed, and hCG is given to trigger ovulation. Careful monitoring has brought the multiple birth rate down by more than half, from 25 to 12 percent.

There is no question that daily monitoring of estrogen levels and ultrasonic examinations have made Humegon/Pergonal treatment safer and so much easier to manage. We now rarely see a patient hospitalized from overstimulated ovaries. Nevertheless, the risks and costs are still sufficient to require that all other avenues of therapy be considered before gonadotropins are used. As a rule, women who have amenorrhea will usually do very well on Humegon/Pergonal, but poorly on clomiphene citrate. Today, we see more and more career women in their early forties who are trying to conceive. Most of them do well on Humegon/Pergonal, a mixture of FSH and LH. A few patients already have elevated levels of LH. For these women, we use a preparation that contains pure FSH and little or no LH, called *Metrodin*. Like Humegon/Pergonal, it is given by injection. I find it helpful to teach the patient and her husband how to prepare the injection and administer either Humegon/Pergonal or Metrodin since therapy usually extends over a period of about 7 to 10 days each cycle.

Humegon/Pergonal has also proven to be an excellent switch in therapy for patients who had not conceived after 6 to 8 cycles of trying with clomiphene citrate. Many of these patients will conceive in the first or second cycle of Humegon/Pergonal use. I think one reason for this is related to the fact that not only cervical mucus but mucus in the uterus and tubes becomes improved with use of Humegon/Pergonal, because the drug induces high levels of estrogen around the time of ovulation. Another factor is that multiple ovulations are induced and the sperm have more targets available to them.

Currently available gonadotropins like Humegon/Pergonal extracted from menopausal urine all contain protein contaminants. Bioengineered pure FSH made from recumberant DNA injected into bacteria allows for a much purer product - one which can be self-administered as a subcutaneous rather than an intramuscular injection. These newer forms have been tested and await FDA approval.

Ovulation Induction and Ovarian Cancer

Ovarian cancer constitutes about 4% of all female cancers. In the general population the lifetime risk is just over 1%, although the risk is up to 50% in certain families in which there seems to be an autosomal dominant form of inheritance. Add to this two additional well documented facts: (1) oral contraceptive agents have a strong protective effect, increasing with duration of use and persisting over a woman's lifetime; (2) never pregnant women (voluntary or involuntary) have about a six-fold increased risk (to 6%).

Against this background of perplexing data, a report appeared in January 1993 suggesting a link between fertility-promoting drugs and development of ovarian cancer. The report was a meta-analysis, a reshuffling of previously published reports between 1956 and 1986 in 12 different epidemiologic surveys, none of which was designed to evaluate this question. Various methods of data collection were employed and definitions of ovarian cancer were inconsistent among investigators. In 3000 ovarian cancer patients only 24 had taken any fertility promoting drugs and the final conclusion was based on 12 patients who had not conceived following therapy. Obviously this is a minuscule base upon which to draw meaningful conclusions. Moreover, no mention was made of another logical conclusion, i.e. infertile women who did conceive following drug therapy, had achieved, besides their main goal of pregnancy, a reduced risk for ovarian cancer.

Then, in 1994 a report which evaluated 3,837 previously treated infertile women was published. There were 11 possible ovarian cancers in the group, with only six actually proven. Nine women had received clomiphene citrate as part of their therapy. No increased risk was noted statistically when the drug had been taken for less than one year as a cumulative experience. Today, few therapists would suggest such a prolonged course.

This issue is being closely scrutinized by clinicians and epidemiologists alike. At the moment, these findings may be only statistical quirks. We are not making light of this issue, but for now there is little reason for alarm.

GONADOTROPIN RELEASING HORMONE (GNRH)

The rate at which gonadotropin releasing hormone (GnRH) is released by the hypothalamus is important for normal function (see chapter 2). For instance, if one injects this agent into the bloodstream as a steady dose, pituitary-ovarian function diminishes. But if given as a rhythmical burst every 90 minutes or so, the hormone proves to be stimulatory to the pituitary to release FSH and LH and thus eventually to stimulate the ovary. It's a delicate balance. Some patients may have a disturbance in the release of GnRH that causes anovulation. If so, clomiphene citrate rarely works. Humegon/ Pergonal will supply the FSH and LH needed, but some patients are exquisitely sensitive to even small doses of Humegon/Pergonal. Medical researchers have tried giving GnRH in 90-minute bursts either intravenously or just below the skin via a small programmable pump. The theory was that this process would be more natural than using Humegon/Pergonal and that since the drug would not bypass the pituitary gland, overstimulation and multiple births could be avoided. However, this method has not worked out as well as hoped. The ovaries still can become overstimulated and multiple births still occur. Although this method of treatment is mildly popular in Europe, it has not caught on in the United States, mostly because patients don't like being attached to a pump - even if it is quite portable and small - for 20 days. At the moment, this treatment is best suited for those women who are difficult to properly regulate on Humegon/Pergonal.

GNRH LOOKALIKES

In some women, particularly those who are close to menopause, FSH levels may be elevated with little daily variation. Addition of Humegon/Pergonal or Metrodin under these circumstances has little effect on the ovary which has become "desensitized" to these high levels of FSH. A novel approach is the use of GnRH synthetic lookalikes (analogs) to shut off the pituitary FSH release and let the ovary become responsive once again to increasing amounts of FSH, starting from a normal baseline. This allows the doctor to use Humegon/Pergonal or Metrodin, for example, without the patient's pituitary gland continuing to release its own FSH and LH, which makes it difficult to adjust the drug dose. This approach has been especially helpful in inducing ovulation in conjunction with *in vitro* fertilization, leading to improvement in the quality and quantity of eggs and pregnancy rates. There are also reports that this approach is helpful for patients with polycystic ovarian disease who do not respond well to other treatment (see chapter 5).

PARLODEL

High prolactin levels not associated with nursing can result from pituitary tumors, the use of drugs (especially tranquilizers), or unknown causes. A simple blood test will help make the diagnosis. Fortunately, the drug *bromocriptine* (Parlodel) works well for suppressing prolactin. If a small pituitary tumor is at fault, bromocriptine will also shrink it, although it may grow again when the drug is stopped. Larger pituitary tumors may have to be removed surgically. It is amazing how patients with this abnormality can slip through diagnostic tests without being identified. One thirty-nine-year-old patient was referred to me after seventeen years without periods (amenorrhea). Testing showed a very high level of prolactin *without* any milky breast discharge. We began bromocriptine, she conceived within five months, and delivered a healthy baby. Two years later, she returned and was once again successful with the same form of treatment. However, a note of caution is in order for women who conceive after bromocriptine therapy. Pregnancy can cause a pituitary tumor that is already there to grow. The growth may threaten the optic nerve which runs past the pituitary gland. Therefore, after bromocriptine therapy we closely monitor women who conceive for any sudden tumor growth. In some countries, physicians routinely avoid this problem by keeping the mother on the drug during pregnancy. No ill effects have been observed in infants born to these mothers. However, this form of therapy during pregnancy has not been approved in the United States.

When beginning therapy with Parlodel many patients experience a stuffy nose, headache, and may have lowered blood pressure, which can cause dizziness if one stands up after sitting for a long time. These side effects are temporary, and usually subside quickly.

A somewhat similar endocrine problem involves an excess of *growth hormone*, usually from a pituitary tumor. In large amounts, *acromegaly* or gigantism results. We know that mild disturbances sometimes mimic symptoms of prolactin excess so we watch for this condition, although it is much rarer.

Ovarian Surgery May Induce Ovulation

The surgical approach to ovulation induction for women with polycystic ovarian disease is *ovarian wedge resection*. Wedge resection involves cutting wedges out of the ovary, like cutting a slice of pie, then suturing the ovary together. I cannot really explain why this procedure works, but it certainly does in over 50 percent of patients. The effect of wedge resection is temporary: If pregnancy does not occur within a year, most patients who have not conceived revert back to their abnormal state. As with most surgery, wedge resection should only be attempted in patients who do not respond to other medical therapy. Risks include the formation of adhesions between the ovaries and the tubes which may result in infertility. A new approach drills small holes in the cysts just below the ovarian surface with a laser or electrical probe under laparoscopic guidance. This should lessen the problem of post operative adhesion formation. So far, early trials by a few different surgeons have been promising. Perhaps this procedure will prove a good alternative to using Humegon/Pergonal for patients who do not respond to clomiphene citrate (Serophene/clomid).

8

The Cervix:
Its Role in Fertility

The cervix is the point of departure for sperm about to ascend into the upper female reproductive tract. Its crypts act as reservoirs for sperm; its normally alkaline mucus secretions protect sperm from the acid environment of the vagina. Changes in the cervix of a congenital nature, or those that occur after disease or surgery, may be responsible for infertility.

Disorders of the Cervix

Women are rarely born with cervical disorders that diminish fertility. Usually these conditions develop later in life following infections, inflammations, and surgery. One exception to this rule is what happened when DES mothers took this drug during their pregnancies. As we discussed in chapter 2, DES daughters often have somewhat distorted cervices. They experience slightly more difficulty conceiving and their abortion rate as well as ectopic pregnancy rate is definitely higher than average.

Sometimes cervical mucus can be acidic rather than alkaline. While the age-old remedy for this was to have the patient take an alkalinizing douche just prior to intercourse, I believe it never really worked because water and mucus do not mix. Patients have had better results with drinking two bicarbonate of soda (Alka-seltzer) tablets in water three times daily for the two or three days preceding expected ovulation, which alkalinizes their secretions. When the acidic cervical mucus becomes more normally alkaline, sperm survival improves and so do the chances of pregnancy. The Alka-seltzer approach does not work for all patients, but your doctor can easily monitor your pH levels without special equipment by measuring the cervical mucus with a simple test strip of pH sensitive paper.

The Inflamed Cervix

Inflammation of the cervix, cervicitis, can kill sperm or inhibit their movement. It can also diminish the amount and the reproductive quality of cervical mucus. To treat cervicitis doctors try to find the responsible organisms so that the appropriate antibiotic can be prescribed. We culture the cervix with a cotton swab and test it in a laboratory. Under normal conditions a variety of microorganisms reside in the cervix without ever causing trouble. Identifying the culprit organism can be difficult. Sometimes, doctors treat patients with tetracycline without ever attempting to identify the offending organism. This is because tetracycline is effective against many organisms, including ureaplasma and chlamydia, both of which are frequent culprits. This is not the ideal way to practice medicine, but it is certainly less costly than identifying each and every organism by doing cultures before attempting treatment. Remember that the sexual partner must be treated too, even if he has no symptoms, to avoid reinfecting the woman. Of the various organisms that most frequently trigger cervicitis, chlamydia is certainly the most important because it is also associated with tubal inflammations that lead to obstruction of the fallopian tubes, even more commonly than gonococcus. While chlamydia, gonorrhea, and ureaplasma can be present without symptoms, chlamydia is more frequently associated with a thick, yellowish, vaginal discharge which actually emanates from the cervix.

Some cases of cervicitis will not respond even to multiple courses of antibiotics because the infection lies deep within the cervical crypts, a condition somewhat analogous to an abscessed tooth. To rout it, it is necessary to get past the inflamed tissue. The trick is to destroy this tissue without harming the mucus-secreting cells that are still healthy. A freezing technique called cryocautery works well for this purpose. It produces no appreciable scarring, and complete healing takes place in about 8 weeks. Hot cautery, which burns away diseased tissue, should be avoided because it produces scar tissue that may actually block the cervix. Also, the amount of tissue destruction is more difficult to control with a hot cautery. We now have lasers to treat the cervix. They are particularly helpful in treating localized disease because the laser vaporizes discrete areas with minimal damage to adjacent normal cells. Newer electric loop procedures seem better than laser methods so far as limiting unwanted damage to normal cervical tissue is concerned.

Cervical Mucus and Ovulation

A significant number of women, for no detectable reason, consistently show poor cervical mucus at ovulation. These women may improve their mucus by taking small doses of estrogen before ovulation. Estrogen, you will recall, increases mucus production and gives it the qualities necessary to allow sperm to move through the cervix. But too much estrogen can block ovulation, which is why birth control pills are so effective. Therapists try to find the right dose to enhance the mucus without blocking ovulation. It takes some trial and error, so don't get discouraged if the treatment lasts several months. Some fertility doctors use potassium iodide drops to enhance mucus production, but I haven't had success with these drops. By the way, antihistamines and certain cough medicines should be avoided around the time of ovulation; these can suppress the production of cervical mucus, just as they suppress mucus production elsewhere in the body. Although popularized in newspapers and magazines, use of certain cough medicines to improve cervical mucus has been reported primarily by a single physician and there are no confirming scientific studies.

The potential adverse effect of clomiphene citrate on cervical mucus may be a consequence of increasing already elevated testosterone levels, but in large part when it occurs, it is primarily due to the drug itself. Estrogen levels at the time of ovulation in patients receiving clomiphene citrate are already higher than usual, and for that reason giving extra estrogen by mouth or by injection to offset the drug effect usually does not help. If mucus quality/quantity remains unsatisfactory for sperm survival, consideration should be given to intrauterine insemination or to an early move to gonadotropin therapy with Humegon/Pergonal or Metrodin.

Cervical Infection and Stenosis

Cervical infection can sometimes cause stenosis, an extreme tightening of the cervical opening. Fertility experts disagree over whether a tight cervix actually interferes with conception. Some believe that no matter how tight the cervix, sperm can get in if menstrual blood can get out. However, I have seen some previously infertile women conceive after no other treatment apart from the surgical opening of the stenotic cervices.

Some cervices - commonly the DES cervix that has been biopsied, or a cervix subjected to a cone biopsy - are difficult to dilate without putting the patient to sleep. After surgery, the cervix must be kept open till healing occurs, or else the cervical tissue can fuse again. This problem can be solved very simply with a device called a stem pessary or a Wylie drain (illustrated in figure 8.1). A physician inserts the device and sutures it in place. Grooves in the Wylie drain allow menstrual flow to pass out until the device is removed in the doctor's office about 2 months later. By then healing has occurred and the cervix remains open.

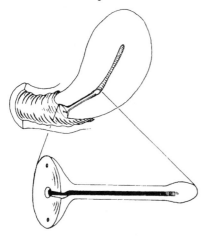

FIGURE 8.1 Use of a sperm pessary following cervical surgery in order to prevent cervical stenosis.

9

Disorders of the Uterus

Infection and Its Aftermath

Infection of the uterine lining, *endometritis*, may occur in conjunction with pregnancy or from an infection acquired sexually, or associated with use of intrauterine devices. Women at highest risk are those who abort, either spontaneously or by induction, and those who require surgery after birth to remove placental fragments from the uterus. Sometimes endometritis can be diagnosed by biopsies and cultures taken directly from the interior of the uterus. The areas of inflammation may be scattered throughout the uterus but can be seen with a hysteroscope. Most of these infections can be cured with commonly used oral antibiotics.

Often, however, the impact of endometritis on fertility comes not from the infection itself, but from its aftermath. The infection may destroy portions of the endometrium, and leave in its place scar tissue (adhesions). This leads to infertility or pregnancy loss by reducing the number of good implantation sites for a blastocyst, and by interfering with the proper blood supply to the uterine lining. Severe infection can develop that can lead to loss of so much of the uterine lining that the patient will become amenorrheic, even though she shows normal BBT charts and hormonal levels. This condition is called *Asherman syndrome*. The diagnosis is made by HSG (figure 9.1) or hysteroscopic examination. Treatment of uterine adhesions consists of first curing any residual active infection with antibiotics and then hysteroscopically removing the adhesions from the uterine wall. When the adhesions are removed, they leave behind bare patches on the uterine wall. Any endometrial tissue which has survived must be stimulated to grow over these "bald spots." To accomplish this, the patient is given large doses of estrogen for about 2 months. The most difficult part of treating Asherman's syndrome comes after surgery. Normally, the uterus resembles an uninflated balloon with the walls in contact with each other. But after surgical repair the walls must not touch one another during healing or they will fuse together and obliterate the uterine cavity. This is the same problem encountered in treating a stenotic cervix. So after snipping away the adhesions through the hysteroscope, the surgeon inserts an intrauterine device (IUD), the same device used in birth control, to hold the uterus open while the endometrium regenerates. When the return of menstruation signals that the healing is complete (about 6 weeks later), the IUD is removed. A follow-up hysteroscopic examination or HSG is taken to assess the results of treatment. About 70 percent of women who are treated for intrauterine adhesions eventually deliver a baby. But this rate is reduced to 40 percent for those who have no periods at all before surgery. It should be mentioned, however, that the same infection that caused the syndrome may also have been present in the fallopian tubes, possibly closing them. Before any corrective surgery is done, a preoperative HSG is done to make sure that at least one tube is open. This type of hysteroscopic surgery is quite difficult, and the operation may actually have to be done in two or three separate sessions. The surgeon often faces dense scar tissue, and to avoid perforating the uterus, laparoscopy is done at the same time so that the surgeon's assistant can warn of impending perforation of the uterus. If perforation occurs it is usually not catastrophic, but the procedure has to be discontinued and the uterus must be allowed to heal before the second procedure can be carried out. These operations are usually performed on an outpatient basis.

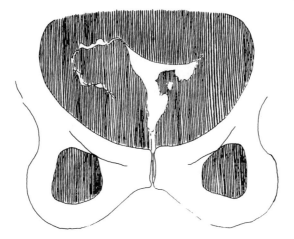

FIGURE 9.1 X-ray appearance of intrauterine adhesions causing a "filling defect" within the uterus. The defect appears as a dark irregular area surrounded by a white dye.

Fibroids: Benign but Troublesome

Benign tumors within the smooth muscle of the uterus are found in a significant percentage of women. These *myomas*, or *fibroids*, are seen in more than 25 percent of women over thirty-five, and seem to occur in black women more often than white. And they seem to be inherited. If your mother had them there is an increased chance you'll get them too. Fibroids do not always cause fertility problems, but when they do, they usually involve pregnancy loss rather than failure to conceive. Whether or not fibroids interfere with conception depends more on their location than on their size; if they grow near the junction of the uterus and the fallopian tube, they can obstruct the tubal entrance.

Fibroids may interfere with reproduction in a variety of ways. A fibroid just under the endometrial lining will frequently be associated with heavy menses. Fibroids in the wall of the uterus can distort and enlarge the cavity (figures 9.2, 9.3, and 9.4). During pregnancy, the high estrogen levels that normally occur can stimulate fibroid growth. A small fibroid that does not appear to be of clinical significance in a nonpregnant state can show tremendous growth during a pregnancy, finally resulting in loss of that pregnancy.

Pregnancy loss occurs when an intruding fibroid causes the placenta to separate from the uterine wall. Distortion of the uterus by the fibroid may also make it irritable, causing contractions and eventually premature labor. If pregnancy reaches an advanced stage, a fibroid blocking the birth canal may force the physician to deliver the child by cesarean section. After delivery, the fibroid may interfere with the ability of the uterus to contract. If so, a hysterectomy (removal of the uterus) may be necessary to control the bleeding. While older birth control pills contained relatively high estrogen doses, the newer agents do not, and studies have shown no stimulation of fibroid growth with use of these agents.

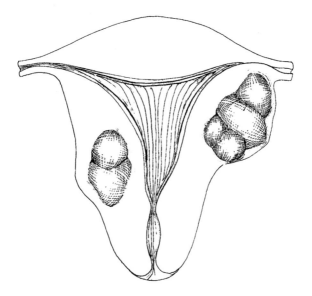

FIGURE 9.2 Uterine myomas, or fibroids. Partial obstruction of the patient's left fallopian tube at its entry into the uterus has occurred, but the shape of the uterine cavity is normal.

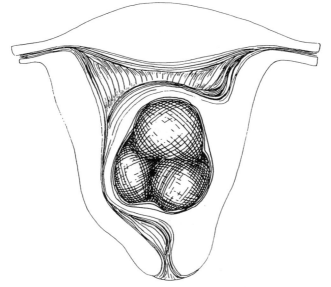

FIGURE 9.3 Myomas distorting the uterine cavity, as shown here, are likely to cause abortion.

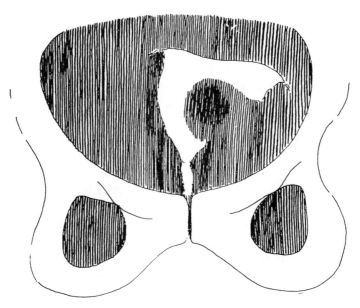

FIGURE 9.4 X-ray picture of uterine distortion caused by myoma.

If a woman is seen in consultation for surgical removal of a myoma, or *myomectomy* (figure 9.5 shows the removal of a large fibroid), the doctor takes into account the age of the patient and her previous pregnancy history. Usually, if the patient is young enough, it is suggested that she try a pregnancy to see if she can deliver first without surgery. If a woman with a large fibroid is over the age of thirty-seven and has never been pregnant, we have other considerations to think about. We know her fertility is beginning to diminish, and the decision to remove her fibroids versus waiting for her to conceive and possibly abort, becomes quite difficult. If the surgery requires multiple or deep incisions, future deliveries will have to be by cesarean section because of the risk of the uterus rupturing during labor. Moreover, adhesions resulting from surgery may cause infertility. Finally, new fibroids grow in 20 to 30 percent of women who have fibroid surgery. Many of these women eventually will require a hysterectomy. Therefore, you can see why there are honest differences of opinion among fertility experts over what to do. Less controversial is the reproductive necessity for myomectomy in women whose fibroids have caused pregnancy loss.

For example, one thirty-four-year-old woman married to a sterile man was referred to us for artificial insemination-donor (AID). Preliminary examination showed that her uterus was enlarged to the size normally seen at 14 weeks of pregnancy and distorted in shape as well. X-ray examination revealed a solitary myoma protruding into the uterine cavity. Because of her age and that finding, we decided to remove the growth before she tried to become pregnant. Subsequently she conceived with AID and delivered her baby without complication by cesarean section. However, the reproductive future for these patients depends on the total bulk of the myomas encountered at surgery. Nevertheless, we have been gratified by high success rates even in women whose fibroids had extended up past the navel.

You may recall our discussion in chapter 7 about GnRH used to shut off the pituitary so that ovulation could more easily be induced. In the absence of Humegon/Pergonal, use of a synthetic GnRH induces a menopausal state with very low estrogen levels. Just as with naturally occurring menopause, the fibroid undergoes

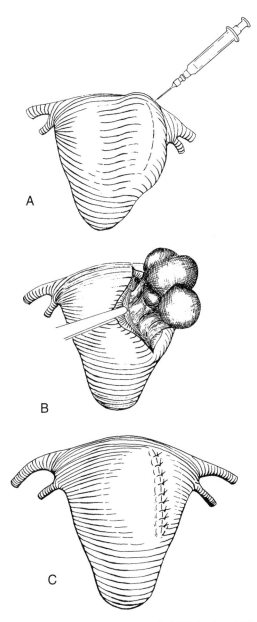

FIGURE 9.5 Removal of uterine myomas (myomectomy). (A) Injection of Pitressin along intended incision to reduce bleeding, (B) Multilobulated myomas "shelled out" through incision, (C) Closure of incision in layers.

tremendous shrinkage, sometimes as much as 60 percent within 3 or 4 months. These drugs are currently available by injection either daily or monthly as a single injection of a long-acting preparation. A synthetic GnRH analog given as a nasal spray works just as well for fibroids. I must strongly emphasize that once therapy stops, the tumors rapidly grow back. But the exciting aspect of this form of treatment is that it can be used prior to surgery to shrink the fibroid tumors, which can then be removed with smaller incisions and less blood loss. Now that we see more women over thirty-five attempting pregnancy, the number of women with fibroid tumors who need surgery has increased. The results of this treatment have been encouraging and more than 70 percent of the women who have been operated on have successful deliveries, although they may require cesarean delivery if incisions had to be made in the uterus to remove the fibroids.

The surgical technique utilized depends on the location, and size of the myoma(s) and the philosophy of the surgeon. Those growths totally within the cavity of the uterus (submucous) can be removed during hysteroscopy as an outpatient procedure. Myomas which grow from the outer surface of the uterus on a stalk can be operated with laparoscopic techniques, also on an outpatient basis.

While skilled laparoscopic surgeons can remove myomas deeply imbedded in the uterine wall, reports of poor healing and uterine rupture during pregnancy in patients treated in this fashion have tempered the ardor of gynecologists to perform all myomectomies (removal of myomas) endoscopically. A small open procedure (a mini laparotomy) allows for a more accurate anatomical reconstruction of the uterus in certain cases. Patients are advised to seek a good fertility surgeon and to let him or her make the decision best suited to the individual. Whether or not subsequent deliveries should be by mandatory cesarean section or a trial of labor depends on the size of the tumors, the number and depth of uterine incisions and finally on the judgement of the surgeon post-operatively as well as the decision of the obstetrician during labor.

Repairing Uterine Abnormalities

Congenital uterine abnormalities were discussed in chapter 2 (and illustrated in figure 2.6). No attempt to repair a bicornuate uterus is made without first observing the outcome of pregnancy. Even a severely distorted uterus may produce a healthy newborn. Surgery generally is reserved for cases of repeated pregnancy loss, usually at least two consecutive losses, unless the age of the patient with at least one loss dictates a more aggressive approach. Figure 9.6 shows the steps in the removal of an intrauterine septum. Figure 9.7 shows how a bicornuate uterus is reunified. Although both conditions have two uterine cavities instead of one, the approach to each is quite different. The septate uterus is more often associated with early pregnancy loss and usually can be surgically corrected on an outpatient basis with a combined laparoscopic and hysteroscopic technique rather than by an open route. Besides the obvious advantage of outpatient surgery, the long-term benefit is also significant in that a normal vaginal delivery can take place. The bicornuate uterus, on the other hand, is usually associated with pregnancy loss later in pregnancy. Its repair requires abdominal and uterine incisions. Patients who have had surgery for a bicornuate uterus will need to have a cesarean section. Surgery for either of these two conditions carries about an 80 percent success rate; as defined by the number of women who subsequently leave the hospital with a baby.

A typical case is that of a twenty-nine-year-old woman referred to us because of repeated pregnancy loss. Each of her previous four pregnancies had ended in a loss at 8 to 14 weeks. Her X-ray picture suggested a septate uterus. This was later confirmed by a laparoscopy/hysteroscopy examination. We then cut the septum using a hysteroscope in an outpatient procedure, and she was sent home the same day. She has since delivered two babies at term without difficulty. The septum went undetected in spite of the fact that she had three dilation and evacuation (D & E) procedures performed at the time of her pregnancy losses. Therefore, we screen all patients with a hysteroscopic examination (because X-ray is not as accurate) who have a history of this type of pregnancy loss. Imaging techniques such as ultrasonography are also helpful in assessment of uterine structure, except during pregnancy.

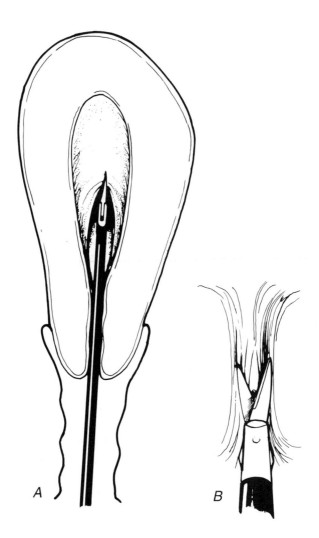

A   *B*

FIGURE 9.6 (A) Hysteroscopy has indicated a septate uterus. Scissors are inserted through an operating channel, (B) A close-up view of the septum showing the scissors being used to cut the septum. The septum is composed mainly of fibroelastic tissue which separates easily when cut.

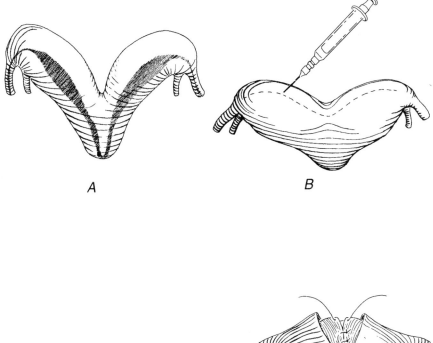

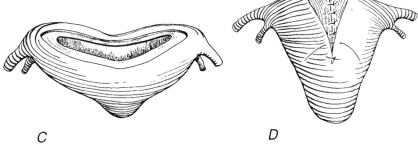

FIGURE 9.7 Steps in repair of bicornuate uterus. (A) Appearance before surgery with two small separate cavities, (B) Injection of Pitressin along incision to control bleeding, (C) Appearance after cavities united, (D) Closure of incision in layers.

Adenomyosis

Adenomyosis is a condition in which endometrial tissue grows into the muscle fibers of the uterine wall. Patients usually experience clear-cut symptoms with this condition because it results in a tender uterus, causing *dysmenorrhea* (painful menses) and *dyspareunia* (painful intercourse). Heavy menses are usually present. Since adenomyosis occurs most frequently in women over thirty-five, it has only been recently recognized as a cause of infertility. The exact way in which fertility is diminished is unknown, but is probably similar to a related condition, endometriosis. Medical treatment is similar to that for endometriosis and is therefore discussed in the next chapter. If medical treatment fails, and if the condition is not widespread, surgical removal of the affected areas is attempted.

Diagnosis of adenomyosis can be quite difficult. Because larger lesions cause uterine distortion and enlargement, it is often mistaken for uterine fibroids, which can also cause pain and heavy menses. While hysteroscopy, and less often, hysterosalpingograms, can suggest the diagnosis, the MRI has proven to be the best diagnostic aid in spite of its expense.

10

Endometriosis

The inner lining of the uterus, the endometrium, is made up of special tissue that undergoes dramatic changes over the course of the menstrual cycle. At the beginning of the cycle estrogen stimulates its growth, or proliferation. At mid-cycle, progesterone matures the endometrial glands which then secrete substances designed to nourish the implanting blastocyst. Small blood vessels increase in diameter and new ones appear to offer a rich vascular point of attachment for the blastocyst. Then, at the end of the cycle, if pregnancy has not occurred the secretory endometrium disintegrates into bloody fragments and a woman's monthly period follows.

How It Occurs

Endometriosis occurs when pieces of this tissue escape the uterus and take root on the surfaces of other organs, usually those in the abdomen. Each month as the ovary sends out signals to the endometrium in the uterus to grow, these renegade tissues also respond and grow. They proliferate, they secrete, and they turn into menses - a menses that has no outlet from the body. Because of this internal bleeding, and for other reasons that are only vaguely understood, endometriosis can pose a serious threat to fertility. In most infertility practices, more than 30 percent of patients evaluated laparoscopically will have documented endometriosis. In fact, endometriosis is one of the leading causes of infertility today.

Endometriosis: Theories and Fact

Gynecologists used to think that endometriosis was primarily a disease of thin, well-to-do white women over thirty years of age. New studies have shown us how ridiculous this notion was, thanks in part to the work of Dr. Donald Chatman in Chicago who showed endometriosis was not rare in the black population. Endometriosis affects teenagers and women from all economic and ethnic backgrounds. For example, Drs. Donald Goldstein and John Leventhal in Boston studied a group of teenagers who had painful periods that were resistant to medication. When no cause could be found for their complaints, the young women's physicians referred them for psychiatric evaluation. At this point, Drs. Goldstein and Leventhal looked at them with a laparoscope and found the cause of their pain - endometriosis. I've taught in the People's Republic of China and I know firsthand that endometriosis is common there, too. For some unknown reason, endometriosis is not common in Israel but strangely often is seen in the United States in Jewish women. There is evidence that endometriosis is inherited. The incidence in the general population is approximately 2 percent, but in sisters and daughters of affected women this jumps to as much as 10 percent and the disease also tends to be more severe in those patients where heredity is a factor.

There is some debate over whether endometriosis is more common today than in years past. Many fertility therapists, myself included, believe that delaying the first pregnancy increases the risk, and it does appear that more couples than ever before are doing just that. But it also seems that the use of the contraceptive pill decreases the risk, and the current popularity of the "pill" may offset the statistical effect of delayed pregnancy. Remember, just 100 years ago, women were either pregnant or breastfeeding during their reproductive years. Both of these states tend to discourage development of the uterine lining in a cyclical fashion. Only recently have women been able to use birth control with any degree of success. The mechanical methods (any method other than hormonal) of contraception or use of rhythm are associated with long durations of repeated ovulation in women who choose to delay pregnancy.

Figures 10.1 through 10.3 show some typical sites for endometriotic implants or *lesions* (a catchall term that is used to describe any abnormality). The special term *endometrioma* describes the presence of endometriosis within an ovary. The ovary becomes enlarged by an ever-expanding space filled with fluid that contains mostly old blood from the endometriosis cells lining the cyst (a fluid-filled space). This particular cyst has been called "chocolate" cyst by gynecologists because of the appearance of its contents. Reproductive surgeons are specially trained to salvage as much normal ovary as possible rather than unnecessarily removing the entire ovary.

FIGURE 10.1 Small endometriotic implants along uterosacral ligaments supporting the uterus.

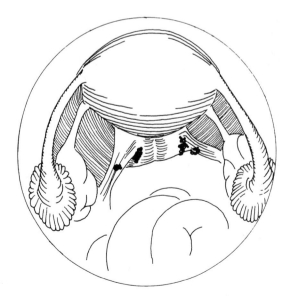

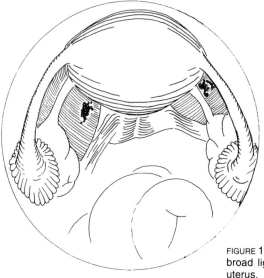

FIGURE 10.2 Endometriotic implants on broad ligament on either side of the uterus.

How Does It Start?

Endometriosis can start in more than one way. The most popular theory is that during menstruation, fragments of the disintegrating endometrium are pushed upward and out the fallopian tubes by uterine contractions. This explanation certainly seems reasonable, since sperm are known to swim against the flow within the tube. Also, it's not unusual to see blood flowing through the tubes of a woman having surgery during menstruation, although most of the time this does not result in endometriosis. Thus, women who have this retrograde menstruation will not develop endometriosis unless there is some predilection for them to do so, as is suggested by the finding that this is, to some extent, an inherited disease. The fact that lesions sometimes appear in such distant sites as the lungs or in the nasal passages suggests that other theories may be necessary to explain this finding. Some experts believe that the endometrial cells can spread via the blood stream or the lymphatic system, or both, in much the same way that some cancers spread (a process called metastasis). Remember that endometriosis is not a cancer but a

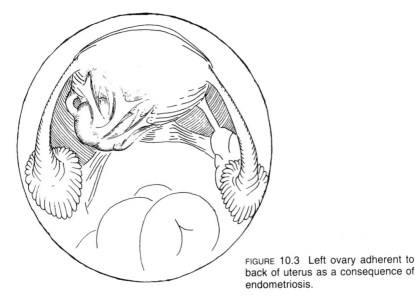

FIGURE 10.3 Left ovary adherent to back of uterus as a consequence of endometriosis.

benign disease, although it can cause considerable pain. Another explanation suggests that the undifferentiated cells lining the peritoneal cavity can be transformed by various stimuli into endometrial cells; this is known as the metaplasia theory.

So that doctors can compare the results of various therapies, a grading system for endometriosis has been established by the American Society for Reproductive Medicine. Without going into details, endometriosis is classified as minimal, mild, moderate and severe (stages I through IV) based on the amount of diseased tissue, its location, and the extent of associated adhesions.

Symptoms Can Be Misleading

Endometriosis is certainly the chameleon, the great imitator, in gynecology. Physicians often mistake the symptoms for such conditions as pelvic inflammatory disease, ovarian cysts, colitis, cystitis, psychosomatic pain, and disorders of the lower back and spine. Because the pelvic nerves may become irritated, pain often radiates down the leg, mimicking lower back disorders. If endometriotic implants are on the surface of the bladder, the pain mimics symptoms of bladder infection or cystitis. Many times, however, very large implants, particularly on the ovaries, cause little or no pain at all and go unnoticed until the patient has an infertility workup. Although an experienced physician can often suspect that this condition exists, most of the time diagnosis is made by laparoscopy (described in chapter 5), although ovarian imaging by ultrasound is quite helpful.

The symptoms of endometriosis may include painful menses, painful coitus, pain with bowel movement, or pain during urination. The severity of the symptoms often does not match the extent of the condition. Very small lesions can cause intense pain, and large ones can be silent. A woman with just a few tiny lesions may experience long-term infertility, whereas a woman with a significant bulk of endometrial implants may conceive successfully without any intervening therapy and carry the pregnancy to term.

Patients often ask if there is a blood test to diagnose endometriosis. Actually, it has been found recently that there is something in the blood of many women with endometriosis that can be used as a diagnostic marker. The problem is that this marker is also present in some women with cancer and some normal women as well. In general, the levels tend to be related to the extent of endometriosis; therefore this marker, called CA 125 antigen, may have some use in following the course of endometriosis after treatment because levels tend to decline with successful treatment. Reappearance of this marker is associated with new activity of endometriosis, which tends to be a recurrent disease in 25 to 30 percent of the patients.

Effect on Fertility

It is not always clear why endometriosis should affect fertility. Some cases seem obvious enough. Severe disease with adhesions and inflammation in the pelvis along with heavy scar tissue formation cause the tubes to become immobilized even though they are open, interfering with ovum and sperm transport. But explaining infertility in cases when just a few implants are found is more difficult. Some researchers think that *prostaglandins* (PGs) may be responsible. These hormone-like substances, that can be found normally everywhere in the body, are intimately involved in inflammatory responses and in the pain which accompanies them. Studies have shown that high concentrations of PGs appear in the menses of women who suffer from dysmenorrhea. These women are often relieved of symptoms when given anti-PG drugs such as Motrin or Anaprox. Although not all women who suffer from dysmenorrhea have endometriosis, perhaps those who do have the disorder become infertile because of high PG levels in the reproductive tract. The PGs might impair fertility by immobilizing sperm, by interfering with ovulation, or by causing a disruption of normal tubal rhythmical contractions. Simple treatment of endometriosis with the antiprostaglandin drugs has not resulted in improvement of fertility. This has led some researchers to think that there may be an immune or antibody factor associated with endometriosis. Other researchers are trying to explain the relationship between minimal endometriosis and infertility by looking at other subtle hormonal and chemical changes. Yet another class of compounds linked to endometriosis and infertility are the interleukins, which the body uses as part of its immunological protective system.

In some studies, when sperm are placed in fluid that has been collected from the abdominal cavity of a woman with endometriosis, their motion becomes impaired compared with placing them in abdominal fluid from normal women. Even after a woman conceives, endometriosis may exert a deleterious effect. Many physicians have reported increased miscarriage rates in women with endometriosis compared with normal pregnant women. There are many more findings and theories I could cite, but it is clear that there is more than one way by which endometriosis impairs fertility. And it is clear that there is a lot about endometriosis we need to learn.

Treatment of Endometriosis

Endometriosis can be treated with drugs, surgery, or a combination of the two. Whether endometriosis can be "cured" depends on how rigidly one employs the definition. Any treatment employed -

whether surgery or drugs - will not alter permanently the body's tendency to form new implants. Generally speaking, the best non-surgical therapy for endometriosis occurs during pregnancy because of natural hormonal changes. This is why women are encouraged to get pregnant soon after therapy has been completed, given the recurrent nature of the disease. Of course, this is the Catch 22 of the situation. Whether or not a particular treatment will result in pregnancy depends upon many factors: the severity of the condition; the state of other fertility factors in the couple; and if surgery is performed, the skill of the surgeon. In the following discussion of treatment, I will give some cure rates that indicate what a couple might expect from therapy. Two facts about endometriosis have important implications for treatment. First, endometriosis is known to subside after menopause because the ovaries no longer secrete enough estrogen to stimulate the lesions. Second, if pregnancy should occur in spite of endometriosis, the condition disappears, often for good. This is because progesterone levels are high and persistent, causing the lesions to melt away.

No Treatment

There are several reports in the medical literature which state that the pregnancy rate in minimal and mild endometriosis is higher with observation alone as opposed to surgery or drug therapy. Initially, it makes sense for doctors to withhold treatment, especially surgery, for these mild cases of endometriosis. Of course, if the diagnosis is made by laparoscopy, treatment can be given at the time that diagnosis is made, as we shall shortly see. By the time a patient sees a fertility doctor she may have been infertile for a considerable period of time, at which point some active treatment becomes desirable. Most of the patients who come to me, for example, have been infertile for almost 5 years. Therefore, decisions on therapy must take into account the age of the partners, duration of infertility, and other reproductive factors.

Hormone Therapy

BIRTH-CONTROL PILLS

One approach to treatment attempts to mimic the hormonal conditions of pregnancy. This can be done with large doses of birth-control pills (estrogens and progestins) taken every day over a period of 6 to 9 months, not allowing a monthly period to occur as contrasted with the usual cyclical use of the pill. This treatment is popular; it has been used for more than 20 years even though it has never been approved as an indication by the FDA for use of the pill. The constant high levels of progestins cause the endometrial implants essentially to burn themselves out. But at such high doses, the estrogen present in the pill sometimes produces *edema* (water retention) along with side effects such as bloating, weight gain, breast tenderness, and sometimes pigmentation of the facial skin. Menstrual-like spotting is common although no menses, as such, occur during treatment.

DEPO-PROVERA ACETATE

Another way to mimic pregnancy and treat endometriosis so that a pregnancy may later occur is to give a woman injections of a long-acting progesterone-like preparation. This is done with Depo-provera acetate at 3-month intervals. Again, the idea is to stop menstruation for 6 to 9 months to allow the lesions to disintegrate. This method avoids some of the side effects seen with contraceptive pill therapy, although bloating and weight gain may still occur. The problem with this form of treatment is that the drug is stored in body fat. As a result, some women, especially those who are obese, may not resume menses for 6 to 18 months after the last injection. This can be disconcerting to the woman who is actively trying to conceive. Therefore, this method is reserved for women for whom pregnancy is not an immediate issue.

Both the "pill" and the Depo-provera acetate methods result in pregnancy about 50 to 55 percent of the time if the extent of the endometriosis is mild, about 35 percent in moderate cases, and about 20 percent in severe cases. Neither of these two forms of treatment work very well for lesions in excess of 3 millimeters in diameter, and they do not seem to be very effective with ovarian endometriosis.

DANAZOL (DANOCRINE)

Another hormonal approach to treatment seeks to mimic menopause; that is, a pseudomenopause is induced with daily doses of oral *danazol* (Danocrine). This drug interferes with the release of FSH and LH by the pituitary gland and also acts directly on the endometriotic lesions. Without the stimulatory action of these gonadotropins, described in chapter 2, the ovaries drastically reduce their output of hormones, and menstruation ceases as it does in menopause. As with the other hormonal therapies, a course of treatment usually lasts 6 to 9 months. Pregnancy rates following this form of therapy seem to be better than using contraceptive pills. Danazol affects the body in much the same way that testosterone and other "male" hormones do. This produces predictable side effects. Most women taking this drug can expect to gain weight, not so much from water retention, but from appetite stimulation. Danazol may also cause rashes, oily skin, acne, and a decrease in breast size. These side effects disappear when the drug is withdrawn. Some women also experience severe muscle cramps and must be taken off the danazol before treatment is completed. Danazol also has the propensity to induce changes in the blood lipids that might lead to acceleration of atherosclerosis with prolonged use. Therefore, if you have a family history of early cardiovascular disease, heart attacks and strokes, you should probably not take this drug. Danazol also may cause alteration in liver metabolism leading to jaundice. If this happens, therapy should be halted at once. These side effects aside, the drug has proven to be an invaluable therapeutic agent for endometriosis. Menses return in about 6 weeks after therapy. Danazol has been the mainstay of drug therapy for endometriosis for many years and has an excellent track record for safety. It is usually well-tolerated since the side effects usually are more of a nuisance than a medical threat, and therapy is limited in duration.

SYNTHETIC GNRH

Another way to induce a pseudomenopause is to use a pharmacologically altered molecule of naturally occurring GnRH (gonadotropin releasing hormone) which we discussed earlier as a treatment for fibroid tumors (see chapter 9). Side effects from this form of treatment are far fewer than with danazol, and the most significant symptom is usually hot flashes which occur only during therapy. During long-term therapy with GnRH, estrogen levels decrease to very low values and the same problems with osteoporosis that occur during menopause may be seen. The process is reversed and bone density is rapidly restored when therapy is stopped. The drug cannot be given orally, but is administered through monthly injections or absorbed through the lining of the nose with a nasal spray used twice each day. Results of GnRH therapy are encouraging in treating even severe cases of endometriosis, resulting in pregnancy rates that are quite comparable to those seen with danazol.

Surgery

Surgery for endometriosis can be minor or extensive, depending upon the size and number of lesions found. If during laparoscopic examination the surgeon finds very small lesions, they can be fulgurated (burned electrically) or treated with a laser. In mild endometriosis pregnancy rates of 50 to 60 percent can be expected from this procedure alone. Nothing is lost by this approach since hormone treatments or further surgery can be used if the patient doesn't get pregnant within a year. Surgery for extensive endometriosis may not be simple. If the bowel has large lesions, it may be necessary for the surgeon to remove a section of the colon. The surgeon often performs an appendectomy because endometriosis is found in the appendix in about 15 percent of the women affected. Extensive surgery on ureters and the bladder may also be required. Fortunately, these severe cases are quite rare, and I mention it here only as warning against delaying treatment once the diagnosis of extensive endometriosis has been made.

In addition to removing endometrial lesions, the surgeon must cut away any adhesions that have formed in order to restore the proper positioning of the tubes and ovaries. The surgeon often can relieve the pain of endometriosis by cutting or lasering the sensory nerves to the uterus. Fortunately, most endometriosis can be approached surgically with the laparoscope. Endometriomas can be surgically removed or drained and destroyed with an electric probe or one of the various lasers that have been designed for use with a laparoscope. In our own practice we have achieved a 49 percent pregnancy rate within just 9 months of follow-up after laparoscopic laser treatment in patients with *moderate* and *severe* endometriosis. Before the advent of the sophisticated equipment necessary to do this, we would have had to resort to open surgery (laparotomy) for these women. The results with a laparoscope are better because there is a tendency to have fewer adhesions form than after open surgery. Also important is the fact that we are now able to treat just as well on an outpatient basis, and women can return to their normal lives within 2 to 3 days, compared with the 4 to 6 weeks of recovery required with the older techniques. In spite of all this sophisticated technology, for some women endometriosis cannot be stopped, and eventually they find themselves facing a hysterectomy and removal of the ovaries. At this point this is the only "cure" we have for these more extreme cases.

Nearly all pregnancies that result from medical or surgical treatment occur within 6 to 18 months after treatment. If pregnancy does not result within that time, the prognosis is not good. The reason is that endometriosis tends to recur. More specifically, the mechanism which leads to the condition in the first place is probably still at work, and what we see are actually new lesions being formed. Fully 25 to 30 percent of these women will need a second surgical procedure, and reproductive success from the second operation occurs in only about 15 to 20 percent of these cases.

Just because you have a severe case of endometriosis is no reason to give up hope of bearing a child. I have seen pregnancies result from treatment even in severe cases. One of my twenty-nine-year-old patients, for example, had extensive implants on her ovaries, colon, and adjacent organs. Major surgery was performed, during which 40 percent of one ovary and 60 percent of the other ovary were removed. At the same time it was necessary to remove a portion of her colon and to reconnect the colon because of a partial obstruction. This patient has had two children since that operation, illustrating that fertility can return even in the most severe cases.

Perhaps equally impressive was the case of a couple in which endometriosis was compounded by other fertility problems. The woman's husband had a *varicocele* (varicose vein) in his scrotum with moderate reduction in sperm motility. We fulgurated the woman's lesions and her husband underwent a varicocele repair. Because it often takes months for a man to experience improvement in seminal quality following surgery of that nature, the woman was placed on danazol to dry up any residual implants. When we took her off the medication 6 months later, menses ensued, but ovulation was associated with poor hormonal production. Then we placed her on a regimen of clomiphene citrate and estrogen. After two cycles on this combined therapy she conceived and eventually carried her pregnancy to term. This case illustrates that multiple approaches may be needed to achieve pregnancy, and that a combination of treatments may be successful even when both partners have major fertility problems.

In conclusion, endometriosis is a progressive disease that adversely effects fertility. There are many ways of treating it. Pain may have no direct relation to the extent of the disease or to infertility. Because of its many faces, it is difficult to recommend a standard approach to treatment. The kind of therapy used must take into account how much pain there is, the age of the partners, duration of infertility, and other reproductive factors - all of which should be discussed with the physician. Generally speaking, the extent of the disease can best be determined by a laparoscopic examination, at which time electrical instruments or lasers are frequently helpful in restoring fertility and in eliminating pain. On the other hand, drug therapy can be used as the primary therapy or together with laparoscopic laser surgery. When the ovaries have been involved, a follow-up evaluation with ultrasonic imaging of the ovaries is very helpful in detecting the presence of new lesions.

11

Tubal Disease and Reversing Sterilization in Women

To make its contribution to fertility, a fallopian tube must catch an egg cast adrift in the pelvis and move it toward the uterus while secreting the fluid that nourishes the egg and capacitates the sperm. The structures that enable the tube to accomplish its mission - the sweeping fimbria, the waving cilia, the secretory cells in the folds of the endosalpinx - are perhaps the most delicate, and least resilient, in the female reproductive system.

Disorders of the Fallopian Tubes

Damaged fallopian tubes are a major cause of infertility in women. Some women are born with damaged tubes, as in the cases of those exposed to DES in utero. Another cause of tubal malfunction present from birth is cystic fibrosis. The same genetic defect that caused a lack of cilial activity in the lung has been found to exist in the fallopian tubes. With improved medical treatment women with cystic fibrosis now reach maturity. Most damage to the fallopian tubes, however, is a result of infection. Tubal infections can be effectively treated with antibiotics, but the inflammation that accompanies infection may cause permanent damage to the specialized cells in the tubal lining.

Ectopic Pregnancy

The aftermath of the infection may pose problems of its own. Adhesions of scar tissue can close the tubal lumen, immobilize the fimbria, and prevent the tube from normally contracting as it should. Post-infection scarring can cause the tube to lose its ability to contract in a wave-like form, similar to that which goes on in the intestinal tract. If scarring is not severe enough to completely prevent conception, it may still increase the risk of tubal, or *ectopic* pregnancy - a dangerous development in which a blastocyst implants in the fallopian tube instead of in the uterus. Surgery is then required to remove the embryo before it develops to a size sufficient to burst the tube. If the tube does rupture, the resulting hemorrhage can be fatal.

Until recently, the reproductive outlook for women following ectopic pregnancy was poor, with only 40 percent of them eventually successful in having a child. The conditions most often leading to ectopic pregnancy, such as a history of previous tubal infection, or prior abdominal surgery, are those that usually affect both tubes. Evidence also shows that the anatomic changes caused by the DES syndrome are not limited to the uterus, since as many as 1 in 10 women conceiving with an abnormal-appearing tubal X-ray (HSG) will have an ectopic pregnancy, whereas the usual incidence of ectopic pregnancy varies between 1 in 90 and 1 in 120. Having one ectopic pregnancy raises the risk for a second occurrence, whether the tube is removed or salvaged. Having an ectopic pregnancy also increases the risk of sterility, not only because of the adhesions caused by surgery, but mainly because the pregnancy may have occurred in the healthier of the two tubes.

Of late, there has been a trend to salvage the affected side if the pregnancy has not caused the tube to rupture, especially because repeat ectopic pregnancy, when it occurs, is equally divided between the first affected tube and the other, indicating that both tubes had some degree of pathology. Whether or not this can be done depends on early diagnosis. Ectopic pregnancy is most often found in the ampullary portion of the tube, less frequently in the isthmus, and rarely directly on the ovary. Occasionally the pregnancy implants in that portion of the tube which runs through the uterine wall. The latter situation is especially dangerous, because it is usually discovered late, and rupture can cause massive internal hemorrhage. The embryo can be removed from the tube without an incision only if it is implanted at the very end (figure 11.1). Usually the tube is slit open along its long axis - *a linear salpingostomy* - the pregnancy tissue extracted, and the tube preserved. This can often be accomplished with a laparoscope and special operating instruments. Some of the newer lasers are particularly helpful because they cut and seal blood

FIGURE 11.1 A fimbrial ectopic pregnancy is shown on the lower left, and an ectopic pregnancy located at the ampullary-isthmic junction on the lower right. The fimbrial ectopic pregnancy can be removed easily with laparoscopic forceps. A laser can be used under laparoscopic guidance to make an incision in the tube over the implantation site of the ectopic pregnancy (upper right). The pregnancy sac can then be extracted using forceps. The tube heals without the need for suture.

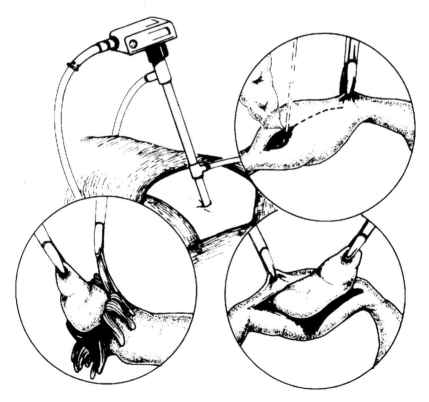

vessels at the same time thereby avoiding heavy bleeding. Another way of dealing with the ectopic pregnancy is with a laparotomy using magnification and fine instruments - microsurgery - though this is not always available for emergency surgery. Tubal pregnancies can be handled by removing the affected piece of the tube, and reconnecting the segments either at that time or at a later date. Pregnancies within the tube rarely can develop to term. Implantation secondarily within the abdomen is possible, but this is rare and results in a high rate of congenital abnormality in the fetus.

One of the newer forms of treatment for ectopic pregnancy is methotrexate, a drug used in high doses for certain malignancies. Reports indicate that when this drug is used in smaller doses it can be a safe and effective therapy for this condition. This form of treatment should be performed only by doctors who are familiar with and comfortable using this drug. Methotrexate causes the pregnancy tissue to disintegrate and no surgery is necessary, but the pregnancy test may remain positive for 60 days and close medical supervision is necessary. This type of medical therapy can be substituted for surgery in selected early cases, or used when surgery has not removed all of the pregnancy tissue. There is some evidence suggesting that the affected tube heals better with a medical approach than a surgical approach.

Most ectopic pregnancies cause pain and intermittent internal bleeding beginning at about 40 to 60 days from the last period. Ectopic pregnancies are often difficult for women to recognize. Typical symptoms of an ectopic pregnancy are occasional light bleeding or spotting, which mimic a normal menstrual period or threatened miscarriage. Lower abdominal pain may be one-sided or diffuse. Internal bleeding causes an irritated diaphragm with pain radiating to the shoulder and neck (as with Rubin's test or following laparoscopy). This occurs because the nerve supply to the diaphragm extends down from this region. Levels of hCG are usually lower than with normal pregnancies, but sometimes show up as entirely normal.

However, even findings of lower hCG levels don't clinch the diagnosis for ectopic pregnancy because most of the time this finding is associated with an impending spontaneous intrauterine abortion.

Usually, early diagnosis is made during laparoscopy when the pregnancy can be seen within the tube. The diagnosis is suggested when an ultrasound reading shows that the uterus is empty. But even that finding can be deceiving because sometimes no pregnancy sac is picked up on ultrasound in women who are about to miscarry. Occasionally, a sac can be seen on ultrasound outside of the uterus and the diagnosis can be made that way. A patient's symptoms are one tipoff to do this study. Another consideration is if the patient is at high risk for ectopic pregnancy; for example prior tubal infection, tubal surgery, or a previous tubal pregnancy. A gentle laparoscopic procedure - where no instruments are inserted into the uterus - will not harm a normal intrauterine pregnancy.

What are the current statistics for those who have had an ectopic pregnancy? Today, about 70 to 80 percent of patients will conceive again. About 70 percent of those will have a successful pregnancy and delivery. The spontaneous abortion rate in pregnancies following ectopic pregnancy is higher than usual for reasons that are not clear. Only 8 to 15 percent of women who have had an ectopic pregnancy will have a second ectopic pregnancy. Early diagnosis and conservative operations for tubal salvage, which surprisingly, do not create any greater risk of a second ectopic pregnancy than removing the tube, seem to be responsible for an increase in later reproductive function. Gentle handling of tissues with minimal disturbance to the unaffected tube also helps. For those who do not conceive following an ectopic pregnancy, corrective tubal surgery results in a normal pregnancy in 30 to 60 percent of cases, depending upon the extent of tubal damage and adhesions. The popularity and success of *in vitro* fertilization has changed the medical profession's approach to ectopic pregnancy; the surgeon now knows that there is always a fall-back position that can be taken if both tubes are so badly damaged that they cannot be repaired.

Pelvic Inflammatory Disease (PID)

An active tubal infection is called *pelvic inflammatory disease*, or PID. We don't try to diagnose PID solely by an office examination and a count of white cells in the blood because any number of conditions produce the same signs and symptoms and thus can masquerade as PID. These include appendicitis, endometriosis, ovarian cysts, and inflammatory bowel diseases such as colitis. Therefore, it is probably best to confirm the diagnosis with a laparoscopic examination of the tubes.

Many organisms can cause PID, with gonococcus being the one that is best known. Both men and women can carry and sexually transmit the disease without experiencing any symptoms of their own. Gonorrhea, like other tubal infections, may "smolder" in pelvic tissues for years before becoming apparent. Women with gonorrhea usually experience lower abdominal pain, fever, and vaginal discharge.

Gonorrhea is diagnosed by taking a culture from the cervix, urethra and/or anus in either sex, or from the tubes themselves if laparoscopy is performed. When culture results confirm the presence of gonorrhea, treatment must be vigorous and prompt to avoid reproductive damage. Women with gonorrhea who are in pain and who have a fever should be hospitalized and given large doses of intravenous antibiotics. Even with good care, 12 to 15 percent of women having one episode of gonorrhea become sterile because of tubal scarring and closure. The incidence of sterility rises with subsequent episodes. The male partner(s) must be treated and recultured following antibiotic therapy.

Chlamydia, not widely recognized as a cause of tubal infection even a few years ago, has proven to be a more common culprit than gonococcus in terms of the number of people in North America infected. Because its symptoms are mild, patients may not realize they have it, even while it closes the fallopian tubes. Like gonorrhea, chlamydial infections are sexually acquired and therefore, both partners must be adequately treated to prevent reinfection. Unlike viral diseases, infections with chlamydia or gonococcus do not confer lifelong immunity afterwards, and a man or woman may become infected again by having sex with an infected partner. Streptococcus and staphylococcus are common bacteria normally found on the skin and sometimes in the vagina, but are capable of causing tubal damage. Any time the skin is breached, or after abortion or delivery, there is some risk of active infection from these organisms. We mentioned the ureaplasma organisms previously. The scientific literature is still unclear whether ureaplasma organisms are harmful to the reproductive tract. It is not uncommon to get a positive culture for these organisms in normal fertile patients, but since they *may* be harmful to the tubes, diagnosed ureaplasma infections should always be treated. Tubal infections can come about indirectly from a ruptured appendix or abdominal surgery not done for gynecological reasons. Tuberculosis is another disease than can strike the tubes, and it nearly always results in sterility. But tuberculosis of the fallopian tubes - common in many parts of the world - is rare in North America.

Women who use an intrauterine device (IUD) for contraception have 4 to 9 times greater chance of getting PID than women who do not. Statistically, this is especially true for women who have more than one sexual partner. The IUD itself is probably not the cause of the infection, but rather, it aggravates infections that would otherwise be mild and not even noticeable. Newer evidence suggests that many IUD-related cases of PID are a consequence of infection acquired as part of the insertion process. However, IUDs are now infrequently used in the United States, and if you've been trying to get pregnant, you've long discarded it.

Tubal Inflammation

Salpingitis isthmica nodosa (SIN) can cause blockage in the isthmus of the tube, the part that connects the tube to the uterine cavity (figure 11.2). This condition is an inflammation, *not* an infection. It is more akin to such chronic inflammatory conditions as arthritis and colitis. Like these other inflammatory disorders, SIN waxes and wanes. Eventually, most affected tubes will become rigid, fibrotic, and closed. The condition can be partially controlled in some women after a steroid solution is administered via the cervix to the tubes to allow pregnancy. This procedure, called *hydrotubation*, can be performed in the physician's office. Most women suffering from this condition must have their tubes surgically repaired or consider *in vitro* fertilization.

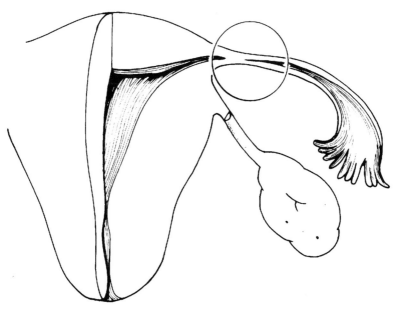

FIGURE 11.2   Point of blockage in salpingitis isthmica nodosa.

Restoring Damaged Tubes with Surgery

No medication can restore severely damaged tubes. Donor tubal transplants are technically possible, but are not done because dangerous drugs have to be used to prevent rejection of the foreign graft material. Prior to the advent of *in vitro* fertilization, surgery was the only hope. The pregnancy rate for tubal surgery is lower than that in other parts of the female reproductive tract. Moreover, surgery can itself increase the risk of tubal pregnancy. From 8 to 15 percent of pregnancies following surgery on severely damaged tubes are ectopic, compared with about 1 percent in the general population. Microsurgical techniques, which employ small instruments, fine suture, and meticulous technique performed with the aid of an operating microscope, have greatly improved the outlook for women with tubal damage. Lasers have also been helpful. But, because of all these factors, and because women want to avoid major surgery as long as they have something to say about it, women increasingly are opting for *in vitro* fertilization techniques as these become more available and more successful throughout the country. But we must not overlook the fact than once a fallopian tube has been repaired sufficiently for it to function normally, a woman can go on to conceive more than once without any intervening therapy. This is not the case with IVF procedures, which must be repeated if the patient wishes to conceive again, unless an embryo freezing technique (to be described later) has been used.

The discussion of the results of tubal surgery that follows includes estimates of how often various procedures will result in pregnancy. But first something should be said about how physicians arrive at these estimates. An excellent surgeon may have a low batting average if he or she accepts the most severe cases for surgery. Conversely a high success rate could mean that a surgeon operates on only those cases that offer a very good prognosis.

Results of Tubal Surgery

An infection can cause the fimbria to adhere to one another, interfering with their ability to pick up the egg. As the infection

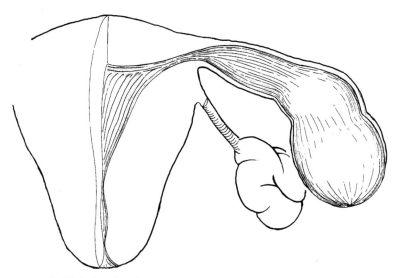

FIGURE 11.3 Dilated hydrosalpinx caused by blockage of the distal end of the tube producing a collection of tubal secretions.

becomes progressively more severe, the end of the tube closes entirely, forming a sac in which fluid accumulates. This sac, illustrated in figure 11.3, is called a *hydrosalpinx*. Results of surgical repair of such tubes are poor. However, the outlook is somewhat better if the infection resulted from a ruptured appendix or abdominal surgery instead of a sexually transmitted disease, because the former do not cause scarring of the endosalpinx.

Almost any closed tube can be opened. But removing all of the damaged tissue may leave a residual stump completely devoid of fimbria. Because the length of the tube is important for conception, a surgeon must often compromise between removing all of the diseased tissue and leaving an adequate amount of tube. Before microsurgery, the pregnancy rate after repair of clubbed tubes was about 15 percent. Using the same criteria for accepting cases, our success rate has almost doubled with microsurgery. Most pregnancies occur 6 to 20 months after surgery, reflecting the long time needed for damaged tubes to heal. Improvement in laparoscopic techniques, especially the ability to concomitantly use a laser, has allowed us to repair many tubes without subjecting the patient to open surgery. This trend parallels that which was discussed with endometriosis surgery. Results of tubal repair done with a laparoscope and a laser are equal to those achieved with open surgery - about a 25 percent pregnancy rate.

Adhesions around the outside of the tube can prevent it from contracting properly and sweeping over the ovary to capture the egg. But if the tube is open, and the endosalpinx is healthy, fertility can be restored with microsurgery about 60 percent of the time. Similar results can be achieved with a laparoscope, provided the adhesions are not so severe as to warrant an open laparotomy.

After open tubal surgery, many physicians prescribe antibiotics over a long-term basis to prevent reinfection and also use various medications to discourage the formation of new adhesions. In spite of these measures, however, many women do reform adhesions or develop new scarring. These adhesions can be removed before they become dense, with the laparoscopy procedure, 4 to 6 weeks after surgery. This is not standard care, but some fertility surgeons have found that this "second look" does increase the chances of pregnancy.

Salpingitis isthmica nodosa is treated surgically by resecting (cutting and removing) the blocked portion of the isthmus and joining the severed ends of the tube. However, if most of the isthmus is affected it is removed and the ampulla is reimplanted through the rear of the uterus with pregnancy resulting in about 40 percent of women (figure 11.4 illustrates these procedures). Tubes that are blocked proximally (at the uterine end) have been treated successfully under fluoroscopic guidance in the radiology department without anesthesia or by hysteroscopy. The procedure involves passing a wire guide and catheter through the cervix and uterus past the point of obstruction. This new procedure shows promise and should be attempted prior to open surgical repair much like the balloon techniques used for blocked coronary arteries.

About 60 to 70 percent of tubes blocked at the uterine end can be opened in this fashion, and pregnancy rates of 30 to 40 percent by the end of the year after successful reestablishment of patency are usual. Some tubes close again but the ectopic rate is surprisingly

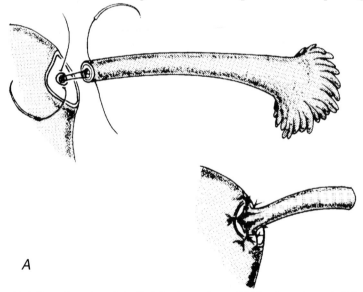

A

FIGURE 11.4 Operations for salpingitis isthmica nodosa. (A) Direct anastomosis (joining) of isthmus to intrauterine portion of the tube after diseased portion removed.

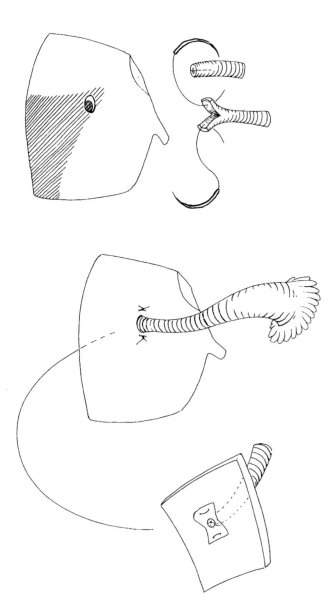

(B) Reimplantation of ampullary portion of the tube into uterus after isthmus removed. Top, opening in back of uterus made with a borer and tube "fishmouthed" open. Middle, tube entering tunnel formed in uterine wall. Bottom, method of suturing tube to uterine wall.

low, and a 30 percent overall yield for a non-operative approach merits a try in almost every case. Failure of attempted tubal cannulization, or inability to conceive within a year after apparent success brings the patient to a decision between open resection and anastomosis or *in vitro* fertilization.

Reversing Sterilization in Women

About 1 million women each year choose sterilization as a form of permanent contraception. Although women who desire sterilization routinely receive preoperative counseling, about 1 percent who decide to have the procedure done change their minds after sterilization and want reversal, usually because of the death of a child or husband, or divorce and remarriage. Whether or not fertility can be restored to these women depends upon the technique by which they were sterilized. In the days before laparoscopy, the Pomeroy method of sterilization was standard (figure 11.5). This procedure is performed through a small abdominal incision. The surgeon forms a small loop in each tube and ties it off. The portion of the tube above the ligature is then cut. When the suture material is absorbed weeks later, the severed ends of the tube pull apart. This technique is still favored for women who choose to be sterilized just after their babies are delivered. Restoring fertility to a woman sterilized in this manner depends on whether or not the remaining tube is sufficiently long.

Another sterilization technique is *fimbriectomy*, shown in figure 11.6. In this procedure an incision is made through the vaginal wall into the abdominal cavity. The tubes are pulled down into the vagina where the fimbria are tied and cut. Chances of restoring fertility to women who have had a fimbriectomy are poor; with the fimbria removed, the mechanism for picking up an egg from the ovary is gone forever. Nevertheless, restoration of an open tube occasionally has resulted in pregnancy without fimbria being present.

There are several laparoscopic sterilization techniques (see figure 11.7). One is electrofulguration (11.7A), in which a section of tube is destroyed by using electrical energy. The length of tube destroyed may be very small or quite large, depending upon the amount of energy used. Other laparoscopic techniques employ clips (11.7B),

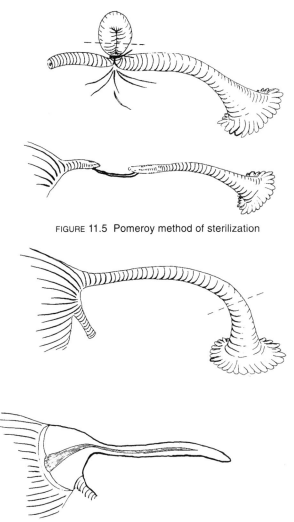

FIGURE 11.5 Pomeroy method of sterilization

FIGURE 11.6 Fimbriectomy sterilization.

or rings (11.7C). The amount of tube destroyed by these devices is usually quite small, and the chances for sterilization reversal are very good, about 75 to 85 percent. When we counsel a couple about sterilization reversal we discuss the risks and estimate the chances for success. To avoid unnecessary surgery, we have to make sure that both husband and wife have reasonably normal fertility in other

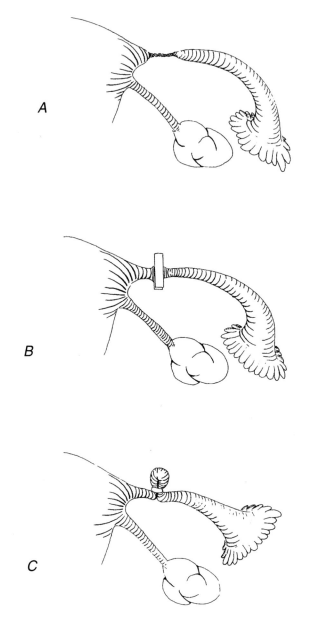

FIGURE 11.7 Laparoscopic sterilizations. (A) Electrofulguration, (B) Clip application, (C) Ring application.

respects. The man should have a semen analysis; the woman's ovulatory function may need to be assessed. An HSG will reveal the location of the blocks in the tubes. Finally, *all* women should have a preoperative laparoscopy. If laparoscopy shows that surgery is feasible, the reversal should be performed under the same anesthesia to save the woman time, money, and emotional stress; if laparoscopy demonstrates anatomy unsuitable for reversal, the patient is discharged without having been subjected to needless major surgery.

Sterilization Reversal Procedures

It is in sterilization reversal that the impact of microsurgery has been most dramatic. The different ways in which the severed ends of the tubes can be joined are illustrated in figure 11.8. The most successful procedure is the isthmus-to-isthmus (11.8a) *anastomosis* (joining). The pregnancy rates following this procedure are very good, usually between 70 and 85 percent.

An isthmus-to-ampullary connection (11.8b) is more difficult to perform because of the unequal diameters involved; it's like trying to join a garden hose to a fire hose. Still, the procedure can restore fertility in more than 50 percent of women.

Ampulla-to-ampulla connections (11.8c) are easier for the surgeon, but the subsequent pregnancy rate is only about 50 percent. The loss of part of the ampulla during the sterilization process decreases the chances for conception, even though the joining is technically successful.

One of the most demanding sterilization reversal procedures is that of joining the isthmus to a portion of tube buried within the uterine wall (11.8d and 11.8e). This is the same operation described earlier for treating salpingitis isthmica nodosa (SIN). It is the operation most often appropriate for reversal of sterilization done originally by electrofulguration. It requires a high-magnification operating microscope, and great patience. The success rates, nevertheless, are high (about 65 percent), provided that there is healthy tube remaining within the uterine wall. If not, the surgeon may resort to the reimplantation technique illustrated in figure 11.4. The pregnancy rate resulting from reversal done in this manner is

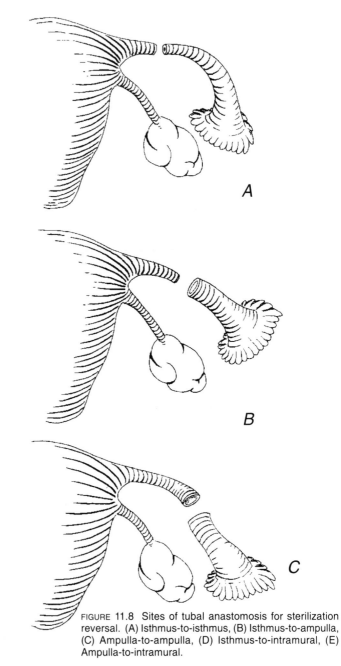

FIGURE 11.8 Sites of tubal anastomosis for sterilization reversal. (A) Isthmus-to-isthmus, (B) Isthmus-to-ampulla, (C) Ampulla-to-ampulla, (D) Isthmus-to-intramural, (E) Ampulla-to-intramural.

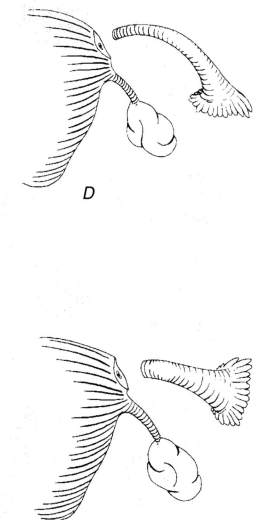

D

E

about 50 percent. Following surgical repair, pregnancy rates in women who had a sterilization procedure reversed are better than the rates seen in women whose tubes were damaged by infection. In the former we have a tube that was basically healthy to begin with, and the technical task becomes one of microscopically removing a little bit of scar tissue and getting a good union of the two segments. In the latter, the tubes have suffered from infection and have multiple areas of scarring and damage that must be handled differently.

A number of surgeons have experimented with laparoscopic repair of tubes previously altered by sterilization. While pregnancies have been recorded, the rate is decidedly less than that achieved with microsurgical techniques.

Regardless of the specific type of repair, success with sterilization reversal usually occurs within 6 to 15 months. My earliest success was with a woman who conceived 23 days after surgery. I reject about 20 percent of cases for actual operation because the preoperative laparoscopy reveals an insufficient length of remaining tube or other pelvic conditions that make restoration of fertility unlikely. There are no hard and fast rules for deciding whether or not to operate. The decision must be tempered by such considerations as age, previous pregnancies, and how fertile a couple is in other respects. Very recently, I reversed a sterilization in a forty-one-year-old woman who had remarried someone without children. For a number of reasons *in vitro* fertilization was not their first choice. While I told her that surgery was not the best approach to her infertility, or the most likely to succeed, she couldn't be convinced not to try it. Only one tube was repairable, but despite her age and the odds against her, she conceived one month later. This illustrates the difficulty in patient selection. I try to give the patient as much information as possible concerning risks and chances of success. Microscopic tubal repair is by definition major abdominal surgery. Operating time, especially with microsurgery, is usually about 2 to 3 hours, but may on occasion last as long as 4 or 5 hours. Generally this surgery is quite safe, and in fact, safer than cesarean section for delivery. One major drawback for some patients is the fact that health insurance may not cover this elective surgery. As is the case with tubes which have been damaged by infection or disease, *in vitro* fertilization offers an alternative form of therapy.

12

Male Infertility

As we know, men normally remain fertile much later in life than women. Men past the age of seventy have been known to sire children, while fertility in a woman of fifty is quite rare. Since the average age of couples who seek fertility guidance from a specialist seems to creep up each year, one might expect infertility to be predominantly a female problem. But this just isn't so. In about 40 percent of couples seeking therapy, infertility arises solely from the man. In another 10 percent, infertility arises from factors affecting both the man and the woman. This is why a semen analysis early in the fertility investigation is so important.

Anatomical Factors

Some men are born with testes that have not descended from the pelvis into the scrotal sac. We briefly discussed this anatomic disorder, called *cryptorchidism*, in chapter 3. The testes must be maintained at about 4° F below normal body temperature. Exposure to excessive heat decreases production of sperm. If this exposure is intense or long lasting, the tubules that produce sperm can suffer permanent damage. This is why cryptorchidism must be corrected early in life.

Unfortunately, even prompt surgical treatment does not ensure adequate function in adulthood. The fact that the testes have failed to descend in the first place implies increased risk of a disorder in fetal testicular development. It is not surprising then that a high proportion of undescended testes are abnormal in other respects. Nevertheless, cryptorchidism should be corrected, if only because persistent exposure to abdominal temperatures also increases the risk of getting a testicular malignancy.

For years, fertility therapists have been advising obese men to lose weight and to switch from jockey shorts to the looser fitting boxer shorts. This advice is based on the commonsense notion that obesity, coupled with restrictive underwear, can raise the scrotal temperature. Although there is no scientific evidence that this advice does any good, it certainly does no harm. However, dietary counseling for the obese infertile man is certainly sounder and a direct treatment.

Varicocele

Some men are infertile because one or more of the veins that carry blood away from the scrotum have become varicose, meaning dilated and enlarged (figure 12.1). Each of these clusters of veins, one on either side of the scrotum, normally has in the wall of each vein valves which cause blood to flow in one direction only - toward the heart. But if a valve fails, gravity in the upright position causes a backflow

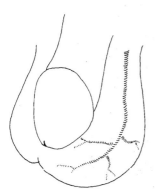

FIGURE 12.1 A left scrotal varicose vein.

of blood and the vein becomes distended to several times its normal width. This, by the way, is the same thing that happens when veins in the legs become varicose.

About 15 percent of adult men have a varicose vein, a varicocele, in the scrotum. Usually, the left vein alone is involved, but some men have a varicocele on the right side as well. Many men with varicocele have normal fertility, but about 30 to 40 percent of men in an infertile marriage have a varicocele. So we see that varicocele is more common in an infertile population. A varicocele can affect sperm count, motility, and morphology, although no one is sure why. Some researchers report that the backflow of warm blood from the abdomen increases scrotal temperature. Others have found that when this blood washes down from the abdomen, it carries with it high amounts of certain adrenal hormones that harm testicular cells.

Varicocele is diagnosed by examining the scrotum while the patient is standing. If varicocele is present, it can be felt in the scrotum. Some are so large that they can be seen by looking at the scrotum. An ultrasonic device that can detect backflow of blood in the vein is often used to aid diagnosis.

The size of the varicocele does not influence the chances for successful treatment. We are still uncertain if the effect of the varicocele on sperm production becomes more severe over time. If it does, this would mean that many normal fertile men with varicocele might eventually experience a reduction of fertility. We have seen men who have sired a child without difficulty in the past, then become infertile presumably because of a varicocele that had existed before the child was conceived. Treatment for the varicocele is a minor surgical procedure that involves tying off the affected veins to stop the backflow of blood into the scrotum. Although the procedure is fairly simple and complications are rare, surgery should not be considered unless the results of post-coital testing or semen analysis are poor, or there is impaired hamster egg penetration. Often, the presence of excellent cervical mucus will offset the effect of varicocele on sperm motility. Thus, if a varicocele is found, the infertile couple may get successful indirect treatment just by improving the woman's cervical mucus, if it has been found to be inadequate. Once again, this underscores the importance of treating the couple as a reproductive unit rather than looking at them strictly as individuals. More will be said about the surgical treatment of varicocele in chapter 13.

Some studies show that semen can be improved without surgery for varicocele. One approach has been that of passing a small device down the vein that opens up in place like an umbrella, essentially serving as an artificial valve. Another approach has been to clot the vein by injection. These two procedures are still relatively new. There is a noninvasive form of therapy that reduces testicular temperature to offset the heat of the varicocele. The man wears an undergarment that cools the scrotum, similar to wearing an athletic supporter filled with ice. It remains to be seen whether early beneficial results reported with this approach hold up in a large number of patients.

Other Anatomical Problems

Retrograde ejaculation of sperm into the bladder, rather than out the urethra, is caused by failure of the bladder sphincter to contract. This condition occurs most frequently in men who have diabetes mellitus, but it can also result from certain urethral procedures, prostate surgery, and the use of some drugs. Diagnosis is made by recovery of sperm in the urine after ejaculation.

Some medications can improve the functioning of the bladder sphincter. Otherwise, sperm can be collected from the bladder if the patient voids following ejaculation. Those sperm can be used for artificial insemination. Because the urine is normally acidic, and sperm do poorly in such an environment, we have the man take sodium bicarbonate tablets, approximately 600 mg three times daily to alkalinize the urine before we collect the sperm. The man should also drink plenty of water to dilute the osmotic content of the urine. After coitus or masturbation, the man urinates into a sterile container. The sperm are separated from the urine in a centrifuge and then suspended in a small volume of balanced salt solution for insemination. This technique is also helpful for men who have had spinal cord injuries that damaged their bladder sphincters. Most men with spinal cord injuries are functionally sterile. They cannot deliver sperm into the woman's reproductive tract, even though sperm production is usually unimpaired. Special electrical techniques have been developed that allow the semen to be collected. These procedures must be done under close medical supervision because the electrical stimulation of the nerves may sometimes cause a temporary, but significant, rise in blood pressure.

If a semen analysis reveals no sperm in the ejaculate, the fructose test described in chapter 5 can determine whether a blockage present in either the vas deferens or the epididymis is the cause. Some men are born with a blockage of this type, usually in the vas. If only an isolated segment is blocked, that part can be removed surgically and the remaining segments rejoined. This usually produces excellent results. Unfortunately, many men born with this abnormality have more than one area of blockage. Correction in such cases may be impossible. In the next chapter, we will describe the method of surgical collection of sperm in these patients.

Hypospadias was described in chapter 1 as a condition in which the urethra opens on the underside of the penis rather than at the tip (figure 12.2). Surgical correction for hypospadias is successful in all but the most severe cases.

Infections and Inflammatory Diseases

Many infections that strike a man's reproductive system threaten fertility by their effects on the ductal system rather than on sperm production. As is often the case in matters of fertility, it's not so

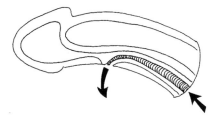

FIGURE 12.2 Hypospadias with urethral opening on the underside of the penis.

much the infections themselves that do the damage, but the scarring left behind. Scar tissue blocking the vas or epididymis can result in permanent sterility.

The body develops no immunity to most of the sexually transmitted diseases. Repeated bouts of gonorrhea, for example, increase the risk of infertility in both men and women. Antibiotics can cure acute infections, but the blockages that result from scarring cannot easily be corrected. The prostate gland is particularly vulnerable to infections, which usually have the effect of decreasing sperm motility.

Mumps, a viral infection that specifically attacks the gonads, can strike people of either sex, but an adult man's testicles are particularly vulnerable because he is constantly making gametes (spermatozoa). As a childhood disease, mumps generally causes no permanent damage; if the disease strikes after puberty, it can destroy forever the ability of the testes to produce sperm. About a quarter of all men who contract mumps after puberty become permanently sterile.

We have already mentioned the ureaplasma organisms in connection with the female reproductive tract. This microorganism has the ability to adhere to individual sperm cells. Whether this in any way harms the sperm is questionable because these organisms are often found in the reproductive tract of fertile men and women who seem none the worse for it. In any case, tetracycline and related antibiotics work well against these organisms. For that reason, treatment is usually started when cultures reveal the presence of these organisms.

Some infections that don't specifically strike the reproductive system can indirectly harm fertility. For the most part these are infections that produce high fevers which are persistent or recurrent. Malaria is a good example. The damage results from fever-induced overheating of the testes. Severe illness, in general, can disturb sperm production because of effects on overall well-being. Examples include such inflammatory diseases as ulcerative colitis, regional enteritis, rheumatoid arthritis, and systemic lupus erythematosis. Some of our patients suffer from these illnesses. The quality of the semen seems to worsen during acute episodes and to improve when the inflammation subsides. In addition, there is now no question that some of the anti-inflammatory drugs, such as Azulfidine (given to patients with bowel disorders), are associated with harmful effects on sperm production.

Other Factors

Trauma

Many infertile men report a childhood incident involving direct physical trauma to the scrotum, and wonder about long-term effects. The truth is that these injuries rarely produce any long-term effect on subsequent fertility. Severe injury may require drainage of the resulting *hematoma* (collection of blood) which may occur as a consequence of broken blood vessels within the scrotal sac. Failure to do so may cause severe pain from increasing pressure which eventually can cause testicular damage.

Infertile or sterile men tend to get frustrated and angry when doctors cannot offer an explanation for the cause of their condition which, unlike female fertility problems, is often uncovered without any suggestive symptoms or history.

Hormones

Some infertile men have deficient amounts of gonadotropins, FSH and LH. Frequently, the deficiency is caused by *Kallman syndrome*, in which the hypothalamus fails to release adequate amounts of GnRH. This hormone, as you will recall, instructs the pituitary to release FSH and LH. One related symptom of Kallman syndrome is the inability to detect odors (anosmia). The condition in a man or a woman is treated with Humegon/Pergonal, the same preparation described in chapter 7 for ovulation induction.

In a woman, prolactin levels high enough to cause disturbance in the menstrual cycle may be accompanied by milky discharge from the nipples. But the same hormone elevation in men rarely offers this telltale sign. Too much prolactin can suppress testosterone production and decrease a man's sex drive. Treatment orally with bromergocryptine is quite effective; the problem lies with diagnosis. Prolactin levels should be checked in any man with reduced seminal quality that is associated with low serum levels of testosterone and a reduced sex drive.

Genetic or Developmental Factors

Every cell in the human body contains a pair of chromosomes that identifies a person's sex. In a woman, this is an XX arrangement. In a man, the combination is XY. *Klinefelter syndrome* refers to a man who has an XXY arrangement (an extra X). These men frequently have poor sexual development with respect to genital structures, beard growth, and body build. Although a few men with this syndrome have proven fertile, most are sterile and, alas, no treatment is possible.

There are a number of rare syndromes involving poor development of the male sexual organs because of a hereditary factor that causes a hormonal receptor defect. The receptor sites in the testes and adjacent structures are defective and will not bind testosterone. Under these circumstances, even though testosterone is normally produced, it cannot get into the cells. The sex organs, which need testosterone to develop normally, do not mature. There is no known therapy for this condition.

Cystic fibrosis, as we mentioned in the discussion of the fallopian tube, has a devastating effect on the respiratory system. Until recently, victims of this disease often did not live through puberty. But today, with better medical care, men as well as women are reaching reproductive age. We now find that many men with this disorder have a closed ductal system or lack the vas deferens.

A somewhat related disorder is *Kartagener syndrome* in which there is a disorder in the formation of cilia throughout the body. This causes its victim to suffer from frequent bouts of pneumonia, since the respiratory system has problems cleansing itself. Frequently unnoticed is the effect on sperm motility. High-power electron microscopy shows an abnormal structure of the sperm tail (flagellum). Females with this syndrome may also be infertile due to altered cilial function in the tube. Although pregnancy has been noted in affected patients of both sexes, the harmful effects of this condition seem to be worse in men.

Drugs

A large segment of the American population continues to use marijuana. For men with normal semen quality, occasional use of this drug poses little or no threat to fertility. But chronic and heavy use can reduce testosterone levels, which suppresses both sperm production and sex drive. In my practice, we urge men with marginal semen quality to refrain from using marijuana. Cocaine, often thought to heighten sexual enjoyment, actually results in diminished sexual function when used regularly.

Tranquilizers, antihypertensive drugs, and other medications can interfere with complex ejaculatory mechanisms. Often, a substitute drug can be found that will accomplish the same therapeutic goal without antifertility side effects.

Calcium channel blocking medications, used for cardiovascular diseases, impair male infertility by reducing the acrosome-capacitation reaction in the sperm, necessary to achieve fertilization potential.

Radiation treatments and various drugs used to treat cancer can directly inhibit sperm production. The effect may be temporary or permanent, depending on the dosage and duration of the treatment. Nitrofurantoin, a drug commonly used to treat urinary infections, can also reduce sperm quality. The fertility inhibiting effects of this and other drugs may last for months because of the amount of time, about 72 days, it takes for new sperm to mature. However, these drugs do not induce changes in the genetic content of the sperm that would lead to abnormal children.

Chapter 2 discussed the DES syndrome and its possible effects on female fertility. Only recently has it become clear that exposure to estrogens within the uterus may also affect the development of reproductive organs in the male fetus as well. It now appears that some "DES sons" exhibit certain abnormalities in the ductal systems which may cause infertility.

Heavy smoking and drinking have been found to be associated with diminished male fertility. Heavy alcohol consumption will cause liver damage, which in turn affects the metabolism of male sex hormones. In general, I suspect that the sum total of all of the pollutants we are exposed to in the air we breathe and in the food we eat adversely effects fertility in everyone.

Immunological Factors

We have come to realize that the body's immune system can manufacture antibodies that attack its own tissues. Such an *autoimmune response* triggers a number of diseases including thyroid and adrenal disorders. Some men manufacture antibodies against their own sperm. The result is sperm agglutination and poor motility. A semen analysis may indicate an immunological factor if sperm stick together, but specific immunological tests are needed to clinch the diagnosis. Post-coital tests with such sperm usually show poor results, even in the presence of excellent cervical mucus. Specific treatment of immunological infertility is discussed in chapter 14.

Nonsurgical Treatments

If a couple's infertility arises solely or partly from a male factor, how might the man's fertility be improved? And when is artificial insemination with his sperm an appropriate therapy?

HORMONAL THERAPIES

Years ago, physicians routinely treated male infertility with thyroid hormone. We now know that there is no justification for giving thyroid hormone to anyone whose thyroid functions are normal. But even today, not all treatments for male infertility are without controversy. An example is "testosterone rebound therapy," designed to achieve a temporary improvement in sperm production. The patient is given large doses of testosterone to suppress release of FSH and LH (just as these gonadotropins can be suppressed in women with doses of estrogen). This can drive the sperm count down to zero. After the testosterone is stopped, the body's attempt to restore hormonal balance may produce a temporary overcorrection, a sort of "spring back" effect that results in a brief enhancement of sperm production. Critics note that some men seem to be permanently *less* fertile after a course of this treatment. Nevertheless, testosterone rebound therapy is still used by some fertility specialists. But the treatment is rapidly disappearing and is no longer routinely recommended.

Low-dose testosterone as a stimulant, rather than as a suppressive, also is used to treat male infertility. This is similar to the use of low dose estrogens to induce ovulation or to increase cervical mucus production. Over a number of years, various drugs similar to clomiphene citrate, such as tamoxifen, have been tried experimentally in men as a treatment for infertility. Generally speaking, although it has improved the fertility of some men, it has not been shown to have any statistical significance when large groups of men were studied under strict scientific conditions for a long period of time. Doctors consider a study reliable when not all of the patients are given the test drug, and the investigators as well as the patients are kept in the dark about which of the patients got the drug and which received an inert preparation (placebo). Later, when the experimental code is broken, these individuals serve as the "control" group. Changes in the variable under observation, in this case the semen quality, are compared between the group receiving treatment and the group getting the placebo. Nevertheless, the semen analysis of about 10 to 15 percent of men who have been treated with these oral drugs has shown significant improvement. It is definitely not a standard method of treatment, and although safe, is not recommended on a routine basis as yet. Let your doctor be your guide.

A very popular method of treatment of infertile men with poor semen analyses has been the use of hCG, the LH substitute which we described in chapter 7. A typical program of hCG treatment might consist of twice-weekly injections for 10 weeks. Results range from dramatic improvement to no improvement at all. At least some improvement occurs in about 20 to 25 percent of cases, but the pregnancy rate is only about 15 percent. Seminal improvement may not last very long, or may persist for months. Patients who have had varicocele repair seem to respond particularly well to hCG, which probably acts as a super stimulus for whatever functioning Leydig cells remain in the testes. This increases the amount of intratesticular testosterone in a way that oral or injectable doses of testosterone cannot. But remember that, although this form of treatment has been used for years, it is not FDA approved.

Humegon/Pergonal, an injectable FSH-LH preparation also discussed in chapter 7, is reserved for men who have hypothalamic or pituitary failure. Since it must be given daily over a period of months to initiate and sustain sperm production and maturation, the cost becomes prohibitive for most couples.

Artificial Insemination-Husband

Artificial insemination-husband (AIH) involves collecting semen from the husband and placing it directly into his wife's cervical canal or vagina at the time of ovulation. AIH can be successful in cases where the man is subfertile but has at least some motile sperm in his ejaculate. Although the insemination itself is a very simple procedure (we sometimes encourage the husband to perform it himself), a program of AIH places a good deal of stress on the couple. For this reason, therapists do not resort to AIH until other logistically easier methods have been exhausted. We shall discuss this in more detail in chapter 15.

Fertility investigators are exploring ways to enhance the quality of the semen specimen used for insemination. For example, some therapists have been performing AIH using a "split ejaculate," that is, using the first drops of semen in the ejaculate to get the most motile sperm. Some researchers have reported that interrupting coitus after the first muscular contraction of orgasm is also associated with a higher pregnancy rate. A popular approach utilizes what is known as a "swim-up" technique. The sperm is washed in a salt solution and centrifuged down into a pellet in a test tube. The most motile sperm will, in time, swim up through the salt solution above, and it is these sperm which are collected for concentration and subsequent insemination. Sperm prepared in this fashion are particularly suited for placement directly within the uterine cavity. The rationale for doing this is that the higher in the reproductive tract the sperm are placed, the greater the number that will eventually be able to surround the egg. Intrauterine insemination (IUI) should cause the woman little or no discomfort other than a mild cramp. There is a small risk of infection with any intrauterine manipulation. Therefore, many doctors will prescribe a broad spectrum antibiotic such as tetracycline for a day or two to prevent infection.

Newer techniques of sperm processing incorporate adding various substances which can improve and maintain sperm motility, thereby adding to the pregnancy rate.

My associates and I recently concluded a study of 302 couples with IUI in 991 cycles. Pregnancy was evaluated according to the indication for the IUI, and compared with pregnancy rates in cycles in which no therapy was given. IUI was best for infertility associated with poor sperm survival in cervical mucus, but with normal sperm motility in semen analysis. In some cases adding Humegon/Pergonal for the wife improve results even more.

A cervical cap with a stem which protrudes from the vagina can be used for inseminations at home. The woman needs to be fitted for this cap which is then used somewhat like a diaphragm. Rather than inhibiting pregnancy, the cap promotes fertility by keeping sperm in contact with the cervix for long periods of time after the husband uses a syringe to deliver sperm up through the stem into the cap which surrounds the cervix. Under these circumstances, the sperm are protected from the normal vaginal acidity. Results with the cap have been good, and it allows patients to perform this therapy at home. Usually the insemination is done once or twice monthly, with urinary LH kits for ovulation detection.

13

Surgical Treatment of Infertility in Men

This chapter is brief for two reasons. First, a man's reproductive system suffers from few diseases whose effects on seminal production or delivery lend themselves to surgical correction. Second, it is unfortunately true that research in male infertility has not yet caught up with the efforts directed toward female infertility. The problems are harder to study, and in truth, urologists have paid less attention to disorders of male fertility than gynecologists have paid to female reproductive difficulties.

Testicular Biopsy

Surgeons generally will not perform an involved fertility operation on a man's ductal system without first taking a testicular biopsy (two exceptions to this rule are vasectomy and vasectomy reversal). The reason is that diseases or congenital abnormalities in the male reproductive tract often affect more than one site. For example, if a man has a poorly developed vas with blockages, his testicles may also be poorly developed and incapable of producing motile sperm. As discussed earlier in chapter 5, taking a tissue sample from the testicle under local anesthesia is a quick and relatively painless procedure. By revealing whether or to what degree the testes are producing sperm, a biopsy can spare the patient the ordeal of unnecessary surgery.

A biopsy taken from a man with a varicocele is sometimes difficult to interpret. Frequently scarring of the tubules can be seen through the microscope, along with disordered sperm production and development. We do not know how a varicocele produces scarring, but we do know that tying off varicose veins often restores fertility, in spite of whatever permanent damage remains in the testes. We can all function well with one healthy kidney, or one quarter of a good liver. It seems that a man's reproductive system often has the same marvelous reserve.

Fertility Surgery

Varicocelectomy

In chapter 12 we discussed the diagnosis and physiology of varicoceles. Fertility specialists still debate whether the size of the varicocele affects the chances for successful surgery, and whether men who are fertile despite a varicocele should be routinely monitored for decreasing seminal quality. The vast majority of varicoceles occur on the left side. Specialists now believe that a right-sided varicocele may also have important effects on fertility. The problem with advising a man to have a surgical repair lies primarily in the fact that the varicocele may not be the only cause of decreased seminal quality. *Varicocelectomy* very simply stated is an operation in which a cluster of varicose veins are surgically ligated (tied). There are alternatives to this procedure - injection of particulate matter to cause clotting in these veins, or the umbrella procedure. These are not totally without risk. The patient should have a thorough discussion of the options with his doctor before any therapeutic decision is made. With increasing frequency, the operative approach is performed on an outpatient basis, or with an overnight stay. A small incision is made very low in the abdomen, in the groin rather than in the scrotum in most men, because the vein branches to form a network of smaller veins that are too numerous to be tied off individually. Doctors are very careful not to damage the testicular artery or the vas, both of which run parallel to the vein. Complications are rare and usually not serious. For this reason, and because the varicocelectomy doesn't worsen the situation, most therapists recommend the operation.

Little or no improvement in sperm count and motility is to be expected for a month or two after surgery. In fact, the semen quality of some men temporarily declines. Usually, 6 months must pass before results can be accurately assessed. It is impossible to predict what an individual's response to varicocelectomy will be. We have seen pregnancy occur a few months after surgery from a forty-four-year-old man who previously had no motile sperm at all in his ejaculate. On the other hand, some men who seemed only minimally infertile before surgery have shown no improvement at all in semen quality, and pregnancy has not occurred. In general, some seminal improvement can be expected after this procedure in about 70 percent of men. Actual pregnancy, however, follows in 45 to 55 percent of cases, provided the wife is reasonably fertile.

Ductal Surgery

Infertility in a man can often be caused by blocked ducts. Blockage of the vas or the epididymis can be due to congenital abnormality or acquired infections. In either case, there are often several areas of blockage. Even sophisticated tests sometimes fail to pinpoint the location of the blockage, so men have to prepare themselves for an operation that may be exploratory only.

The channels of the vas and the epididymis are extremely narrow, barely visible to the naked eye. However, microsurgical techniques have made it much easier to work with these structures. The operating microscope allows accurate placement of fine sutures when joining remaining segments after the blocked portion has been removed. Microsurgery is most successful when only an isolated segment is blocked. Extensive areas of damage are much more difficult, and sometimes impossible, to correct. If blockage occurs in the epididymis, the structure in which the sperm acquire motility, there may be a long lag time between successful surgery and conception; it can take as long as two years before sperm acquire good motility. The exact reason for this is still unclear. But newer surgical procedures are being developed to help men who can produce normal sperm, but whose sperm transport mechanisms remain unrestored. A *spermatocele* can be constructed in which the sperm from the microscopic tubules empty into a small reservoir surgically created within the scrotum. This area can be tapped with a fine needle to collect sperm suitable for intrauterine insemination. This form of treatment is just undergoing early trials, and more experience is needed to decide if it will really work. Results to date have not been impressive. In some men, the vas is not formed and no real corrective surgery is possible. Sperm can be taken directly from the small tubules at the time of surgery and used right then with *in vitro* fertilization techniques to bring about pregnancy. This is very exciting for two reasons. First, it used to be thought that sperm taken from the tubules were too immature to fertilize. Second, even though a permanent correction cannot be made, pregnancy can be achieved. However, only a small amount of sperm can be collected in this fashion; these sperm can be frozen, but lose motility on thawing. Coupled with the ability to inject a single sperm directly into the egg as part of a microscopic IVF technique, pregnancies are being achieved with recovery of only a few sperm, and motility is not a factor.

Bilateral Absence Of The Vas Deferens

This is a specialized case and one which brings together clinically the talents of the urologist, gynecologist and geneticist. Most of the time, people with one recessive gene are carriers for that specific disease and are otherwise normal. This is not true for men who carry one copy of the gene responsible for cystic fibrosis. These men who have normal lung function, are born without the vas but have normal sperm production within the testes. The problem of course is the mechanical block to sperm transport. Usually the construction of a satisfactory channel is impossible surgically, and the actual surgery consists of getting sperm from the testicular tubules with those sperm then being used for *in vitro* fertilization. Under these conditions the genetic status of the male and his wife, who may also be a recessive carrier without any symptoms, must be ascertained prior to any active therapy since a child with cystic fibrosis could be the undesired product of this treatment. If the wife is negative as a carrier, the child will be either completely normal, a female carrier, or a male with the same fertility problem but not a cystic fibrosis patient. If she is positive, early embryos achieved via IVF can have a genetic diagnosis made prior to insertion into the uterus by removing one or two cells (blastomeres).

One problem is that the recessive gene has more than one form and even with advanced genetic diagnosis, current evaluations are limited to about a 90 percent accuracy. It is recommended that screening procedures be done in the male relatives of affected men.

Vasectomy Reversal

Sterilization by vasectomy is the most popular and effective method of permanent contraception. Severing and sealing the vas is a simple procedure that is quickly performed either in a physician's office or in an operating room. But anastomosis (rejoining) of the vas to restore fertility is not so simple. The surgeon must find the severed ends of the vas, trim the scar tissue, and rejoin the two segments (figure 13.1). Like the ductal surgery described previously, vasectomy reversal requires perfection that is difficult to achieve with conventional surgical techniques. Again, microsurgery is used to achieve better results. Sperm will reappear in the ejaculate in about 90 percent of men undergoing this procedure. The actual pregnancy rate for vasectomy reversal, however, is only about 50 percent.

Whether vasectomy reversal succeeds in restoring fertility depends on the manner in which the sterilization was performed, the skill of the surgeon performing the reversal, and the elapsed time between sterilization and the reversal attempt. Generally, the chances for success diminish with time, and the outlook is poor for achieving pregnancy if sterilization was performed more than five

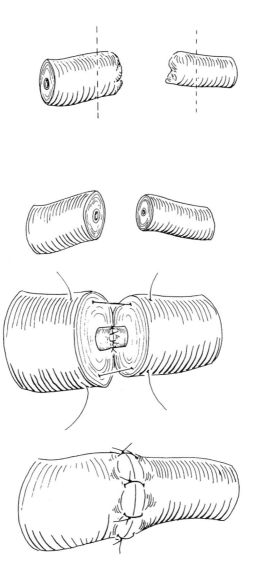

FIGURE 13.1 Vasectomy reversal. Top to bottom, trimming of scarred ends, alignment, anastomosis of the two segments.

years prior to reversal. The most probable reason for this is the formation of sperm antibodies.

Remember that vasectomy does not affect sperm production. Sperm trapped within the sealed vas disintegrate after time and become resorbed in the epididymis. But some sperm can leak out of the severed ends and get into the bloodstream. If this happens, the immune system may mistake the sperm for invading antigens and begin to manufacture antibodies against them. It is likely that the chance of antibody formation against sperm increases over time, and this would explain the five-year effect. This explanation would account for the discrepancy between the percentages of cases in which sperm reappear in the ejaculate and the actual pregnancy rate resulting from reversal. The sperm in the ejaculate are often completely coated with antibodies, and I have begun to recommend that an antibody test be done prior to the operation. If high levels of sperm antibodies are detected, I usually tell the man not to expect a good result with restoration of fertility. Although the pregnancy rate is lower in the presence of antisperm antibodies, it is certainly not zero. Whether antibodies are present or not, it normally takes 6 to 24 months after successful vasectomy reversal before sperm acquire normal motility.

14

Immunological Infertility

The body's immune system protects it against invasion by harmful microorganisms and other irritants, all of which are known collectively as *antigens*. When the immune system detects one of these foreign substances, it identifies precisely which type of antigen it is, and then manufactures the specific antibody to fight off the intruder. If there has been contact with that antigen before, the response is very rapid. If it is a new antigen, never before encountered by the body, some time passes before antibodies can be detected. Do you remember our discussion in chapter 2 of the lock-and-key mechanism, the way hormones bind to their target cells? The same type of pattern applies in immunology. The surface of a given antigen has its own chemical and physical "lock." The immune system manufactures antibodies that have just the right physical-chemical structure to form the perfect "key." These antibodies can then bind specifically to the antigen and render it harmless (figure 14.1). In this way, our bodies fight off most viral and bacterial diseases without the help of medication.

Occasionally, our immune systems become a nuisance, or even a danger to good health. People with respiratory allergies produce antibodies against certain pollens. When these pollens from various plant sources are present in the air, the body reacts as if it were

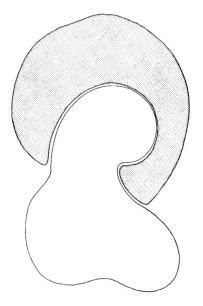

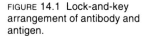

FIGURE 14.1 Lock-and-key
arrangement of antibody and
antigen.

fighting off a disease. This produces the familiar symptoms of hay
fever. Some people are allergic to certain foods. This immune system,
designed to protect us, can also become a threat when an organ is
transplanted from another person. It recognizes the transplanted
organ as "foreign" and manufactures antibodies to fight it. This is
why the tissues of an organ donor must have antigenic properties as
similar as possible to those of the recipient. If the match is less than
perfect, powerful *immunosuppressive* drugs must be given to protect
the organ against attack from the recipient's immune system.

Some people even manufacture antibodies against their own
tissues. Such an autoimmune response can cause a variety of
illnesses, including rheumatoid arthritis and some forms of diabetes.
Autoimmune disease can occasionally cause infertility in men. There
is also some evidence that certain forms of premature menopause
may be due to antibodies directed against ovarian tissue.

One might think that all women should form antibodies against
sperm. Sperm, after all, do contain foreign protein. The truth of the
matter is that only about 2 percent of infertile women have an
"allergic" reaction to sperm. Those women form antibodies which
may be directed specifically against sperm from their husband but

usually against all sperm. As mentioned in chapter 13, men who have had a vasectomy often manufacture antibodies against their own sperm. Sperm antibodies can be found in some men with no history of genito-urinary disease or surgery for reasons that are still unknown.

Diagnosis

Identifying the immunologically infertile couple is not easy. The doctor can get a hint that there is trouble from a post-coital test that shows poor sperm motility in what appears to be normal mucus. If, in time the sperm agglutinate (stick together), or begin to move in very erratic patterns, or both, the doctor is closer to a diagnosis. On the other hand, we have seen patients, both men and women, with high antisperm antibody titers, who show no apparent defect on the post-coital examination. Yet another pattern exists, one in which we see no sperm at all in the cervical mucus, even a few hours after intercourse. Our bodies have scavenger cells known as phagocytes which are responsible for cleaning up the debris of dead cells anywhere in the body. When sperm are attacked by antibodies, the phagocytes then view these cells as trash which must be removed. In some cases, this process is so efficient that examination of cervical mucus only a few hours after intercourse fails to show any sperm whatsoever.

A hint that there are sperm antibodies can also come from a Kurzrok-Miller test which uses donor cervical mucus and donor semen to evaluate the corresponding substance from the infertile couple. If the woman has significant antibody activity, her mucus will tend to immobilize the sperm of the fertile donors. On the other hand, if the problem resides with the man, his sperm won't adequately penetrate excellent mucus from a fertile woman donor.

To make matters more complicated, different antibodies show different forms of behavior. For instance, the two most important antibodies in reproductive infertility are immunoglobulin G (IgG) and immunoglobulin A (IgA). IgG tends to be more easily measurable in the blood, while IgA is a more locally occurring antibody. Going back to our example of people who have allergies to pollen, high levels of IgA are often found in their nasal mucus even if blood tests for sensitivity are negative. Not only are there different types of antibodies confounding things, but we must add to the puzzle the fact that some antibodies will cause the sperm to agglutinate, while other antibodies will immobilize the sperm. Antibodies attach to different points on the sperm. Those that attach directly to the sperm head and neck are thought to impede egg penetration, while those that attach to the tail interfere more with motility.

The older methods of sperm antibody detection relied on several blood tests that were primarily agglutination tests, so named because the end point was testing sperm against blood samples that would cause them to stick together. Some of these tests showed primarily a head-to-head pattern (figure 14.2), while others showed tail-to-tail agglutination (figure 14.3). The problem with the agglutination tests was that they were not very specific; some fertile couples showed a positive antibody reaction in both partners. Moreover, either partner might show a positive reaction in one test system, but not in another. Some tests, such as the Isojima and the Friberg tests, are more accurate in detecting antibody problems that seem to be related to infertility. These tests depend upon immobilization rather than agglutination to show a positive result.

We routinely use a test developed by Dr. Richard Bronson in New York, which we described previously, called the immunobead test. It employs plastic microspheres coated with rabbit antibody to test

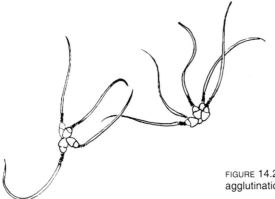

FIGURE 14.2 Head-to-head sperm agglutination.

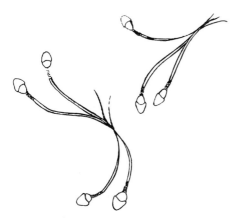

FIGURE 14.3 Tail-to-tail sperm agglutination.

the semen and blood of the man, and the blood of the woman. The results can be quantitated and compared with a repeat analysis in the laboratory after treatment. Sperm antibodies, when they are present, may be found in semen or blood, or both.

Treatment

Treatment for immunological infertility is complicated and difficult. The powerful drugs used to suppress the immune system against organ transplants are too dangerous to be used in a nonlife-threatening situation. They cause the body to become prone to infections, and perhaps cancer, and interfere with sperm production and ovulation. Therefore, use of these immunosuppressive drugs for immunological infertility is out of the question at this time.

If it is the woman who manufactures sperm antibodies, treatment may consist of her avoiding all contact with sperm. This means that the man must use condoms during intercourse and avoid depositing semen *anywhere* in the woman's body. It is hoped that with avoidance of repeated exposure to sperm, the stimulus for antibody production, the woman's antibody levels will eventually drop enough to permit conception. If reappraisal after 6 months shows that antibody levels indeed have declined, the partners are encouraged to have intercourse without a condom - but only at the time of ovulation. The results of this form of treatment are spotty, with some therapists reporting excellent results, others disappointing results.

If the man produces antibodies against his own sperm, the necessary treatment involves drug use because it is impossible to remove the antigen (sperm) from his body. Steroid drugs similar to cortisone can be given in this instance. The drug can also be given to a woman who shows antibodies directed against sperm. There is no universal program of steroid treatment. Some centers use high doses over a short term, while others use low doses over a long term. Steroids can have serious side effects. At high dose steroids can induce the formation of a peptic ulcer, diabetes mellitus, or psychosis. Even if high doses are used for a short time they may lead to degeneration of the hip years later that could require artificial hip replacement. Steroidal treatment, then, is to be used only after you've discussed the potential risks with your therapist.

An alternative treatment is to wash the sperm with a salt solution to remove the prostaglandins present in the semen, collect those sperm whose motility seems to be unaffected by the antibodies, and use these for artificial insemination. We (and others) have had some success in utilizing a special technique of sperm processing in which some of the antibodies can be removed from the sperm prior to intrauterine insemination. But the antibodies tend to be tightly attached and vigorous efforts at separation result in rupture of the sperm.

Men or women with sperm antibodies have achieved pregnancy after the diagnosis had been made, but before it was treated. Statistically though, the outlook gets worse as time goes on. This is one of the conditions for which *in vitro* fertilization and its related therapies has proven helpful. Even with high levels of antibodies, affected sperm placed in large numbers in a Petri dish around an egg have successfully caused fertilization. When the woman is allergic to sperm, it helps to promote fertilization if we take an egg out of the body and place it in a balanced salt solution free from circulating antibodies present in her body fluids.

15

Artificial Insemination

For many couples unable to bear children, adoption long has provided a very satisfying alternative. Most people have no trouble loving and receiving joy from a baby not genetically their own. However, the number of babies available for adoption has decreased in recent years. Widespread use of various contraceptive agents and legalized abortion now allow women to avoid having babies when they are not ready to have them. Just as important, the fertility rate in general has declined for reasons we discussed in chapter 1. All of these factors have increased the demand for adoption while reducing the pool of adoptable babies. The difficulty in adopting has increased interest in artificial insemination as a solution to infertility.

In artificial insemination sperm are collected and deposited directly into the woman's vagina, cervical canal, or uterine cavity. The sperm may be the husband's (AIH) or a donor's (AID). Artificial insemination is not new. In 1799, in England, Dr. John Hunter performed the first recorded AIH. The first successful AIH in the United States was performed by the gynecologist J. Marion Sims in 1866.

Who May Be Helped By AIH?

Candidates for AIH usually have some seminal problem. Pregnancy has not occurred with intercourse because the man has low semen volume but normal sperm concentration and motility, for example. In fact, most fertility disorders in men that do not involve sperm quality or quantity can be treated quite effectively with AIH. Two such disorders are hypospadias and retrograde ejaculation. When AIH is used as therapy because of reductions in sperm concentration and/or motility, results are still good but less impressive. AIH should be considered by couples who have problems that inhibit the frequency of intercourse, if the marriage is on good ground in other respects. The list below indicates these and other causes of infertility which might be overcome with AIH. While AIH is usually used to treat subfertile men with fertile wives, AIH may be of use in overcoming infertility that has resulted from poor cervical mucus and immunological factors.

Indications for AIH
Male Factors
> Low seminal volume
> Low sperm concentration
> Decreased sperm motility
> Nonliquification of sperm
> Excessive or diminished seminal volume
> Autoimmune sperm antibodies
> Sperm clumping and agglutination
> Retrograde ejaculation
> Anatomical reasons
> Sexual dysfunction
> Poor sperm penetration assay results

Female Factors
> Cervical abnormalities
> Poor cervical mucus
> Sperm antibodies
> Sexual dysfunction

Combined Factors
   Unexplained or continued poor post-coital tests
   Unexplained infertility

Coital Counseling

Artificial insemination can make great demands on a couple. The woman may need to maintain a BBT chart to monitor ovulation or use the ovulation detection kits. She may be inseminated once or twice in each menstrual cycle. If she has a full-time job, this can be difficult. The man must be ready to produce a semen specimen on demand, and to abstain from coitus for an appropriate interval to ensure the best possible specimen. Thus AIH will be, at best, sexually disruptive for the couple. At worst, we have seen men become disturbed to the point of impotence. Therefore, before starting any AIH program, the fertility therapist should provide counseling to prepare couples for coping with these problems.

The Cap: An Alternative To AIH

These drawbacks to AIH make the cap technique, which we discussed earlier, attractive. It is done privately at home once or twice a month, around the time of the LH surge, as indicated by the urine testing kit. Men feel more relaxed about it, and usually have no difficulty producing the specimen with their spouses' help. The couple allows about 20 minutes for liquifaction to take place before the specimen is drawn into a syringe and transferred, via the stem, into the cervical cap inside the woman. The couple may then go to bed and remove the device the next morning. While this approach may not be as good as an office insemination, there is no question that it is much easier and cheaper. So why not try it?

The AIH Procedure

COLLECTING THE SPECIMEN

Successful AIH requires great care in collecting the specimen. The couple should avoid coitus for 48 to 72 hours prior to collection so that the best possible specimen will be obtained. To collect several specimens and store them for future use is rarely helpful, because sperm from subfertile men do not survive the process of freezing and thawing very well. Chapter 12 discussed how semen can be collected from men with retrograde ejaculation, as well as other aspects of specimen collection for AIH. On the other hand, if the problem is primarily the woman's it is quite acceptable to use frozen sperm, provided that adequate motility exists after thawing.

If the man simply cannot bring himself to masturbate he may have intercourse at home using a special plastic condom, which can then be brought into the office. The sperm of some men do not stay motile long enough to allow the specimen to be produced at home and delivered to the laboratory later. These men may have to produce the specimen in the physician's office.

TIMING OF AIH

Naturally, the best time for a woman to receive AIH is just before ovulation. But we have seen how difficult it is to pinpoint the precise moment ovulation starts. Unless the woman ovulates at the same time each month, the physician may not be able to schedule AIH for any particular day. Therefore, we try to create an office-based insemination program that is flexible enough to accommodate patients who call to report the results of the urine LH test, and expect that the insemination will be done within 24 hours. Most programs report greatest success when IVI is performed during the day following the LH kit change (i.e. the day of ovulation). Some physicians use serial ultrasonic examinations to time insemination. When timed tightly, multiple inseminations add nothing to the pregnancy rate but increased cost and inconvenience. Weekends are always a problem with respect to having adequate laboratory facilities. If you are lucky, your therapist or physician will be involved in an *in vitro* fertilization program that functions 7 days a week with access to laboratory facilities. This is an important point to discuss with your doctor; the exact workings and accessibility of this program should be made clear from the beginning.

INSEMINATION

Artificial insemination is a simple and painless procedure performed in the office without anesthesia. The woman positions herself in the same way as for a routine gynecologic examination, lying on her back with her feet in stirrups. The vagina is opened with a speculum and the cervix exposed. For cervical insemination, the semen is drawn up through a pipette or syringe, inserted into the opening of the cervix, and delivered into the cervical canal. To ensure that the semen stays in contact with the cervix, the physician may place a cap over the cervix, which the woman removes later that day. Some doctors insert a plastic-coated tampon for the same purpose. While there is some debate over whether either of these devices improves the pregnancy rate, there is no argument over the fact that these methods avoid annoying leakage of fluid when the patient stands up following insemination.

If the woman has poor cervical mucus, the doctor may consider delivering the semen directly into the uterine cavity. Many doctors feel such *intrauterine insemination* is generally more successful than cervical insemination. The chief indication for this form of insemination is the finding of poor or even absent cervical mucus resistant to any form of therapy. Previous cervical cone biopsy may have so distorted the cervix as to interfere with sperm deposition or migration, or both. In addition, some investigators claim great success with this method when the problem is primarily one of low sperm numbers or motility, or both, since all of the motile sperm in an ejaculate can be placed within the uterine cavity. Because the seminal fluid contains high levels of prostaglandins, it is necessary to wash the specimen and replace the semen with salt solution before the sperm are inserted into the uterine cavity. This prevents the uterine lining from absorbing prostaglandins, and avoids a reaction of nausea, severe cramps, abdominal pain, and diarrhea that can follow such absorption.

How Successful Is AIH?

Why should artificial insemination lead to better pregnancy rates than intercourse? Under normal conditions, less than 10 percent of all the sperm deposited into the vagina reach the cervix. Placing sperm directly into the cervical canal increases the number of sperm that may migrate through the reproductive tract. A good method of determining the success rate of AIH is to compare the spontaneous pregnancy rate of couples who drop out of an AIH program against the AIH pregnancy rate. Dr. Frances Batzer and I performed a survey that revealed a spontaneous pregnancy rate of 12.2 percent in such a population versus an overall AIH pregnancy rate of 17.5 percent. This is not a great difference. But a review of 100 of our own case histories revealed why AIH might *appear* to be less helpful than it actually is. The reason is simply that many couples become discouraged and drop out of therapy too soon. In fact, our pregnancy rate was 28 percent after 3 months of insemination and 41 percent at 6 months with *cervical* insemination. This last figure is a reasonable success rate for infertile patients in whom other therapies have failed. Therefore, we encourage couples to stay with therapy for at least 6 to 9 months.

How effective is artificial insemination when done as an intrauterine procedure? In our practice we found that pregnancy rates ranged from 17 to 63 percent at 6 months, depending on the reason for insemination. For example, when a woman had poor cervical mucus, we had success rates of 60 percent, whereas if the sperm had poor motility, the success rate was only 17 percent. Many centers have abandoned AIH in favor of IUI, feeling that improved pregnancy rates justify the additional laboratory time and costs.

Seminal problems are complex. Low sperm numbers and poor motility are often not the only defects a patient may have. Often there is impairment of sperm *function* as well. This is why we recommend the hamster egg penetration assay. It allows us to differentiate the potentially normal fertile man with a low sperm count from others who have similar counts but who have sperm that are not efficient in penetrating an egg. It is not rare to have poor hamster egg penetration with a semen specimen that is normal in all other respects. We do know that when there are any motile sperm, pregnancy can occur even though numbers may be small. Therefore, we first offer artificial insemination using the husband's sperm before going on to discuss high-tech-assisted reproduction such as *in vitro* fertilization or insemination using donor sperm (AID).

AID

AID has been performed on humans in the United States since 1882, when Dr. Joseph Pancoast at Jefferson Hospital in Philadelphia carried out the first procedure. While AID has become commonplace in veterinary medicine, its use with humans has not been as readily accepted. Some orthodox religions forbid their members to use AID. Nevertheless, an increasing number of couples are entering AID programs. Because of the private nature of AID, statistics are difficult to obtain. From informal surveys of known providers of this service, the best estimate suggests that perhaps 14,000 babies conceived through AID are born each year in the United States.

When Is AID Indicated?

The list on the following page indicates various circumstances under which AID might be considered appropriate. Most couples enter AID programs because the man is infertile. Exceptions include Rh problems, genetic disease, and those cases where a woman produces antibodies specifically against her partner's sperm. Of course if a woman produces antibodies against all sperm, AID will be of no help.

Couples who know that the husband carries a dominant gene for an inheritable disease may choose AID rather than natural conception. It's easy to understand why, when it is documented that inherited diseases passed on by a dominant gene affect 50 percent of the offspring.

As methods of prenatal diagnosis improve, it will be possible in more cases to make an intrauterine diagnosis on the fetus. If the genetic disease in question is found to be present, the patient's alternatives are either to abort the pregnancy or carry it. But a new answer to the problem is on the horizon whereby a fetus at risk for an inherited disease can be treated in utero. Experiments in people will soon begin whereby normal genetic material can be "spliced" into fetuses or even adults who lack certain genetic information, or who have faulty genetic material. We are still to learn if this genetic engineering will be widely accepted. Fundamentalist sects will, no doubt, oppose it.

Indications for AID
Complete absence of sperm (Azoospermia)
Severe reduction in sperm concentration and/or motility
Isolated sperm defects
Immunologic infertility
Genetic Disease
Rh disease (Erythroblastosis)
Previous male sterilization
Ejaculation failure
Poor sperm penetration assay results
Single women

Each year, more than a million American men are sterilized by vasectomy. This, coupled with the current high divorce rate in the United States, has produced a sizeable group of remarried sterile men who wish to have children. But vasectomy reversal affords only about a 50 percent chance of restoring fertility. Therefore, many couples choose AID instead of surgery, or after a failed attempt at sterilization reversal. Some men with retrograde ejaculation choose AID rather than endure the procedures by which sperm must be recovered from the bladder.

After a long period of infertility, in which the only finding is non-penetration of hamster eggs by sperm, it still becomes reasonable to shift to donor insemination if other methods of treatment including *in vitro* fertilization have been given a chance. But many times we find that couples opt for AID rather than go through the complicated process of *in vitro* fertilization. With IVF it is the female who really bears the brunt of the treatment - employed really to indirectly treat the man. Before the advent of the newer forms of therapy, the decision to treat or not treat, and what form the treatment should take, was often made simple by the fact that there were limited choices. Today, we usually have more than one way to deal with a particular problem. This introduces the element of choice not only to the physician, but more importantly, to the couple. These decisions are sometimes quite difficult to make, and one should take sufficient time to weigh the pros and cons of the various therapies available.

AID for single women is the most controversial of the indications for the procedure. About 10 percent of all women receiving AID are single. Over 30 percent of children in our country are raised by a single parent. Recent demographic surveys show that 40 percent of children were delivered to nonmarried women in all socio-economic groups. Most of the single women who come for AID are career women who never had the time or the inclination to get married or cultivate a steady long-term relationship. As these women get into their late thirties, they find that they really want to have a child and that they can provide for a child. Within an AID program, they can have a donor who is screened for various genetic and psychological factors. Because the arrangement is anonymous, there is no other person who may have an emotional or legal hold on the child. Recent social and psychologic studies show that children raised in these single-parent homes are for the most part happy children who perform well in society. This is also true of children raised in lesbian homes; studies show that the psychosexual orientation of both girls and boys in these circumstances is at least as "normal" with respect to sexual preference as in the general society. It is imperative that these women have a good self-awareness of their needs and motives for raising a child. If the physician is concerned about any particular patient, the doctor can insist that she have psychological screening before entering the AID program. Most practices in the United States flatly refuse insemination by donor in a single patient.

Selecting A Donor

One of the most important things for a physician and a couple to consider before beginning an AID program is the selection of the sperm donor. Couples become quite concerned about the choice of a donor, and rightly so. It is the donor who contributes half of the genetic makeup of the child. Medical schools are thought to be an excellent source of donors. Medical students are presumed to be bright, responsible, and at relatively low risk of transmitting sexually acquired diseases. Graduate students in the various arts and sciences are also frequent donors. The image of a semen donor as one who masturbates for money is terribly distorted. Yes, there is payment, but money is not the incentive. These men are well-motivated, responsible people who know that they are giving the gift of life to infertile couples. I recall one of our donors who could not keep his specimen collection appointment because he had to take his own wife, who was in labor, to the hospital. Yet he still took pains to have his specimen delivered to us for use by a childless couple.

Because patients and donors usually never meet, the awesome responsibility of selecting a donor rests upon the physician. We first review both the personal and family medical histories of each prospective donor. In this way, we eliminate, as much as possible, candidates who may carry a gene for inheritable disease. Second, we perform a semen analysis. We want semen donors to be very fertile, with sperm concentration, motility, and morphology all within the higher ranges of normal. We select a donor who looks like the husband and is from the same ethnic background. Donors are screened for genetic diseases, of course. Jewish donors, for example, are Tay-Sachs screened; black donors are screened for sickle cell disease; Italians, Greeks, and others of Mediterranean background are tested for thalassemia. Cultural patterns greatly affect AID practices. Colleagues in India tell me that not infrequently, insemination is done with a specimen taken from a pooled collection donated by the brothers of the sterile husband. While the biological advantages are obvious, the potential for psychological problems makes this an uncommon approach in our society, but one which is becoming more popular. Sperm from a brother can be collected, frozen, and shipped to the center for thawing and insemination.

While donor insemination began as an anonymous procedure, recent surveys of infertility patients have shown an increasing preference for use of a sibling as the semen donor - a choice actually favored more by the affected males but also endorsed to a great extent by the spouse. Obviously, competent psychologic evaluation and counseling is a necessity. In addition, although previous experience was overwhelming in favor of failure to disclose to the child the exact circumstances of the pregnancy initiation, recent surveys show that this philosophy is changing as well. The father of the affected male in selected cases has also served as the sperm donor provided that the seminal quality is reasonable.

Sexually Transmitted Diseases

The main concern we have today is not so much that the donor look like the husband; it is avoiding the risk of sexually transmitted disease. The American Society for Reproductive Medicine has issued some guidelines that cover donor screening. Blood tests are taken for syphilis, cytomegalic inclusion virus, and the virus causing acquired immune deficiency syndrome (AIDS - the well-known acronym for the disease, not AID, the artificial insemination program acronym), as well as for hepatitis. Although the hepatitis virus has been found in essentially all body secretions, there seems to be very little evidence that it is, in fact, transmitted by exposure to semen. Direct urethral cultures are made from the donors for the presence of gonorrhea, chlamydial infection, and ureaplasma organisms. Obviously, prospective donors whose life-styles put them at high risk for these infectious agents, are not included in an AID program, even if their culture results are negative. These tests should be repeated at no more than 6-month intervals.

One way of getting around the problem of infection is to use only frozen semen for these programs. This allows an individual donor to provide a multitude of specimens that can be stored indefinitely. Six months after the last collection, testing can be repeated, and if negative, the semen can be used clinically with great but not complete confidence. The reason for the delay is the incubation time necessary to get a valid reading on the blood. Recently, it has been discovered that some men continue to test negative for HIV in blood a year or more after isolation of that agent from their semen. What this discovery has meant in the field of fertility is that use of frozen semen from a negative donor, who has tested negative 6 months later, is not foolproof, although it does dramatically reduce the risk of contact with HIV. Still, at the time that this is being written I know of no woman in the United States who has become HIV positive after insemination with thawed sperm properly quarantined and tested. The American Society for Reproductive Medicine, with input from the Centers for Disease Control in Atlanta, GA, has recommended that frozen sperm released after at least a 6-month incubation period from a retested negative donor (as mentioned above) is advised for all patients. In other words, use of fresh semen is strongly discouraged.

The problem with this approach is that frozen sperm are not so efficient at achieving pregnancy as fresh sperm. It usually takes twice as long to conceive, and some women never conceive with frozen sperm. Obviously we need to develop methods of sperm freezing and thawing that will give us better specimens for use in our patients. Many laboratories are currently engaged in research along these lines. Even better would be developing an inexpensive blood test for HIV that does not depend on the detection of antibodies, the basis for the currently employed tests. Best of all for our purposes would be a test for the HIV in semen itself that could be quickly performed on each fresh specimen.

I feel it is important to screen the recipient with the same tests with which we screen the donor. We have seen a number of women who carry, in an asymptomatic form, chlamydia or other infectious agents, including the hepatitis virus. If these women later develop the clinical form of the disease without having been cultured prior to AID, it is impossible to say whether they brought the infection with them, or whether they acquired it from the donor. So we test recipients beforehand for everything that donors are tested for. Because hepatitis and HIV can be found in semen, we test the husband for this when we are using his semen for AIH as a safeguard for our laboratory personnel.

Commercial services supply frozen semen for physicians who don't do their own banking because they find it too costly and time consuming, and because a good pool of donors is difficult to find. Doctors and patients have to trust the screening procedures to unknown parties. Patients in smaller communities may have to rely on commercial frozen specimens for ethnic matches. Whether justified or not, there is some fingernail-biting over this. Fertility specialists in a large city, especially if they are near a university, can draw on many racial and ethnic groups and, therefore, have little trouble with matching donors to the husband. Pregnancies have resulted from sperm stored as long as 10 years.

About 13 percent of our inseminations are for patients wanting a second AID child. For this reason, it is worthwhile to freeze many specimens from a donor so that they can be used at a later time. It's not simple to freeze sperm. The sperm must be placed in a special protective solution and frozen at a low temperature in liquid nitrogen. The thawing process is just as precise, and it is here that most of the damage to sperm motility occurs. Artificial insemination with donor sperm has become more complicated and costly because there is so much donor screening and testing to be done. Each round of screening may cost up to $300 for the tests, and most programs will limit the number of babies from a particular donor, especially within a small community for obvious reasons. Added to the burden is the fact that most medical insurance carriers do not cover this form of treatment because it is considered indirect therapy for male fertility. The usual cost of donor insemination can be anywhere from $200 to $600 a month. Without insurance coverage it takes its financial toll. On the other hand, since pregnancy usually occurs rather rapidly as we shall shortly see, the overall cost of becoming pregnant is not unreasonable, and it is certainly much less than the cost of adoption.

Insemination Schedule And Results

AID used to be performed twice monthly at 48 hour intervals in an attempt to bracket expected ovulation. The strong recommendations from the Center for Disease Control (CDC) and the American Society for Reproductive Medicine (ASRM) for use of frozen-thawed, quarantined sperm has had the result of stimulating more accurate prediction of ovulation. Coupled with the expense of sperm freezing, thawing and processing, most donor insemination is performed once each cycle as an IUI, timed with an LH kit or ultrasound. Some practices, however, continue to recommend two inseminations, usually at a 24 hour interval.

The success rate among women who enter an AID program is approximately 75 percent. In our own practice, it has taken women about 3.5 months to conceive with *fresh* semen. This rate is now 5.5 months for patients receiving frozen semen. As I tell our patients, do not be surprised if you conceive in the first month, but also do not be disappointed if it takes 6 months or so. Some of the failures are caused by reproductive problems in the women. If 6 months go by without pregnancy, especially in a woman with apparently normal ovulatory function, a more detailed workup is indicated. Fully 20 percent of all patients who are ovulating normally will have some ovulatory disturbance during the AID program. This is proof that psychological stress does indeed play a part in this particular treatment.

Psychological And Legal Aspects

PSYCHOLOGICAL FACTORS
Certainly the psychological burden of AID cannot be underestimated. For the working woman, it means leaving her job one or two days each month and fielding curious questions from colleagues and superiors. Women can certainly expect to be depressed, when, at day 28 or so, menses occur. Husbands must reconcile themselves to the fact that babies born from AID will not be "theirs" genetically. They must be willing partners in AID and should not be coerced either by their wives or their physicians. We have frequently encouraged the husband to perform the actual insemination under our supervision. This is a way of including him physically in initiating pregnancy. It is normal for a man to have great ambivalence about AID. He may want a child desperately, but there are feelings of inadequacy that may haunt him. Psychological counseling during this difficult time is frequently helpful, and we actually insist on a psychologic screening for the couple. Most men surprisingly show psychological health during this period. In fact, the visit to initiate AID is made more often at the urging of the man than the woman. This is especially true if the man knew he was sterile before he got married. Next to *in vitro* fertilization, AID is the

most emotionally rewarding procedure that I perform. The warm letters and the pictures of newborn infants received from these couples remind me that I have had a hand in starting a pregnancy that otherwise would not have occurred.

LEGAL ISSUES

The legal status of AID in the United States is hardly clearcut. Thirty-five states have imposed some form of regulation, while many others have chosen to ignore the issue. For example, some states require full adoption procedures for the AID baby. In general, there exists medical and legal pressure to standardize the screening of donors, and this tends to limit the number of institutions where AID is performed. In most states, the legal aspects mainly deal with the consent of both partners to the procedure. Most physicians believe that there should be a document that makes clear that the donor gives up any legal claim to the resulting child. For the protection of the donor, the couple must also agree not to attempt to identify the donor. The way in which your child was conceived can be a well-kept family secret. That's the view of most physicians and psychologists. There is a growing minority view which states that the child should be told about how the pregnancy was initiated when he or she is old enough to handle this emotionally. Information on the location of AID providers in a given area can be obtained by writing the American Society for Reproductive Medicine, 1209 Montgomery Hwy., Birmingham, Alabama 35216-2809.

16

Reproductive High Technology

In this chapter the new technologies of assisted reproduction will be discussed. We now have the ability to donate gametes from both sexes (eggs as well as sperm). Embryos can be implanted into women who have made no genetic contribution to the embryos, and surrogate motherhood has become a reality. Whether some or all of these technological answers to the problem of continuing infertility should actually be employed must still be decided by our society.

Surrogate Parenting

In surrogate parenting, a couple in which the wife is infertile enters into a legal agreement with another woman (the surrogate mother) who consents to be inseminated with the husband's sperm. The surrogate mother carries the pregnancy to term, and after delivery, gives the baby up to the infertile couple for adoption. Obviously, the scientific technology that makes surrogate parenting possible is not new. This is simply a matter of artificially inseminating a woman who has agreed to become pregnant under these conditions. Another way to view this is, that like the semen donor, the surrogate mother donates the gamete. However, in terms of legal and emotional issues, the situation is more complex with surrogate parenting, since the surrogate also carries and delivers the product of the pregnancy.

What this technology calls into question is the whole issue of how one should define motherhood and fatherhood. Is the mother the woman whose egg is involved in the pregnancy, she who carries and delivers the baby, or should the term "mother" be reserved for the person who raises and nurtures the child? These are questions not easily answered by either the legal profession or society. By way of illustrating how complicated this dilemma is, imagine a more extreme scenario. It is technically possible to use sperm from a donor, egg from a donor, and to produce an embryo that would be inserted into the uterus of yet another woman. Under these circumstances, who would be the father and who would be the mother?

Several commissions that have studied these problems have concluded that surrogate parenting is not a procedure easily recommended. For example, in a recent summary of new technology in assisted reproduction, the American Society for Reproductive Medicine did not give its approval to surrogate parenting programs. Some states have even legislated against surrogate parenting programs, although most states have no laws to cover this issue.

From a legal point of view, even the best contracted agreement is fraught with problems. As was evidenced in the well-publicized Mary Beth Whitehead case, there is always the threat that the surrogate will change her mind and decide to keep the baby. This haunts all who are involved in these programs and see surrogate parenting as the last hope for some couples. Psychological testing of prospective surrogate mothers does not always succeed in screening out those women who may change their minds. These tests are given before the insemination and even though a woman might be completely willing to give up the baby at that time, there may be no way for a psychological test to measure the ambivalence that may surface over the course of the pregnancy.

There is no end to the controversy over surrogate parenting. At one extreme are those who argue that it is a form of prostitution; others believe that in a free society a woman should be allowed to use her body as she wishes. It seems ironic to me that in certain situations our society actively encourages women to give up their babies for adoption rather than have an abortion, while at the same time it castigates those who would willingly conceive a pregnancy to help a sterile couple. But because money is involved, and agencies for surrogate parenting may be profit-making, the general opinion about this fertility treatment is negative.

Many surrogate mothers, I am told, have a sense of well-being during pregnancy and enjoy pregnancy as its own reward. Money alone has not seemed to be the major motivation for these women, particularly if you calculate what they are making hourly over the 9 months of pregnancy! I have yet to see any battery of psychological tests that is capable of measuring altruism, but I suspect that some of these women are actually motivated by compassion for those who cannot produce their own families.

We don't know how many surrogate parent arrangements are made each year. The number is quite small; the arrangement does not seem to be a popular solution to infertility, probably because of the legal problems involved and because it is difficult to find a suitable surrogate. One reason for this is that the situation cannot be anonymous. The couple must actually choose the surrogate, and because identities are known, there is a great fear that even years after delivery the surrogate mother may want to play some role in the life of the child. This becomes a difficult problem for all concerned.

Embryo Flushing

Embryo flushing helps a sterile woman carry and deliver a baby formed from her husband's sperm and the egg of another woman. As in the case of surrogate parenting, the husband's sperm is used to inseminate a woman who has agreed to the process and who has been chosen by the couple. In this technique, a catheter is placed into the uterus of the surrogate soon after the embryo has entered her uterus. A flushing action with warm salt solution is used to dislodge and retrieve the embryo, which is then implanted in the uterus of the sterile woman with a catheter.

To successfully accomplish this procedure, it is essential that the two women have their menstrual cycles well synchronized, so that the uterine lining of the recipient will accept the embryo and allow it to implant. Embryo flushing has its drawbacks; it is possible to flush the embryo up into the tube of the surrogate, where it may implant and cause an ectopic pregnancy. In general, the process of embryo flushing is not an overly efficient one. More often than not the embryo fails to implant in the recipient. There is also the risk of an ectopic pregnancy in the recipient if the embryo is carried up into the tube while it is being transferred to the uterus. This is another procedure which has not been widely approved by fertility specialists and clinics. It does circumvent the psychological problems encountered in surrogate parenting, because the surrogate is pregnant for only a few days and is not involved with the delivery process. Certainly there is a psychological benefit to the sterile woman, who can experience the joy of carrying and delivering her baby even though she has no genetic input into the offspring. At the moment, this procedure, which is commonly used in veterinary medicine for genetic engineering, does not seem to be destined for widespread use with humans.

In Vitro Fertilization And Embryo Transfer (IVF-ET)

Since no substitute has ever been found for the human fallopian tube, women with severely damaged tubes and women without tubes could not hope to bear children until recently. Now, through *in vitro fertilization* (IVF), it is possible to bypass the fallopian tubes entirely. In *in vitro fertilization*, eggs are surgically removed from the patient's ovaries, transferred to a Petri dish, and fertilized by the husband's sperm. The embryo is later put back into the uterus and a normal pregnancy ensues.

The birth of the first baby conceived *in vitro*, Louise Brown in 1978, capped more than a decade of work by the British team of Robert Edwards and Patrick Steptoe. Following the initial American success at the Eastern Virginia School of Medicine in December, 1981, under the direction of Drs. Howard and Georgeanna Jones, many centers have opened in this country.

Some insurance carriers are beginning to cover *in vitro* fertilization since it became an approved form of treatment endorsed by the American Society for Reproductive Medicine. However, there has been a history of poor funding for this procedure by many insurance companies and prepaid medical programs. This is truly misguided because on a dollar-and-cents basis, a cycle of *in vitro* fertilization costs less than major surgery and hospital care for tubal repair. Since pregnancy rates are similar, the "per-baby" cost of IVF is less than that following surgery.

Egg Retrieval For IVF

Through the use of ovulation-inducing drugs such as Humegon/ Pergonal, it is possible to cause many eggs to develop in a given cycle. For IVF, this is the key to success. During the stimulation interval, as this is called, the patient's estrogen production is closely monitored and serial ultrasonic examinations are performed to identify the number and size of developing follicles. At a point when the lead follicles are starting to show maturity, and estrogen levels are satisfactory, hCG is given to promote the final stages of maturation leading up to ovulation. About 34 hours after hCG is given by injection, eggs are collected. Initially this was done laparoscopically. It has been possible to use improved ultrasonic instrumentation to avoid this operation and the use of general anesthesia. Instead, a local anesthetic is used and the patient is mildly sedated while the eggs are retrieved through the vagina with an ultrasonically guided needle (figure 16.1). The ovaries usually sit low in the pelvis right over the vagina, and it is actually easy to perform the egg retrieval. The vaginal approach also avoids complications sometimes caused by the laparoscopy procedure. Doctors are extremely careful during this procedure to avoid damaging major blood vessels and organs in the lower pelvis, or triggering an infection. However, the procedure is not without risk.

Today, although initially used in women for therapy of endometriosis, GnRH analogs find wide use as "down-regulators" of pituitary function in IVF cycles. Normally the communications which exist between the pituitary gland and the ovary and its

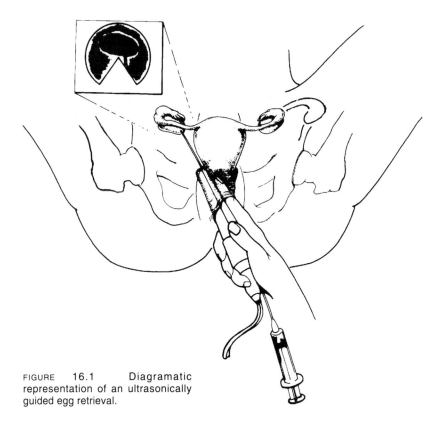

FIGURE   16.1   Diagramatic
representation of an ultrasonically
guided egg retrieval.

hormonal products are such that as the single developing follicle releases more estrogen into the circulation, the pituitary senses both the level and the rate of rise and responds by releasing LH necessary to bring about actual ovulation. During stimulation cycles with IVF,

FIGURE 16.2 Fertilization of egg by sperm in Petri dish.

where a maximum number of eggs is desired, even more so than in-office Humegon/Pergonal cycles, the greatly augmented estrogen levels emanating from multiple follicles can fool the pituitary into releasing LH at a time when the eggs are still immature. Therefore, temporary inhibition of pituitary LH release prevents this chain of events which is the leading cause for cycle cancellation prior to egg collection.

The removed eggs are not all mature; in fact, it is common to have eggs in various stages of development. The husband's semen specimen is then collected and prepared in a sterile fashion to eliminate any foreign matter and to collect the most motile sperm. Mature eggs are then exposed to the sperm (figure 16.2), while immature eggs are allowed to ripen fully in a laboratory incubator for insemination hours later. After fertilization has occurred, and cellular division has begun, the embryos are put back into the uterus (figure 16.3).

Infertility Problems That Can Be Solved By IVF

Although infertility caused by closed tubes was the original reason IVF was performed, it soon became clear that couples with other kinds of infertility problems could successfully have children using this approach. Some of these problems are listed below:

Seminal deficiencies, whether in count, motility, or in egg penetration as demonstrated in the hamster test, will frequently yield to *in vitro* techniques.

The presence of high titers of sperm antibodies, whether manufactured by the man or the woman. Since IVF allows the eggs in the Petri dish to be surrounded by large numbers of sperm, fertilization is more likely to take place, or, the sperm can be directly injected into the egg.

Anatomical problems such as having one tube on one side and one ovary on the other in a woman who has not conceived through the mechanism of transmigration.

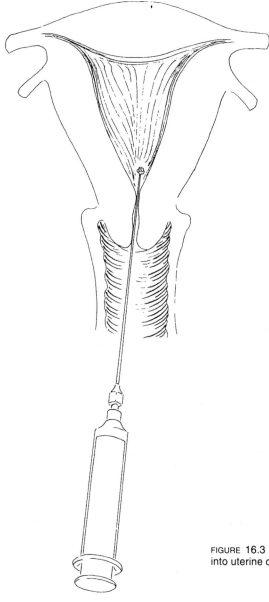

FIGURE 16.3 Introduction of embryo into uterine cavity via cervix.

Infertility even after adequate medical and/or surgical treatment of endometriosis.

Severe pelvic adhesive disease where surgery is either of no help or would make the adhesions worse.

Infertility for no apparent reason. The success of *in vitro* fertilization for these couples is probably based on some undiagnosed defect in the sperm, or in the tubal transport of the sperm and/or eggs.

IVF Statistics

Prior to GnRH use, which usually is begun about one week prior to the expected menses in the cycle preceding ovarian stimulation, IVF centers reported cancellation rates of 13 percent to 27 percent. Most of the cancellations were a consequence of premature LH surges. Even with GnRH analog use some patients have poor stimulation profiles of dropping estrogen levels or adverse ultrasound patterns causing cancellation in 5 to 10 percent of cycles prior to egg retrieval.

The chance of conception in an IVF cycle still remains less than ideal. Conception rates greatly depend on the number of embryos replaced within the uterus. That is, pregnancy is more likely to happen if two embryos are replaced instead of one. The maximum potential for pregnancy is reached when between 3 and 4 embryos are replaced. If more are replaced, the only thing that increases is the chance of having a multiple pregnancy.

The overall pregnancy rate within a given program depends on many factors:

A good laboratory team to mix gametes and nurture embryos.

Patient selection - the best results can be expected in a young population whose infertility is based on tubal disorders. When a large number of patients are infertile men, a lower proportion of eggs are fertilized, and therefore fewer embryos are replaced. Women in the program over age thirty-seven will also statistically reduce pregnancy yield.

Be cautious of the statistics you hear from IVF clinics; they can be misleading. If a pregnancy test 10 to 12 days after fertilization is positive, but the patient menstruates at the normal time, the test is not in error; these are not "false positive" tests, but represent early pregnancy loss, a very common phenomenon. Reputable IVF clinics do not report these transient or "chemical" pregnancies in their success statistics. At reliable clinics, pregnancy success rates are determined using two factors: at least two positive pregnancy tests, and ultrasonic evidence of a fetal sac. Nevertheless, the spontaneous abortion rate in IVF programs is a bit higher than in the general population. This may be due to a number of factors, including the hormonal changes brought about by the stimulation cycle itself, the age of the patient, and certainly the process of artificially inserting the embryos into the uterus through the cervix. Spontaneous abortion rates for IVF and GIFT are also artificially high because pregnancy testing is done so early; not only are patients very anxious for results, but since progesterone is often given in the early part of pregnancy for support, early pregnancy testing is essential.

IVF SUCCESS RATES

What are the chances for success? Each year, IVF clinics, who are members of the Society for Assisted Reproductive Technology (SART), a subsection of the American Society for Reproductive Medicine, report statistics into a central registry. Results are segregated according to female age of 40 or less and whether a seminal factor is present or not. A total of 28,984 stimulated cycles were initiated for the calendar year 1992. Table 16.1 summarized the results as *deliveries* rather than pregnancies since this is the reproductive bottom line.

TABLE 16.1

	Female < 40		Female ≥ 40	
	Male Factor			
	NO (%)	YES (%)	NO (%)	YES (%)
DELIVERY RATE				
Per Retrieval	20	15	7	5

To be noted as well is the fact that overall while there were 67% of deliveries liveborn as single gestations, there were also 26% twins, 6% triplets and less than 0.5% quadruplets or more.

About 15% of cycles were cancelled before retrieval. Of those cycles reaching egg retrieval, 88% led to a transfer of embryo(s).

One reason for low pregnancy rates in stimulated cycles is that the embryos developing in the laboratory are out of phase with the development of the endometrium. This occurs because the ovulation stimulation needed to produce so many eggs causes the lining of the uterus to mature too quickly in some cases. The embryos in the laboratory incubator, on the other hand, develop more slowly than they would in the body. One way to avoid this discrepancy is to use frozen embryos, a subject which will be discussed later in this chapter.

In some cases there are a large number of fertilized eggs (embryos). Most clinics limit the number of embryos inserted in the uterus because of an increase in multiple pregnancies associated with large numbers of embryo replacement. The problem is that the embryo which appears to be developing normally at this early stage may fail to divide in the next stage of cleavage. We desperately need a method of assessing the health of the early (2- to 8-cell) embryo so that if we have a choice, the embryo most likely to continue growth would be chosen for return to the uterus. Then we could increase the pregnancy rate and decrease the multiple birth rate.

Embryo Freezing

In cases where there are many embryos, they can be cryopreserved - frozen - for replacement in another cycle. Scientists are just beginning to understand the nuances of freezing and thawing human embryos. Like sperm, human embryos can probably be stored for years. However, the use of frozen embryos creates other problems and questions. For example, how much research should be done on these early embryos? Who owns the embryos in case of divorce, and who has the right to donate the frozen embryos to another couple? Once again technical advances have outdistanced the ability of our legal, ethical, and governing bodies to handle this situation. Donation of a frozen embryo to another couple produces a person with two biological parents and two nurturing parents. Scientists, clinicians and would-be parents are often impatient with review boards who govern IVF policies. Still, social and ethical issues must be considered before these procedures become common clinical practice.

In any case, it is already apparent that use of frozen embryos will add to the overall pregnancy rate and will reduce multiple pregnancies by allowing us to replace fewer embryos in the uterus during a natural cycle. One common concern is that there might be a higher risk of congenital abnormalities in infants who began life as frozen embryos; this has not proven to be the case. In fact, one could argue that only the most vigorous embryos survive the freezing and thawing procedure, and that the abnormality rate may actually be less than for those pregnancies conceived during the cycle of stimulation. For 1992 there were 6,243 embryo thawing procedures as reported to SART. Of those, 5,708 succeeded in transfer of at least one embryo into the uterus with a liveborn rate of 12 percent. Freezing not only increases the immediate yield per retrieval but allows couples to return years later for another pregnancy without reinitiating the entire process. The time limit in freezing of human embryos is unknown but success has been achieved after four years.

FREEZING EGGS?

You might ask, "Why not freeze eggs?" This would eliminate the moral and ethical dilemmas associated with freezing embryos, but the sad truth is that we do not yet have satisfactory methods for egg freezing and thawing that begin to compare with our existing methods of freezing sperm. The fact that freezing eggs is difficult with all animal species probably means that it will be difficult to achieve with humans too. Nevertheless, there are some encouraging results beginning to accrue from experiments in which immature eggs are obtained and frozen and later matured in culture systems after thawing with subsequent fertilization.

Multiple Pregnancy

The multiple pregnancy yield in most IVF clinics is somewhere in the neighborhood of 20 to 25 percent but may reach over 30 percent in clinics replacing large numbers of embryos. Most of these are twins, but triplets and quadruplets have been reported. As a rule, no one gets frantic about twins, especially when the couple has been infertile for a long time, or when the woman is approaching a point in her life after which she would rather not get pregnant. With good obstetrical care, having twins is not as risky as it used to be. Our colleagues in the hospital nurseries have made dramatic improvements in caring for premature newborns - which is the basic problem associated with the birth of twins. But pregnancy with triplets or more carries with it not only great discomfort for the mother, but a high risk of losing the entire pregnancy and an even higher risk of marked prematurity. Not infrequently (about 15 to 20 percent) one or more of the fetuses will be absorbed early in the pregnancy. We know this by following the pregnancies with ultrasound which may show 3 sacs early in pregnancy then show a spontaneous reduction to 2 or even 1. This usually occurs by week 8.

Selective Reduction

The issue is what can be done and what should be done when our technology is responsible for too much of a cure? The chances of carrying triplets or quadruplets to a successful outcome are poor. It is possible early in pregnancy with the aid of ultrasound to pass a needle through the vagina and the uterine wall into selected sacs and to inject a salt solution which will cause fetal demise. Although frequently called "selective reduction," this is really selective abortion. Couples who have chosen this remedy usually do so with the rationalization that some fetuses are being sacrificed so that others may be born. In most cases the goal is to leave a twin pregnancy. We had such a case at our fertility institute. It occurred in a woman who had 4 eggs replaced in a GIFT cycle. She had 6 sacs on ultrasonic examination. At least 1 sac contained 2 fetuses so that we knew that splitting of the embryos into identical twins was at least partially responsible for the problem.   After a great deal of counseling and soul searching, the couple opted for embryo reduction and she delivered a healthy boy and a healthy girl at term.

Donor Eggs

Some women who have a premature menopause or who have lost ovaries from certain diseases need donor eggs. Donor eggs like donor sperm also help high-risk patients avoid passing on a genetic defect to their child. One aspect of "high-tech" pregnancies is that women without ovarian function who carry a fetus in the absence of their own hormonal function have to be supplemented through the early part of the pregnancy with estrogen as well as with progesterone. We know that high doses of estrogen can lead to DES abnormalities in the offspring. Today we carefully monitor estrogen so as not to exceed the physiological levels of a regular pregnancy. When the placenta has developed, in about the 8th week, estrogen supplements can be tapered or even discontinued because ovarian hormonal production is no longer needed. Just as with a semen donor, the egg donor can be a relative or a close friend. A major source of oocyte donation a few short years ago was a woman within the program who agreed to donate her excess eggs, usually anonymously, but sometimes with a financial arrangement being made to lessen her cost of the cycle. But as freezing protocols have improved, women are understandably less willing to reduce their individual chance for pregnancy by donating any eggs potentially fertilizable. Therefore, some IVF programs recruit volunteer, paid egg donors who are vigorously screened just as with sperm donors. Psychologic assessment and counseling to both donor and recipient is recommended, and is usually mandatory whether or not they are known to each other. Some of the reasons for egg donor gestations are listed on the following page.

TABLE 16.2
Congenitally Absent Ovaries
Ovaries Without Function
Surgically Removed Ovaries
Premature Ovarian Failure
Spontaneous or Caused by Radiotherapy, Chemotherapy or
   Autoimmune Disease
Hereditable Disorders
Advanced Maternal Age
Repetitive IVF Failure
Ovaries Inaccessible for Egg Retrieval

Women successfully treated for Hodgkin's Disease even as
teenagers may lose ovarian function permanently as a result of
chemotherapy. Other women may suffer spontaneous premature
menopause even during the third decade of life.

Clinics around the world have been successful in establishing
donor egg pregnancies in women through 60 years of age. With
proper hormonal support the uterus will sustain a pregnancy even
in this age group. But sociological issues become more important.
Is this really a wise therapeutic option? Consider the scenario of a
10 year old child whose father has recently died and whose mother
has Alzheimer's Disease. For this and other reasons we limit
maternal age to 48 in our program. Pregnancy in an older patient
may become a life-threatening event.

"Carriers" Instead Of Surrogate Mothers

Some women are born with normal ovaries but no uterus, as was
discussed with Rokitansky syndrome. Other women may have had
a hysterectomy but still have functioning ovaries. Many women
have a uterus that may not function well reproductively, as with the
DES syndrome, or a uterus with multiple fibroids, or a uterus that is
scarred. Still others may have had certain diseases that would
interfere with a successful pregnancy. For some, a pregnancy would
even be life-threatening. There is clearly a sizeable number of women
who would benefit from an artificial uterus that would nurture and

support a growing fetus. However, although the artificial uterus is still in the realm of science fiction, a different solution to these problems does exist today.

There are cases in which couples have relied on another woman (the "carrier") to carry their child through an entire pregnancy. Unlike a surrogate mother, the "carrier" makes no genetic contribution to the fetus. Interesting from a physiological point of view is the fact that the carrier's immune system does not reject the donated fetus. It would seem the reason for this is that the interior of the uterus is, to some extent, immunologically isolated from the rest of the body.

Because of the genetically inert role played by the carrier, society may be more accepting of this form of parenting. Still, the carrier cannot be anonymous. The couple must choose a woman who is willing to play this role. She preferably should be someone who has had a successful pregnancy in the past and, of course, she has to be willing to sign legal documents. In addition, the psychological assessment and counseling must be of high quality because of the nature of the arrangement being even more intimate and emotional than egg donation. Reasons for carrier gestation include:

TABLE 16.3 - Uterine Absence - Congenital or Surgical

Reproductively Impaired Uterus

DES Syndrome	Cervical Incompetence
Fibroids	Congenital Abnormality
Adenomyosis	Uterine Scar Tissue

Medical Conditions

Diabetes Mellitus	Heart Disease
Immunologic Factors	Kidney Disease
Liver Disorders	Pulmonary Insufficiency

In general, the legal complexities of all high-tech pregnancies cannot be alleviated until the states redefine their laws concerning parenthood and make the necessary accommodations for technological advances.

Sperm Micromanipulation

Not surprisingly, advances in human reproduction have developed through animal studies. In many animal species it is possible to insert a single sperm into the egg and bring about the birth of a normal animal. This process has now been duplicated in humans in the laboratory by drilling a small hole in the outer covering of the egg that makes it easier for a sperm to penetrate the outer layer and to eventually fertilize the egg. The problem with this is again one of "too much" cure. If more than one sperm enters the egg, excessive genetic material is delivered, and this abnormal embryo is invariably aborted. Excessive manipulation of an egg may damage its ability to limit actual fertilization by one sperm. Even more exciting is the great success achieved with actually inserting a single sperm into the interior of the egg. This process known as intracytoplasmic sperm injection (ICSI) was pioneered in Brussels and is now in use throughout the world. It is exceedingly difficult to master in a technological sense since damage to the egg by the insertional process is an ever present danger. Early results show great promise in terms of normal liveborn infants. The process affords hope to couples who otherwise might have to seek a sperm donor as the only option for pregnancy. Even immature sperm from the testes and ducts rather than sperm in the ejaculate can be used for this purpose. Active manipulation of individual sperm cells and egg drilling are very "hot" areas of IVF-related research, but a theoretical problem causes fertility specialists to pause and consider the following. Nature may filter out very abnormal sperm from penetrating the egg and causing fertilization that would lead to a markedly defective fetus. This would presumably be at a chromosomal level, and it has never been shown that there is any relationship between chromosomal normalcy and the ability of the sperm to fertilize. Still there is a fear that by removing the natural selection barriers, we might help cause an increase in abnormal conceptions. Therefore, it is understandable that research in this area is progressing carefully.

Preimplantational Genetics

In general, IVF research has shown that as many as 22 percent of early four cell embryos which appear normal are genetically unbalanced, which means they are nonviable for an ongoing pregnancy. This probably is true for all pregnancies and explains in part the relatively high spontaneous abortion rate seen when pregnancy is diagnosed very early such as in the last two days *prior* to the expected onset of menses.

Added to this are couples with known genetic risks such as cystic fibrosis. Current technology allows for diagnosis early in pregnancy with a villus biopsy with induced abortion as one of the alternatives when results show an affected fetus.

But a few laboratories have been successful in establishing genetic diagnoses prior to embryo implantation. Couples at risk may have an IVF cycle with egg retrieval and fertilization. The resultant embryos at the four to eight cell stage can have one or two of these cells removed with the micromanipulator and in most cases development will proceed without a deleterious effect. These cells can be subjected to a rapid genetic diagnostic process with genetic probes for specific chromosomes and also for normal gene function as with the case of cystic fibrosis. Then only the normal embryos will be implanted.

This process represents a wonderful marriage between IVF programs and geneticists and promises to yield great relief for those who have already had a child with a genetically determined major defect. Here again, societal values must be respected and the fear of genetic engineering carried to an extreme must be considered.

Gamete Intrafallopian Transfer: The GIFT Procedure

The GIFT procedure, an acronym for gamete intrafallopian transfer, involves placing eggs and sperm into the fallopian tubes. The pregnancy rate of the GIFT procedure is higher than in standard IVF programs. Table 16.4 shows GIFT statistics for our program at Pennsylvania Hospital for the calendar year 1992:

TABLE 16.4
GIFT AT PENNSYLVANIA HOSPITAL 1992

	Women < 40		Women ≥ 40	
	Male Factor			
	NO (%)	YES (%)	NO (%)	YES (%)
DELIVERY RATE				
Per Initiated Cycle	27	43	13	38
Per Transfer	36	50	17	38

This rate reflects results from one of the better GIFT programs in the country, but more important, adding a full menu of technological services allows the patients to be placed into the category best suited to their unique reproductive problem. Thus, we can allocate severe seminal problems to IVF up to and through intracytoplasmic sperm injection (ICSI) with micromanipulation, while those with lesser problems may have GIFT procedures with a relatively high expectation of success.

There are a number of possible reasons for the low yield of pregnancy in IVF cycles. One is that the endometrial lining is stimulated to develop in a rapid fashion, but the fetus in the laboratory incubator is developing more slowly. Another is that embryos are being replaced into the uterus at an arbitrary time - a time sooner after ovulation than normal. So if a fallopian tube is healthy, the woman's incubator obviously is more physiologically normal than the laboratory's. Indications for GIFT are the same as for *in vitro* fertilization except for tubal disease. Of course, the patient has to have at least one normal tube. The stimulation protocol is the same, but eggs are retrieved with the help of a laparoscope rather than through the vagina with the aid of ultrasound (figure 16.4). The sperm and eggs are mixed in the laboratory and immediately inserted into the far end of the fallopian tube (figure 16.4). It is possible to approach the tube from the uterine end, and this is another active area of research. Getting a small catheter through the cervix and uterus out into the tube without causing tubal damage is difficult. Were this not the case, the GIFT procedure could be done as an office procedure, and indeed, may be done this way in the near future as instrumental techniques are improved.

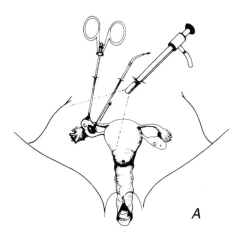

A

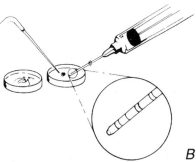

B

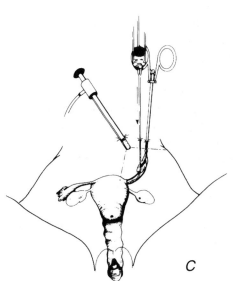

C

FIGURE 16.4   (A) Laparoscopic retrieval of ovum as prelude to GIFT, (B) Catheter loading of eggs and sperm, (C) Placement of catheter within tube.

As this text is drafted we are beginning a program of microlaparoscopy in which eggs will be retrieved via transvaginal ultrasonography as with IVF, mixed with sperm, and placed into the far ends of the tubes using a tiny laparoscope with local anesthesia with the goal of performing the entire procedure in the IVF laboratory-retrieval suite in order to avoid costs of operating room theaters and general anesthesia.

In our GIFT program, the pregnancy rate for couples with unexplained infertility who have not conceived with all other methods of therapy is 57 percent per try! Obviously, we are overcoming some defect in egg pick-up, or sperm transport or function, or both, which had not been diagnosed with currently available methods. Most clinics will place two eggs in each of two normal fallopian tubes along with sufficient numbers of sperm to insure fertilization. As with IVF programs, the likelihood of multiple pregnancies is increased with the number of eggs replaced. Another advantage of the GIFT procedure over IVF is that women whose cervices have been distorted from congenital abnormalities or prior surgery can avoid embryo replacement through that route. The disadvantage of GIFT is, if pregnancy does not occur, one doesn't really know if fertilization has taken place. For this reason, we frequently will take some eggs - if we get more than 4 - and attempt fertilization in the laboratory. If fertilization occurs, the embryos can be frozen and stored for future use.

The GIFT procedure has been used successfully throughout the world, and represents a special advance in those countries whose orthodox religions forbid IVF on the grounds that conception occurs outside of the body. The eggs and sperm are mixed and immediately returned to the body, satisfying religious criticism.

When GIFT was first introduced, there was concern that it would result in high rates of tubal pregnancy. This has not happened, probably because most clinics exclude women who have had previous tubal surgery or tubal infection. Spontaneous abortion rates and multiple pregnancy rates are similar to those seen with IVF. GIFT can be combined with other therapeutic procedures performed laparoscopically such as laser treatment of endometriosis and lysis (cutting) of adhesions. Under these circumstances it becomes a more economically attractive process.

ZIFT

ZIFT stands for zygote intrafallopian transfer, and further adds to the alphabet soup confusion with these "high-tech" methods of reproduction. In ZIFT, eggs are collected, usually with the help of ultrasound, and fertilized. In a day or two, the early embryos that have resulted from fertilization of these eggs are placed at the far end of the tube with the help of a laparoscope, or in the midportion of the tube via a uterine ultrasonic approach. The rationale for doing these two procedures is that the pregnancy rate will improve because ZIFT has certain theoretical advantages over IVF and GIFT. Through ZIFT, early embryos can be placed in the tube for a more normally timed entry into the uterus than can be accomplished with IVF incubator-uterine placement. Although this technique has its proponents, I am not at all sure it is worth subjecting a woman to two procedures when one will suffice. Moreover, early reports suggest disturbingly high multiple pregnancy rates. Tubal embryo transfer (TET) is similar to ZIFT except that placement into the tube(s) is made a bit later allowing for zygotes to cleave to a later (embryo) stage in order to have a selection process built into the procedure.

Direct Intraperitoneal Insemination

Fertility doctors are able to bring about pregnancy by directly inseminating sperm into the peritoneal cavity through the top of the vagina, an approach similar to collecting eggs from the ovary with ultrasound. As in the GIFT procedure, the tubes must be functioning normally. Bypassing the cervix and uterine cavity, sperm are free to swim in the peritoneal fluid and find their way into the fallopian tube. The number of patients treated in this fashion is still small, but the procedure would seem to be useful for infertility caused by decreased seminal factors, immunological infertility, decreased mucus production or anatomical abnormality. The risk of infection is quite small, and proper washing of the sperm prevents prostaglandin reactions. Often, this procedure is recommended when a GIFT cycle is cancelled because of unfavorable hormonal patterns. Under those conditions, a pregnancy rate of 12 to 18 percent per insemination can be expected.

17

Pregnancy Loss and the Effect of Age on Reproduction

Fertility implies the ability not only to conceive but also to carry a pregnancy to term. The ultimate goal is to bring a healthy baby into the world. Some couples conceive with relative ease yet remain childless because pregnancies repeatedly end in spontaneous abortion. Others are prone to give birth to babies with congenital abnormalities. This chapter discusses threats to fertility that occur *after* conception. Since the likelihood of a successful pregnancy is affected by the ages of the partners, I also will briefly discuss the role age plays in reproduction.

Pregnancy Loss

Spontaneous Abortion

You might be surprised to learn how often spontaneous abortion occurs among normal women. The proportion of pregnancies lost in the first few weeks is very high, but then settles down to a lower figure after 8 weeks. The actual abortion rate, as was pointed out earlier, depends upon how early in pregnancy the test is conducted. Many pregnancies abort so soon after conception that the woman has a normal period and without knowing that she had conceived.

Studies show that when pregnancy tests are done *before* the expected period, there is an overall abortion rate of about 50 percent in an average population. If, on the other hand, we study a population in which the first pregnancy test is performed at 2 weeks after the missed period, that abortion rate figure becomes 15 to 20 percent. Most abortions that occur at this time result from a *blighted ovum*, also called empty sac pregnancy. The term describes a blastocyst that fails to develop past an elementary stage, usually because of a chance chromosomal abnormality within the blastocyst. This is not to be confused with chromosomal abnormalities in either parent that may be responsible for repeated pregnancy loss. Fortunately, empty sac pregnancies carry no particular risk of repeated occurrence. The diagnosis is made when no fetal outline is seen within the sac during ultrasonic examination. The nonfetal part of the pregnancy, the *trophoblastic tissue*, continues to secrete hCG for a while, and this can mislead us into thinking that we have a healthy pregnancy. Eventually this production drops, bleeding occurs, and the uterine lining sloughs off.

Spontaneous abortions are classified as complete, incomplete, or missed. *Complete abortion* means that essentially all of the fetal tissue has been expelled from the uterus. Most abortions that occur spontaneously within the first 8 weeks are complete. With an *incomplete abortion* part of the tissue remains in the uterus. One sign of incomplete abortion is persistent bleeding, often accompanied by painful cramps. When the tissue remains in the uterus there is a risk of infection and scarring. A *missed abortion* means that the uterus has failed to expel the dead fetus; the woman continues to carry the fetus even though it has ceased to develop. One *iatrogenic* (caused by physician) cause of missed abortion is the overzealous use of hormones to support an early pregnancy. Any *necrotic* (dead) tissue that remains within the uterus, whether from an incomplete or missed abortion, should be removed. If necrotic fetal tissue remains in the uterus for a long time, it could lead to a blood-clotting deficiency and trigger extensive hemorrhage.

The most common method of removing tissue from the uterus is a surgical procedure commonly known as a D & C (dilation and curettage), although it is more properly termed a D & E (dilation and evacuation) when performed during pregnancy. The cervix is stretched with graduated dilators to give access to the uterus. Tissue can be removed by scraping the uterine wall with a sharp instrument called a curette. A more commonly used method is to insert a cannula (which resembles a vacuum cleaner attachment) into the uterus and suck the fetal tissue out. This device separates the tissue from the uterine wall along a natural plane of cleavage. Most gynecologists feel this is better than having to scrape blindly with a curette that could go too deep, or not deep enough. We turn to the curette when we know suction won't work - when the fetal tissue becomes very sticky and adheres to the uterus.

If a missed abortion has occurred beyond 14 weeks, emptying the uterus may be difficult. Special instruments and techniques must be used for pregnancy losses that occur between 13 and 27 weeks of pregnancy (mid-trimester). Patients frequently ask how long they should wait after a pregnancy loss before trying again. Our customary answer is to wait for one or two normal periods, but new data suggest that this may be an overly conservative view.

Recurrent Pregnancy Loss

Repeated reproductive wastage is a problem in many respects more anguishing than inability to conceive. Definitions vary but the one most widely accepted is loss of a pregnancy before 28 weeks in three consecutive gestational efforts. The definition is relaxed for purposes of diagnostic workup depending on the age of the couple and their index of anxiety and frustration. The chance of a spontaneous abortion occurring in the first pregnancy is 15 to 20 percent if a pregnancy test is done 2 weeks after the missed menses. The figure of 16 percent is usually chosen and is increased from older studies which clustered around 12 percent. This is a consequence of earlier pregnancy testing and also reflects the demographic shift in our country to later initiation of reproduction which carries with it both relative infertility and increased abortion rate.

With one abortion the risk in the next pregnancy is only slightly increased - just bordering on statistical significance since most of these couples will be "normal" reproductively. With each pregnancy an individual statistic event, the risk of 2 consecutive losses becomes 16 percent x 16 percent or 2.6 percent. But after 2 consecutive losses, actual records show the loss rate in the third to be 19 to 33 percent and the loss becomes 30 to 50 percent after 3 consecutive losses with the spread of results largely a consequence of small number studies and different population groups observed.

Table 17.1 details the reasons behind repeated pregnancy loss divided into a column of those conditions generally accepted as being causally linked and into a column of other disorders which may or may not be responsible for pregnancy wastage. Embryo aneuploidy refers to the embryo having an imbalanced chromosomal status such as an entire set of extra chromosomes, (69 instead of 46) or an extra chromosome as with Down Syndrome where there is trisomy for chromosome 21. These errors arise during the fertilization process and early zygote division and strictly speaking, should not recur over and above chance if the parents have normal chromosomal arrangement, but there are certain cases where there seems to be a repetitive phenomenon. Gamete errors refers to intrinsic chromosomal derangements in sperm or eggs, noting that it is here that the age effect is most marked.

In actual practice a diagnosis for repeated (3) pregnancy loss is made in only about half the cases. The later the loss occurs, i.e. especially after 13 weeks, the more likely recurrence, because many of these are a consequence of unchanging uterine/cervical anatomic defects or phospholipid antibody problems. Also, the risk is greater with each succeeding pregnancy if the couple has never had a successful outcome.

TABLE 17.1

RECURRENT PREGNANCY LOSS CAUSES

DEFINITE	PROBABLE/POSSIBLE

Chromosome
    Embryo (aneuploidy)
    Gamete errors ♂ or ♀
    Parental translocation ♂ or ♀	

Immunologic
    Phospholipid-cardiolipin antibodies
	Immunologic
	    HLA Compatibility

Hormonal
    Corpus luteum deficiency
    Diabetes Mellitus (poorly controlled)
    Thyroid disorders
	Hormonal
	    Polycystic Ovarian Syndrome

Anatomic
    Incompetent cervix
    Congenital Uterine Anomalies
        Septa, Bircornuate,
        Unicollate, etc.
    Myoma Uteri
    DES Syndrome
    Intrauterine adhesions
	Anatomic
	    Uterine Polyps

Infectious (not acute)	Infectious
	    Ureaplasma
	    Any Chronic Endometritis

Other
    Active (Untreated) Endometriosis
	Other
	    Environmental toxin -
	    caffeine, nicotine, alcohol

Genetic Causes Of Repeated Pregnancy Loss

Role Of The Chromosomes

If a woman has three or more successive miscarriages, there is only a 3 percent chance that either she or her husband has a chromosomal abnormality. The chances of this are much greater if, in addition to repeated loss, she has already given birth to a child with congenital defects. Several types of chromosomal abnormalities can occur. Those of you who are familiar with genetics will find the following discussion quite basic.

Chromosomes are rod-shaped structures that contain individual genes. It is the genes that determine the physical features that we inherit, such as the color of our eyes and hair. Genes also determine our predisposition to disease, and to some extent, our intelligence. Each chromosome contains thousands of genes. Recent research shows that many of the traits formerly thought to be controlled by environment actually are determined by the genes.

The building blocks of the genes are segments of deoxyribonucleic acid (DNA). Every cell in the human body, except for the germ cells (sperm and eggs), normally contains 46 chromosomes which exist in pairs - 22 pairs of *autosomes* and two *sex chromosomes*. The sex chromosomes, naturally, determine a person's sex, but also carry considerable additional genetic information. This is the reason why some diseases are sex-linked. A man normally has XY sex chromosomes, while a woman has XX sex chromosomes. Sperm and eggs contain only half the number of chromosomes that other cells have; 22 single autosomes and one sex chromosome. The sex chromosome in an egg is always an X. In sperm, it may be an X or Y. At conception, the single chromosomes of the sperm become paired with those of the egg, thus restoring the full complement of 22 autosomal pairs and two sex chromosomes to the developing fetus.

Although chromosomes are extremely tiny, they can be studied with a special staining technique called banding which makes them visible under a powerful microscope. Figure 17.1 illustrates the banding of a white blood cell that has a normal chromosome content. This procedure allows us to examine the chromosomes closely to

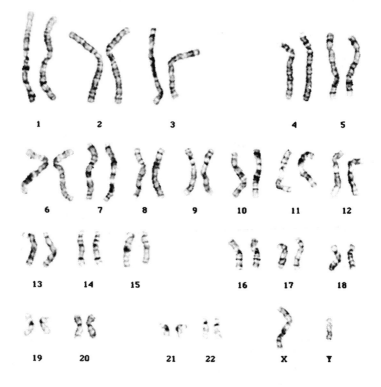

FIGURE 17.1 A normal karyotype analysis of a male patient. (Courtesy of Dr. Albert Yuzpe.)

diagnose subtle changes or abnormalities that can cause disease or malformed offspring. Science has not yet been successful in examining the chromosome on the level of the individual gene. Most of the disorders that are inherited occur because of changes at the molecular level within the gene. Therefore, clinical genetic counseling must function on a statistical basis in many instances, using collected data to determine whether the trait is recessive or dominant in character in order to predict risks of inheritance.

During conception and soon thereafter, any number of genetic "errors" may occur in the blastocyst. One of these genetic errors is *trisomy*, which means that one of the chromosome "pairs" actually consists of three chromosomes. Fetuses with trisomy generally do not survive the pregnancy. However, if trisomy affects the number 21 chromosome pair, the fetus may survive to be born with the Down syndrome of mental retardation and other physical deformity. Another genetic error, *triploidy*, occurs when there are three sets of chromosomes instead of two. Triploidy results when an egg is fertilized by two sperm. Triploid embryos are incompatible with live birth. Occasionally, one of the chromosomes belonging to a pair is completely absent, an error called *deletion*. It's worth repeating that with the exception of those cases where some trisomic fetuses survive, the major genetic errors described here virtually always result in fetal death. They are not the cause of such birth defects as cleft palate and clubfoot, which are not attributable to simple genetic factors. Human reproduction permits very few errors. All but the most subtle will result in early miscarriage.

How can two apparently normal people have a genetic cause for repeated pregnancy loss? Some people carry the proper amount of chromosomal material, but it is arranged in a fashion that predisposes them to reproductive difficulty. Such arrangements are called *translocations*, and they can be passed on to the fetus. Figure 17.2 illustrates two of the most common types of translocation. A *reciprocal translocation* is one in which pieces are actually exchanged between two chromosomes. If the same piece from each chromosome is exchanged, the translocation is "balanced" and results in a perfectly normal baby - but like one parent, an individual who will be prone to reproductive loss. Nearly all unbalanced translocations abort.

The *Robertsonian*, or *fusion*, type of translocation involves the attachment of one chromosome to another, with loss of small fragments from each. As shown in figure 17.2, this can result in a lethal *monosomy* (one chromosome where there should be two), an unbalanced surplus of that chromosome (also lethal), and a normal "balanced" state.

Couples can be screened for chromosomal abnormalities with *karyotyping*, using a sophisticated banding technique. Since karyotyping is expensive, it should not be performed except in cases of repeated wastage. One great advantage of diagnosing translocations in either partner is that it eliminates unnecessary use of hormonal support for a pregnancy. Unfortunately, there is no treatment for abnormal chromosomal states. Couples with such a condition should console themselves with the understanding that, given time, a healthy combination of genetic material will result in a normal child, or a child with a balanced translocation who will function normally. Unfortunately, the couple may have to go through a series of pregnancy losses first.

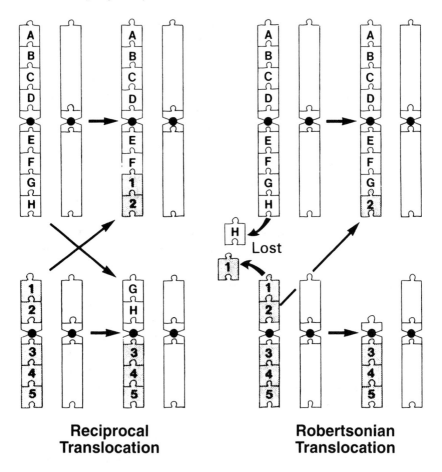

Reciprocal Translocation

Robertsonian Translocation

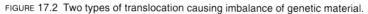

FIGURE 17.2 Two types of translocation causing imbalance of genetic material.

Genetic Testing During Pregnancy

Should genetic sampling be done during pregnancy? It is advised in women who are over thirty-five years of age, or in women who have given birth to an abnormal child in the past.

Two Approaches

AMNIOCENTESIS

The classic approach, as shown in figure 17.3 is *amniocentesis*, which is done about 16 weeks after the last menstruation. With this method, the fetus is located and examined with ultrasound, as is the placenta. Under local anesthesia, a needle is passed through the abdominal

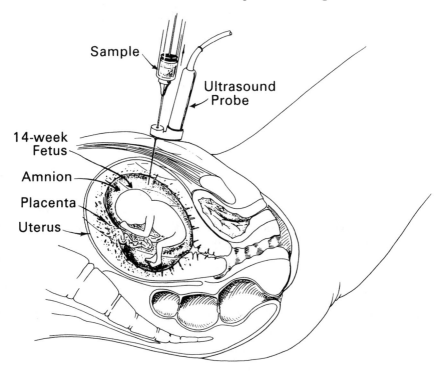

FIGURE 17.3 Amniocentesis. Under ultrasonic guidance amniotic fluid is withdrawn for chromosomal evaluation and biochemical testing.

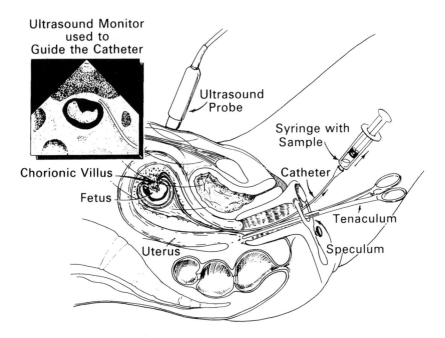

Ultrasound Monitor
used to
Guide the Catheter

Ultrasound
Probe

Syringe with
Sample

Chorionic Villus

Catheter

Fetus

Tenaculum

Uterus

Speculum

FIGURE 17.4 Chorionic villus sampling. Under ultrasonic guidance chorionic villi are obtained for rapid genetic assessment.

wall and uterus into the pregnancy sac. A small amount of amniotic fluid is withdrawn from the sac. The cells from the fluid are grown in tissue culture and, in 2 to 3 weeks, genetic information is available. While the procedure can be done earlier than 16 weeks, it is more difficult because there isn't as much amniotic fluid.

CHORIONIC VILLUS SAMPLING

This approach, shown in figure 17.4, is usually performed in the eighth to tenth week of pregnancy. An ultrasonic probe is placed into the vagina. A small biopsy needle is passed through the cervix into the tissue surrounding the fetus - the *chorionic villi* - which have the same genetic component as the fetus. Results are available in days.

While chorionic villus sampling (CVS) has the advantage of being able to be performed earlier and being able to provide results sooner, amniocentesis provides more overall information than CVS because the ultrasonic examination is conducted later in pregnancy. Nongenetic defects in the fetus, such as spina bifida (a malfunction of the spinal column) and hydrocephaly (a blockage in the central nervous system compartments) can be diagnosed at 16 weeks of gestation but not at 8. The critical issue is safety. About 2 to 4 pregnancies are disrupted in every 1,000 amniocentesis procedures. The best estimate of risk with CVS is about 2 percent, but determining a true risk figure with CVS is complicated by spontaneous abortions. When the spontaneous abortion rate is considered, there is little difference in safety between the two methods. Of late however, there have been some disquieting reports of abnormalities appearing in newborns subjected to CVS. These problems range from malformations in the extremities to facial bony developmental changes and are thought to result from vascular injury occurring during the biopsy process which causes the vessels that should eventually supply blood to these developing areas to be damaged. Therefore, we now recommend amniocentesis instead. These reports emanated from a few specific clinics, and may represent direct trauma not seen in other specific clinics. If you are facing a genetic study, it would be wise to obtain specific site information about malformations and miscarriages occurring after the diagnostic procedure, whether it be CVS or amniocentesis.

TABLE 17.2

RATE OF CHROMOSOMAL ABNORMALITIES PER 1,000 LIVE BIRTHS ACCORDING TO MATERNAL AGE

MATERNAL AGE	DOWN SYNDROME	ALL OTHERS	TOTAL
25	0.8	1.3	2.1
26	0.9	1.3	2.2
27	0.9	1.3	2.2
28	0.9	1.4	2.3
29	1.0	1.4	2.4
30	1.1	1.5	2.6
31	1.2	1.5	2.7
32	1.3	1.8	3.1
33	1.6	1.9	3.5
34	2.2	1.9	4.1
35	3.2	2.5	5.7
36	4.1	2.5	6.6
37	5.2	3.0	8.2
38	6.7	3.2	9.9
39	8.6	3.7	12.3
40	10.8	5.1	15.9
41	14.3	6.3	20.6
42	18.4	8.1	26.5
43	25.1	8.1	33.2
44	32	10	42
45	40	15	55
46	52	17	69
47	70	21	91
48	90	26	116
49	112	38	150

Source: Compiled by the author.

Age And Reproduction

In terms of reproductive capability, age is clearly kinder to men than to women. But when does age begin to affect a woman's fertility? AID clinics in France recently pooled results of their studies of female fertility as a function of age. Analysis of the combined statistics indicated that age had no affect on fertility before thirty, but that women were 13 percent less likely to conceive at thirty-five than at thirty. In the United States about 20 percent of women over thirty-five who want to conceive cannot. Moreover, a British study documented reduced fertility after the age of twenty-seven, although the reduction was very mild. These findings seriously challenge the long-held idea that there is little change in female fertility until after thirty-five. In certain orders of the Amish, no contraception is ever employed and the median number of pregnancies is as high as 12 with live-births in the 8 to 9 range. In these populations, the median age for the last liveborn is usually between 38-40, although 6 to 9 percent have live-births between ages 40-44. This is a distinct subset of our population with respect to habits of living in which women neither smoke, drink, and usually avoid caffeine, and the data therefore, may not apply to other groups. But assuming that pregnancy occurs, what effect does a woman's age have on fetal development? The more advanced a woman's age, the greater the likelihood that she will transmit a genetic error to the fetus. Table 17.2 on the preceding page gives the relationship between maternal age, Down syndrome, and other lesser-known genetic abnormalities. The table shows that at age thirty-four and beyond, Down syndrome outnumbers all other genetic defects among *live births*. But even at age thirty-nine, the risk of Down syndrome is only about 8.6 per thousand *live births* - less than 1 percent. Women hoping to conceive in their late thirties and even early forties should take comfort in knowing that their chances of giving birth to a genetically normal baby remain excellent.

Most other genetically linked birth defects are not so disabling as Down syndrome. They usually result in an individual who possesses normal intelligence, but who may be sterile. Examples are *Turner syndrome*, in which the affected woman has only a single X chromosome, and *Klinefelter syndrome*, in which the affected man has an XXY arrangement of sex chromosomes.

Other Causes Of Repeated Pregnancy Loss

Environment And Disease

Several environmental factors can affect human chromosomes. It is known that use of the drug LSD produces chromosomal breaks in the cells of the users, but no one has reported an increase in the deformity rate among offspring of people who use the drug. Ionizing radiation can damage a fetus exposed to it while in the womb, but the children of people who have received previous X-ray treatments do not have a higher incidence of genetic damage. This is especially important because many people treated for malignancy at a young age are cured and go on to have children. The relationship between viruses and repeated genetic errors is unknown. But we do know that contracting the viral infection rubella (German measles) during pregnancy places only that pregnancy at risk.

Other diseases can affect pregnancy outcome through nongenetic mechanisms. Women with chronic disease of the cardiovascular system or kidneys and those with diabetes mellitus are more prone to pregnancy loss. Indeed, for some of these women pregnancy itself can be life threatening. The evidence is clear that use of nicotine is associated not only with an element of mild infertility, but also with earlier menopause. Thus, it is clear that the ovary and its related organs are sensitive to the influence of nicotine and other noxious agents absorbed from cigarette smoke. Nicotine has the ability to cause spasm of blood vessels, and this is true for the small blood vessels in the placenta as well. Smoking mothers tend to have babies of reduced birth weight because of poor nutrition, and early fetal loss on this basis is also increased. There is no question that use of alcohol can injure the fetus and "fetal alcohol syndrome" is now well established as a legitimate diagnosis. The problem here is that no threshold has been described. Is an occasional cocktail or wine with dinner - customs practiced all over the world - injurious? Because obstetricians don't know, they advise on the safe side, and tell women to refrain from alcohol throughout pregnancy.

Major weight swings can not only interfere with ovulation but also may produce problems during pregnancy. For example, fasting or dramatic reduction of calorie intake may lead to metabolic acidosis, particularly in women with diabetic tendencies; the metabolic change may be harmful to the fetus. There is really very little evidence to indicate that vegetarian diets have any positive or negative effect on conception, although some investigators think they are not helpful. Vitamin and iron supplements during pregnancy, however, are especially important for women who adhere to these restrictive diets. Clearly, folic acid, found in vitamin supplements, when initiated early in pregnancy, offers protection against spina bifida.

Immunological Factors

Immunological factors that affect pregnancy fall generally into two main categories. The first is a paradoxical response and is sometimes difficult to understand. Normally, husbands and wives have great genetic dissimilarity. On the surface of all of our tissues are protein antigens known as transplantation antigens. This is why a skin graft that is not matched perfectly or taken from a very close relative will slough off and be rejected. In reproduction, the very dissimilar nature between the two partners causes the formation of what is known as *blocking antibodies*, which are directed against the fetal tissue.

The blocking antibodies made by the woman are incomplete antibodies. By that we mean they occupy receptor sites on tissues and cause no harm. If the husband has an antigen makeup similar to his wife's, the blocking antibodies will not be produced. Instead, active antibodies may develop to those antigenic sites that are not held in common by both partners, which could cause abortion. Even in this situation, however, there's a quite easy method of treatment. The husband's white blood cells are used to vaccinate the wife so that she can become sensitized to them. It is like other vaccinations except that an antibody response that offers protection for only 6 months or so is produced. In one striking case, a couple consulted us after 13 consecutive pregnancy losses without a diagnosis. On testing, we found the very same abnormality just described. After vaccination, the woman delivered a normal infant in her next pregnancy. Recent reports, however, have cast doubt on this form of therapy as being effective over and above coincidence. The issue her is clouded by small sample size reports, different patient selection and non-standardized protocols for treatment.

Women with autoimmune diseases related to a disorder of collagen, such as rheumatoid arthritis and systemic lupus erythematosus, frequently have a class of antibodies that are collectively known as the *cardiolipins*, members of the phospholipid group that may be associated with pregnancy loss. This is due to the antibody effect on the growing and newly formed blood vessels at the site of implantation and in the placenta. The treatment for this has been to use small doses of aspirin in early pregnancy - 80 mg daily - which is the dose of a baby aspirin. As the pregnancy continues, some patients then are fully anticoagulated with heparin by daily injection which keeps the blood vessels in the placenta open and free of vascular clotting. The salvage rate with this treatment is also very impressive, and part of an assessment for reproductive wastage should include a workup for these antibodies, especially if the woman's uterine architecture is normal, and if she has no chromosomal defects. The cardiolipin antibodies have been found also in women who do not have any other indication of collagen disorders.

Inadequate Luteal Phase

After ovulation, the corpus luteum secretes progesterone to prepare the endometrium for an implanting blastocyst. But in some women, either the corpus luteum fails to produce enough progesterone, or the uterine lining responds poorly to normal amounts of this hormone. In either case, a blastocyst may fail to implant properly after conception. This condition is known as the *inadequate luteal phase*.

Sometimes the BBT chart suggests this diagnosis when a slow or erratic temperature increase is noted after ovulation, or when the temperature elevation lasts for less than 12 days from the lowest temperature reading to the next menses. However, an endometrial biopsy taken during the second half of the cycle, sometimes in conjunction with serum testing of progesterone concentration, is necessary for a "true" diagnosis. The confusing issue is that sometimes the progesterone values are low in the face of normal endometrial biopsies, and vice versa. A sample of endometrial tissue is removed from the uterus by a simple procedure done in the doctor's office. The sample is examined by a pathologist who determines the endometrial stage of development in the menstrual cycle. This is subjective in nature, and therefore an abnormal biopsy is not diagnosed unless the lining seems to be more than 2 days behind in its normal development. Normal fertile patients may have a single biopsy which shows such a lag, but to make a diagnosis of an inadequate luteal phase, some authorities insist that two biopsies be done, both in untreated cycles, and that another biopsy be done during a treated cycle to see if there is improvement. In the past the acquisition of the specimen was rather uncomfortable, but introduction of new small suction instruments has made this procedure quite tolerable. If progesterone levels are taken during the cycle, blood is best drawn at the peak point of production, which is usually between 6 and 8 days following the LH surge in a nonpregnant cycle. If pregnancy occurs, progesterone values begin to increase rather than decrease. However, progesterone normally has a wide normal range, and diagnosis through a blood test will be made only in the most obvious cases. By now it should be clear to you that this diagnosis often rests on somewhat shaky ground.

The inadequate luteal phase can be treated very simply by adding progesterone following ovulation. Because progesterone is broken down in the gastrointestinal tract, this is usually given in the form of vaginally absorbed suppositories instead of the usual tablet form. Some doctors have gotten pharmacies to make up micronized progesterone tablets that can be taken by mouth and absorbed well enough to avoid use of the vaginal route, which admittedly can be a messy nuisance when the suppository liquifies. Progesterone can be given by injection. Regardless of how it is administered, natural progesterone rather than a synthetic molecule is used. There is no question in my mind that it is safe for the fetus. Yet this therapy remains unapproved by the FDA.

This kind of treatment has been seen by many as "closing the barn door after the horse has already left." Most of us feel that events that occur before ovulation influence the function of the corpus luteum after ovulation. So, many doctors treat with ovarian stimulants even though the patient may be already ovulating, albeit not normally. Regardless of the type of therapy used, if pregnancy does occur, most physicians agree that progesterone should be given as a supplement for the first 8 to 10 weeks of pregnancy, or until ultrasound shows fetal heart motion. The same mechanisms responsible for the inadequate function of the corpus luteum shortly after ovulation may still be at play during the early phases of the pregnancy. Human progesterone given as a supplement is entirely safe and may be a good insurance policy. Several studies of drug therapy for inadequate luteal phase report term pregnancy rates of 70 to 80 percent. These claims are somewhat difficult to evaluate because in most cases patient controls (that is, those who weren't treated) were not compared with the treated ones. To make matters more difficult, investigators use different criteria to make a diagnosis. The truth is that luteal phase inadequacy is probably overdiagnosed, although it certainly exists as a clinical entity.

Anatomical Factors

A woman with a septate or bicornuate uterus (described in chapter 2) may have perfect menstrual function, but be unable to carry a pregnancy to "the point of viability" - 28 to 30 weeks in most newborn nurseries. However, corrective surgery usually should not be attempted until the outcome of at least one pregnancy has been observed. Even a uterus that seems very distorted may be able to perform in a satisfactory fashion. After 2 or 3 losses, especially late in the first trimester (10 to 13 weeks) or early in the second, the condition should be surgically corrected, using the techniques described in chapter 9.

　Probably 2 percent of all women have some structural uterine abnormality. Many of these women experience no reproductive problems. However, because the urinary tract develops in concert with genital structures, such women are usually screened for various urinary tract abnormalities. These include the presence of a horseshoe kidney, pelvic kidney, solitary kidney, or duplication of the ureter.

Some women have two completely separate uteri and cervices. They usually do well reproductively and do not need any uterine repair. The septate uterus is by far the most common of the conditions that we see associated with pregnancy loss. Success rates - defined by a live infant born in the next pregnancy - are about 75 to 80 percent following a simple hysteroscopic procedure. The bicornuate uterus demands a more major surgical procedure, but success after restoration of a normal uterine cavity is also quite high.

Fibroid tumors in the uterus, called myomas, are another cause of repeated miscarriages. The hormonal stimulus of pregnancy enlarges myomas until they encroach upon the fetus. They can also cause uterine irritability with resulting uterine contractions leading to abortion or separation of the placenta from the uterine wall. Evaluating the reproductive importance of myomas (women often have more than one) in a nonpregnant woman can be difficult since they shrink after a pregnancy is lost. Surgical removal of myomas was described in chapter 9. The reproductive success rate after surgery is high, usually over 70 percent, although the baby may have to be delivered by cesarean section if the mother had deep incisions in the uterus.

Although the uterus expands tremendously during pregnancy, the cervix normally remains shut in order to contain the fetus. An *incompetent* cervix is one that cannot remain closed against the pressure of the growing fetus. As a result, the amniotic sac will balloon out from the uterus and eventually rupture, causing an abortion or early delivery. Premature rupture of the membranes is also associated with risk of intrauterine infection. Women may be born with an incompetent cervix, as in cases of the DES syndrome. Often, however, the condition is acquired during the course of life. One cause is previous delivery of a very large baby. Another is frequent voluntary abortion, associated with excessive cervical dilation, which tears the fibers in the cervix. The diagnosis is made when the patient is not pregnant, if a doctor can insert a small dilator or a hysteroscope into the uterus without any resistance from the cervix. An HSG also suggests the diagnosis if a wide pattern of dye is seen in the cervical canal.

Treatment consists of reinforcing the cervix with sutures or bands of synthetic material. The procedure, known as a *cerclage*, is usually performed during pregnancy between weeks 12 and 17. Waiting this long avoids unnecessarily treating a woman with a blighted ovum or an otherwise unhealthy fetus. Moreover, the uterus is likely to be less irritable between 13 and 16 weeks into pregnancy, and cerclage at that time carries a lower risk of inducing abortion. Following surgery the patient is usually given bed rest for a short while, and then told to restrict her activities for the rest of the pregnancy. If the uterus is also irritable, uterine relaxing drugs may be necessary. About 70 to 80 percent of these patients will deliver infants mature enough to survive the hospital nursery experience without difficulty.

The DES syndrome gained prominence because of the increased risk of cervical and vaginal malignancy in women who were exposed to various estrogens in utero. It later became apparent that the fertility of many of these DES daughters was impaired, not so much through difficulty in conceiving, as through miscarriage. In particular, the rate of second trimester pregnancy loss for DES daughters is about 3 times the normal rate. One reason for the high miscarriage rate is that many DES daughters are born with incompetent cervices. Another reason is that some of these women have small, distorted uterine cavities, often T-shaped, and often too irritable to sustain pregnancy. Treatment consists of cerclage, reduced activity, uterine relaxants, and sometimes progesterone compounds. The success of the treatment depends on the severity of the DES syndrome.

All the uterine and cervical abnormalities described here can be diagnosed with hysterosalpingography, and confirmed with hysteroscopy, as described in chapter 5.

Infections

Various infections during pregnancy can kill the fetus or affect its development, but it is unclear if any organism is implicated in chronic pregnancy loss. Toxoplasmosis is a disease acquired from a cat parasite. Patients who first contract this during pregnancy will frequently lose that pregnancy or have a child with central nervous system damage. It is rare, however, for patients who already have had the illness, which for the adult is rather mild, to have a recurrence during subsequent pregnancies. Doctors cannot come to an agreement on whether or not ureaplasma organisms cause miscarriages. The organisms are common, and can be cultured from 20 to 40 percent of patients in North America, depending on the socioeconomic group studied. Treatment with tetracyclines is effective. Diagnosis of this infection during pregnancy alters the treatment in that tetracycline should not be given after the first few weeks of pregnancy because it permanently stains the secondary teeth of the fetus, and causes bone abnormalities. Fortunately, we have other antibiotics that can be safely administered during pregnancy.

Cytomegalic inclusion virus (CMV) is another infection which usually is of little consequence except when it occurs in a pregnant patient. As with other viral illnesses, exposure usually results in continuing immunity to the mother thereafter.

Workup

The workup for repeated pregnancy loss depends primarily on the timing of the loss and the partners' medical histories. We also consider the degree of anxiety the couple shows and their ages. Loss of two pregnancies for a twenty-seven-year-old woman presents a different problem than for a woman in her late thirties. In general, a familial history of reproductive difficulty suggests a genetic cause. Losses occurring early in pregnancy also point to a genetic factor as does previous delivery of an offspring with congenital abnormalities. On the other hand, losses later in pregnancy, between 10 and 20 weeks, suggest a uterine problem. Losses after that time may indicate cervical incompetence.

If genetic screening is called for, both partners must be tested. But genetics is a difficult science to master, and I have seen great grief caused by inaccurate genetic counseling. Large medical centers usually have well-trained staffs but couples should not be afraid to ask for the credentials of anyone who is about to pronounce the status of their reproductive future.

We have discussed specific treatments as we examined the causes of pregnancy loss, but at this point some general comments may be helpful. About 20 percent of all pregnancies will be associated with some bleeding early in the pregnancy. Of these, half will develop normally; the other half will spontaneously abort. There is a myth that putting the patient to bed can help avoid spontaneous abortion. Although bed rest may be important late in pregnancy, advice to go to bed and elevate your feet to avoid early spontaneous abortion is without scientific support. This is not to say that you should engage in strenuous sports if there is a high risk of early pregnancy loss. Also, intercourse does not need to be restricted early in the pregnancy. Later in the pregnancy there is some evidence, although it is fragmentary, that female orgasm may trigger uterine contractions in an irritable uterus.

Monitoring Pregnancy

Patients and physicians alike are interested in ways to predict the outcome of pregnancy or to obtain an early warning that a pregnancy will abort. One method is to measure the hormone hCG, secreted by the developing blastocyst after implantation. The level of hCG rises in a predictable way through the first forty days of pregnancy. Normally, the values should double approximately every 2.2 days. A fall off from the normal curve is suggestive of impending abortion, or an ectopic pregnancy. This fall off of hormonal production occurs well before the onset of any symptoms, such as cramps or bleeding. It is reassuring for patients to know that when normal values are found, 90 percent of patients continue with the pregnancy. By day 25 after ovulation, vaginal ultrasonic devices allow us to follow the pregnancy by indirect fetal inspection, first of the sac, and then of the fetus itself. Fetal heart motion should usually be seen by 35 days or sooner after ovulation (7 weeks after the last menses). Once fetal heart motion is seen, the abortion rate is dramatically reduced to less than 7 percent. A combination of hCG testing and ultrasonography provides a highly accurate method for monitoring a pregnancy. This is especially important for couples who have had earlier losses; they want to know what to expect with this pregnancy. Diagnostic ultrasound can also be used to rule out many fetal anatomical or structural defects such as hydrocephalus and spina bifida. It is a noninvasive and safe way of observing the fetus throughout its development.

18

Resolution

The word "resolve" describes an attitude of determination with which people decide to face a problem and deal with it. The word also means to bring a situation to a conclusion. Both meanings in turn apply to the infertile couple. First, the couple resolves to conquer infertility by entering a program of treatment. Resolve is what it takes to endure the stress of a protracted workup. After treatment has run its course, the couple's situation is brought to a resolution. That resolution may be the birth of a child. But when treatment has failed, resolution must take other forms.

The advent of assisted reproduction, or high-technology reproduction, has given couples choices that they never had before. Certainly donor insemination has been with us for years, and has helped bring many children into this world who otherwise could not have been conceived. We are now faced with the prospects of surrogate parenting, egg donors, pregnancy carriers, and embryo freezing. What was science fiction just a few years ago has now become standard routine in the laboratory. Whether these technologies are to become standard within the community is up to society. Too often decisions are made in a vacuum by bureaucrats pressured by minority groups of vocal people who have not known the pangs of despair associated with infertility or repeated pregnancy loss. Childless couples cry out for tolerance of procedures which might not be acceptable to their critics, but which these couples desperately need. Development of *in vitro* fertilization techniques and improvement in pregnancy yields have been responsible for a dramatic reduction of operations on fallopian tubes that could not really be repaired. Although still condemned by some orthodox religious groups, *in vitro* fertilization has been accepted largely in North America as a legitimate ethical form of therapy for those couples who seek it. Every fertility specialist becomes acquainted with hundred of vignettes, each unique, and each involving intense emotions that can range from despair to final elation. The thread common to all of these stories is an attitude of resolve, a determination to endure temperature charts, endless testing, timed coitus, post-operative pain, and the physical and emotional side effects associated with various therapies. Fortunately, more couples than ever before can now achieve a happy resolution. Ovulation disorders respond to treatment in more than 60 percent of cases. Those who fail to conceive with the first line treatment of clomiphene citrate will usually do so with use of Humegon, Pergonal or other more powerful drugs. Surgical therapy for tubal disease still does not have an impressive success rate, and probably never will, given the wide range of tubal damage. Use of laser surgery is helpful, but not a magic wand. *In vitro* fertilization, originally designed to cope with this problem, has, in fact, proven miraculous for these patients. In our in vitro program, 53% of the patients under age 40 are pregnant after 2 cycles at a combined cost of less than one tubal repair surgical procedure.

The relationship between endometriosis and infertility continues to be an enigma. Satisfactory treatment with drugs, surgery, or a combination of the two, results in pregnancy 30 to 75 percent of the time, depending upon the severity of the disease. Our understanding of immunological infertility, although rapidly improving, is still severely limited. *In vitro* fertilization techniques, advanced insemination techniques, and cautious use of steroid drugs are reasonable approaches to treatment. GIFT seems to be an excellent choice for couples with infertility on almost any basis except tubal, when lesser methods have been unsuccessful. Our pregnancy rate for GIFT in women < 40 is 43% for the first completed cycle.

Finally, we are beginning to see some improvement in pregnancy rates with advanced methods of artificial insemination using the husband's semen. Placement of a large number of sperm in the reproductive tract seems to be associated with improved pregnancy yield. Fertility investigators continue to look for ways to enhance the quality of the semen specimen used for insemination, and are seeking methods of improving motility of the sperm before, rather than after, collection.

It is in the area of male infertility that IVF has had a surprisingly beneficial effect. Less severe problems are frequently solved with GIFT, but we have been astonished by some of the pregnancies that have occurred in our IVF laboratory with semen containing very few sperm and with rather poor motility. New methods of egg-sperm micromanipulation will probably increase the number of successful pregnancies in this group even more. Improved techniques of stimulation during *in vitro* fertilization cycles will result not only in collection of more eggs, but eggs also of better quality and in a more synchronized stage of development. At the moment, embryo freezing is in its infancy. Freezing of embryos does introduce medical-legal problems that we don't have with the storage of unfertilized eggs. But we must add to that the practical fact that techniques for the freezing and thawing of eggs have not been overly successful in preserving their ability to fertilize and divide normally.

Once a definitive diagnosis is made and a program of treatment is begun, how soon should infertile couples expect to conceive? The answer depends on both the treatment involved and the specific features of the individual case. If, for example, the goal of treatment is to induce ovulation, each shift in treatment, each new approach that is tried, is really beginning treatment all over again. Thus, the absence of pregnancy after a few months of a particular therapy is no cause for alarm. Many factors influence the therapeutic decisions as to how long a particular therapy should be employed before moving on to something else. Among the considerations are the age of both partners, the diagnosis and duration of infertility, and the personal experience that the physician has had with pregnancy rates per month (fecundity) with this particular therapy. Generally speaking, if clomiphene citrate is being given for ovulation induction and pregnancy has not ensued within six to eight cycles, in spite of apparent good ovulation response, the scene is set for use of human gonadotropins. With the latter agents, most fertility clinics report that pregnancy rates flatten out after the fourth cycle; this is the usual time limit employed for use of Metrodin, Humegon or Pergonal although pregnancies do occur in some patients with continued use. Of great interest are IVF statistics, if for no other reason than the cost and effort involved. Although there is some dissention in the literature, most programs report that pregnancy rates through the first three cycles are roughly equal. This means that if one does not conceive in the first cycle, the chances in the succeeding two IVF cycles are still about the same as that expected with the first. Exceptions to this are repeated failure to fertilize and failure to retrieve any normal looking oocytes coupled with poor embryo development in succeeding cycles which would suggest a recurrent problem. On the other hand, the average elapsed time between successful repair of damaged tubes and conception can be as long as 16 months. For sterilization reversal on otherwise healthy tubes, elapsed time is usually under 6 months. Remember, even fertile couples may require a year or more to conceive. Therefore, patients and doctors should refrain from setting any arbitrary time limit on therapy. During treatment, patients should not hesitate to ask questions. Since results rarely occur overnight, patients need to understand the nature of their problem and what sort of treatment is available to them. If a diagnosis is difficult, or if treatment is not successful, your doctor may recommend consultation with another expert. If you desire a second opinion, get one without worrying about bruising the ego of your present therapist. If the consultant concurs with the strategies already employed, you and your therapist are reassured. Often a fresh eye will generate a new idea that will lead to success.

Lifestyle And Infertility

Not infrequently patients ask whether previous lifestyles in some way have been responsible for their present infertility problem. Certainly one of the legacies of the sexual revolution has been a dramatic increase in sexually transmitted disease. This has led to tubal damage in women and parallel ductal damage in men, and probably has increased infertility to a small degree. Previous IUD use has been associated with increased pelvic infection, but it is important to note that in most cases the presence of the device served to magnify rather than initiate a sexually transmitted infectious disease.

Dietary indiscretions in the past and even drug abuse seem to have little effect on fertility in the future unless those habits reemerge. Large upward and downward swings in weight in women over a short period of time are frequently associated with abnormalities of ovulation. The same holds true for vigorous exercise, which should be modulated if there is any suspicion that ovulation is being impaired.

Perhaps the people who express the greatest guilt are those women who previously have voluntarily terminated a pregnancy, and wish to know if this is the cause of their present status. Unless they developed an infection at the time of abortion that caused tubal damage, or uterine adhesions, both of which occur rarely, the answer is a resounding no.

Alternatives For Infertility

The overall success rate for fertility therapy is in excess of 60 percent. For the majority of infertile couples, then, resolution is straightforward and completely satisfactory. But what of the couples for whom therapy fails? They, too, must resolve their situation at some point. There comes a time when, after all attempts to achieve fertility have failed, the couple must look elsewhere to fulfill their dreams. Adoption becomes a resolution for many people. This can be arranged through government agencies, religious institutions, or private sources. Adoption laws vary from state to state and waiting lists are long everywhere. Therefore, it may be a good idea for a couple to get on an adoption list while still in therapy, especially if the prognosis for successful pregnancy is not good.

If is extraordinary how many people are determined to have "their own" baby or none at all. But that attitude need not be written in stone. Very often, people mature emotionally during an infertility workup and treatment course. We live in an age where many people acquire instant families through remarriage. Most have no trouble loving and caring for children from another marriage. Parenting is an art that is quite distinct from the ability to procreate.

For some people, resolution means remaining childless and diverting some of their emotional energies toward rewarding interests - careers, hobbies, pets, or humanitarian service. Many people become foster parents in response to their own infertility. In some cases, marriages grow stronger from the ordeal of unsuccessful therapy as the couple learns to lean on one another for emotional support. On the other hand, it is quite true that some marriages are destroyed by this problem. In a world that is subject to overcrowding, the anguish of infertile couples is frequently ignored. Their pain is intense and long standing. I hope this book proves informative and helpful to them.